# Praise for the works of Jeremy Naydler

### Temple of the Cosmos

*"A book that breaks new ground, a scholarly yet esoteric approach to an ancient culture and religion."*

**Critical Review**

*". . . not only evokes the atmosphere of the myths, but re-creates that all too rare relationship with them that enables us to understand what it means to be part of ongoing cosmic processes as sacred realities."*

**I. M. Oderberg, *Sunrise: Theosophical Perspectives***

*"The reader experiences living issues rather than the cold reconstructions of a guide book."*

**Clement Salaman, *Temenos Academy Review***

### Shamanic Wisdom in the Pyramid Texts

*"A model of how to engage with religious literature and, still more widely, with the sacred dimension of life. . . . Serves as a mirror to our own consciousness, reflecting back to us objective spiritual realities which have fallen out of contemporary discourse, and waking us up to deeper layers of our own humanity. . . . An essential book for all of us who long to experience the greater possibilities of the human psyche."*

**Jules Cashford, *Temenos Academy Review***

*"An invaluable contribution to the dialogue about the mysteries of ancient Egypt."*

**Rosicrucian Digest**

# The
# FUTURE
## *of the*
# ANCIENT
# WORLD

## Essays on the History
## of Consciousness

JEREMY NAYDLER

Inner Traditions
Rochester, Vermont • Toronto, Canada

Inner Traditions
One Park Street
Rochester, Vermont 05767
www.InnerTraditions.com

**Library of Congress Cataloging-in-Publication Data**

Naydler, Jeremy.
  The future of the ancient world : essays on the history of consciousness / Jeremy
Naydler.
    p. cm.
  Includes bibliographical references and index.
  ISBN 978-1-59477-292-4 (pbk.)
  1. Spirituality. 2. Consciousness—Religious aspects.  I. Title.
  BL624.N39 2009
  200.93—dc22

                                                                    2009003690

Printed and bound in the United States by Lake Book Manufacturing

10    9    8    7    6    5    4    3    2    1

Text design by Jon Desautels
Text layout by Virginia Scott Bowman
This book was typeset in Garamond Premiere Pro with Apolline and Agenda as
display typefaces

To send correspondence to the author of this book, mail a first-class letter to the
author c/o Inner Traditions • Bear & Company, One Park Street, Rochester, VT
05767, and we will forward the communication.

*This book is dedicated to Patrick Gordon*

# CONTENTS

# INTRODUCTION

Why should we concern ourselves with the past, especially the rather distant past of bygone civilizations like ancient Egypt and Mesopotamia, Greece and Rome? The reason, I believe, is that our relationship to the past is at the same time a relationship to ourselves. It is a relationship to a dimension of ourselves that we have become largely unconscious of today. It nevertheless calls to us from hidden depths. By heeding this call, we come to recognize that the depths of the past lie within us, and that the voice that sounds from these depths is our own voice, which we have for too long neglected.

Were we to heed this voice, we would hear it telling us that today's "common sense" view of the world in which what is real is equated with what has material existence and is therefore best known and understood through the methods of contemporary materialistic science is a narrow and sadly reduced view of the world compared to that of the ancients (and is therefore best known and understood through the methods of contemporary science). We would also hear it telling us that our modern standards of what is normal, acceptable, and sane are not absolute or beyond question, because they would have been regarded by people in ancient times as quite the opposite. We might also hear this voice remonstrating with us over our cherished belief in progress, by means of which we permit ourselves to look with condescension, if not disdain, upon cultures prior to our own and thereby bolster up a dismissive

1

attitude to an important dimension of human experience. Today this dimension of experience, for so long suppressed, seems increasingly to impinge upon our lives and to demand our attention.

There is, then, the possibility that we might learn something from the past, if we approach it with due respect. This is not to say that we should idolize the past. Ancient consciousness placed supreme value on maintaining contact with the spirit world through divination, sacrifice, worship, ritual, and visionary experience. Modern consciousness, by contrast, has replaced deference toward the world of spirit with deference to rational analysis and "evidence-based" research that excludes any notion of nonphysical aspects of reality. At the same time, however, modernity has come to place great value on the ideal of individual freedom. In retrospect, we may judge that the ancients lacked any corresponding ideal of freedom—indeed, they would have regarded it as sacrilegious. The path of the historical development of consciousness has been neither one of simple progress nor of decline, but rather a process of gains and losses. We have gained a degree of mental focus and alacrity, and we have gained freedom, but in the process we have lost the relatedness that existed in antiquity to the world of spirit.

Today there is a deep longing in our culture to reconnect to this spiritual world, for we are not whole without it. But our longing cannot be satisfied by embracing religious belief alone, no matter how emotional the embrace, for our longing is at root a hunger and thirst for the *experience* of interior realities. If, however, we are to forge a new relationship to the invisible world of spirit based on experience, what will distinguish it from the past is the modern necessity that it be based on our own autonomy as free individuals, able to think, decide, and act for ourselves. The ideal toward which we need to work today is that of a future reconnection with the realm of spirit in which we retain our capacity to think discriminatively and in which we retain our individual moral autonomy. Only thereby will the "ancient world" acquire an appropriate and authentic future.

This book collects together twelve essays written between 1993 and 2007. It takes a more varied approach to the cultures of antiquity than either of the two previous books that I have written on the culture and religious life of ancient Egypt. *Temple of the Cosmos* (1996) gave an overview of the ancient Egyptian experience of the sacred and was intended to be a general introduction to the consciousness of the ancient Egyptians, which was so highly attuned to the spirit world. *Shamanic Wisdom in the Pyramid Texts* (2005) was a more narrowly focused study that offered a new interpretation of the ancient Egyptian Pyramid Texts and the mystical and initiatory rituals described therein. The present book, whose twelve essays were written before, during, and after the publication of these two books, ranges beyond the culture of Egypt to the cultures of Mesopotamia, Crete, Greece, and Rome, as well as reflecting on the significance of early Christianity. More explicitly than the two previous volumes, it aims to bring the consciousness that prevailed in ancient times into relationship with our situation now. The underlying purpose of these essays is to try to shed light on the historical development of human consciousness, from antiquity to the present day, and from the present into the future. Over the years during which these essays were written, I have felt inwardly compelled to return again and again to this subject, each time approaching it freshly from a different standpoint. It has seemed to me that without understanding the historical development of consciousness, we cannot make sense of the manifold crises facing contemporary culture, nor begin effectively to answer the core philosophical and existential questions that all of us need to address: Where have we come from? Where are we going? Why are we here? What must we do?

All the essays originated as an illustrated lecture or talk. Their translation into the written word, with line drawings replacing the original color images, usually followed closely on the heels of the lecture, and so something of the original oral delivery is preserved in the text. The essays, however, were never intended to form a single unified text and I have felt that it would be a mistake to attempt to mold them into one, as the integrity of each would be compromised if it were constrained to serve an artificial whole. They naturally constitute a "unity in diversity" insofar as all the essays grapple with the overriding question of the evolution of human consciousness and seek to clarify what our stance should be today in relation to this question. For this reason, in preparing them for publication in a single volume, they have received only minimal editing, and I have left them, each to stand on its own ground. Each essay may therefore be read as an independent piece; yet each is also a mirror to the others, catching and reflecting a different aspect of the cultural and spiritual biography in which we all share.

JANUARY 2009

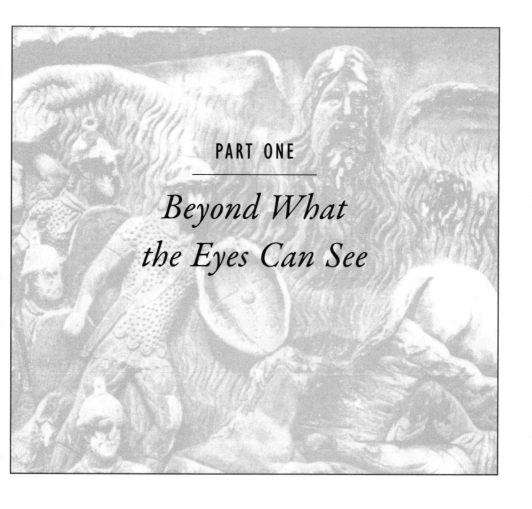

PART ONE

*Beyond What
the Eyes Can See*

# 1

## THE RESTITUTION OF THE EAR

The heart makes of its owner a hearer or a nonhearer.

Ptahhotep

*This essay traces the historical process by which the sense of sight usurped the sense of hearing as the primary metaphor of human mental functions. It argues that through the reinstatement of listening rather than looking as the basis of our model for relating to the world, it becomes possible for a more open, responsive, and participative relationship with nature to arise.*

*The essay is based on a talk given for the Oxford Centre for Human Relations on November 23, 1993, entitled "The Seeing and Listening Mind."[1]*

### IN QUEST OF THE MIND'S EAR

We have become so accustomed to thinking of our mental processes under the metaphor of the sense of sight that we scarcely notice we do it—let alone reflect on its significance. Words abound in our vocabulary, which express functions of the mind in terms of visual functions: we have "views," we "look" at things from a certain "perspective," we "speculate," we "focus" on some issue, are "short-sighted," "far-sighted,"

6

or even "visionary," and when we have gained "insight" into someone's "point of view" we "see" what they mean. And so on.

Why is it that the sense of sight has assumed this role of the model on which we tend to represent to ourselves the workings of our minds? What is the deeper meaning of the fact that our modern Western consciousness finds in the visual experience—rather than the experience of touch, taste, smell, or hearing—the one that most closely approximates our experience of thinking and understanding?

For it has not always been so. In the ancient civilization of Sumeria, which flourished in Iraq during the late fourth and early third millenniums BC, it would seem that the *ear* was felt to be the sense-organ, which corresponded in its functioning most closely to that of the mind. Enki, the Sumerian god of wisdom, who was said to know all things, was described as "he whose ears are wide open" (see fig. 1.1).[2] And when the great goddess Inanna contemplated her initiatory journey into the underworld, we read that she "opened her ear to the Great Below."[3] The words for "the mind" and "the ear" were in fact identical.[4]

Whereas for us the sensory metaphor most often associated with wisdom is "far-sightedness," implying a practical ability to plan effectively for the future, for the Sumerians the equivalent expression

*Fig. 1.1. The god Enki, in his watery abode, the Abzu. Akkadian cylinder seal, 2340 BC.*

would have been "depth of ear" implying a more contemplative, more inward attunement to the spiritual forces active in the present. The image evoked by the expression "far-sightedness" is that of a commanding hilltop view of a landscape spread out before the "mind's eye"; the image that the expression "depth of ear" gives rise to is that of the still, silent waters of a lake or well below the earth's surface, which—appropriately—was the abode of Enki, god of wisdom.

In ancient Egypt, too, a comparable association was made between the ear, or the act of hearing, and our mental faculties. In the Old Kingdom Instructions of Ptahhotep, we read how

The fool who does not hear can do nothing at all.
He sees knowledge in ignorance.[5]

And again:

He who hears is beloved of God,
he whom God hates does not hear.[6]

The divine gift of hearing is the basis of perception of spiritual truth. It is the ear rather than the eye, which opens the mind toward the deepest level of reality. And the descriptions of various ancient Egyptian deities—especially the god Ptah—as being "great of hearing" or as having "hearing ears" attest not only to their responsiveness to their human petitioners, but equally to the depth of their divine understanding and compassion (see fig. 1.2).

Whereas the eye shows us the surfaces of things—their extension in space, their form and color—the ear reveals to us that which is hidden from the eye. The ear, unlike the eye, is physiologically a very internal organ; and what is expressed in sound pertains more to the inner nature of a thing or creature. The sound an animal makes gives us an experience of what is happening in its soul, which no amount of looking would communicate to us.

In listening, the mind must quieten itself to a point of stillness and

*Fig. 1.2. Worship of the god Ptah, who is "great of hearing." Note the ears above and behind the god, Nineteenth Dynasty, Egypt.*

attentiveness. Listening is a receptive, participative activity in which we allow certain qualities of the being to whom we are listening to resound within us. The functioning of the eye is quite different. Instead of this built-in contemplative quality, there is a kind of pragmatism entailed by the eye's demand for distance between us and the object of our gaze. The eye asks us to engage in a practical, instrumental relationship to the world, whereas the ear seems to invite us to overcome our separation from objects that the eye locates "out there" and to involve ourselves with them in a more participative form of knowing.

## THE RISE OF THE EYE

It was the Greeks who first introduced the eye as the primary metaphor of mental functions. Already, in Homer, we begin to suspect as much when the "bright-eyed" Athena intervenes in the thought processes of various heroes. In chapter 1 of the *Iliad* she causes Achilles to reflect instead of following his initial violent impulse to attack Agamemnon; and it is significant that it is she who is the deity closest to the wily Odysseus, inspiring him with his clever plans. Athena's symbolic animal was, aptly enough, the wide-eyed owl (fig. 1.3).

*Fig. 1.3. The goddess Athena, and her wide-eyed owl.*
*From an Athenian coin, fifth century BC.*

The genius of the Greek language is still more revealing than its mythology, especially as the former evolved to accommodate more abstract and philosophical concepts. By the fourth century BC, the verb *idein* was used equally to express seeing and knowing, the congruence of meaning being so complete that the past *oida* was used both in the sense of "I have seen" and "I know." For the Greeks, when one has *seen*, one knows. This coalescence of meaning was retained in the derivative noun *idea*, which expressed both the inner nature of a thing (what kind of thing it is) and its visible form or appearance. Similarly the noun *theoria* denoted both contemplation and beholding or observing. Its verb *theorein* was employed to describe both the activity of spectators at public games and festivals, and that of the philosopher.[7] Clearly, for the Greeks the activity of thinking was felt to imply a distancing of self from object, similar to that which arises between observer and observed in the exercise of the sense of sight.

At the same time the sense of sight itself became the dominant sense, the arbiter and judge of the real. It is a curious and highly significant fact that for over two thousand years before the Greek era began, the portrayal of people and objects in the great cultures of the ancient Near East was not as the eye sees them. The visual arts in pre-Greek civilization, while using the eye as a medium, were not constrained by the eye's view of the world. A single object might be portrayed from several different viewpoints at once, to accord with symbolic principles of representation. For example, the typical way of representing a human being in Egyptian painting was with a side view of the feet, front view of the trunk, side view of the head, and front view of the eye (fig. 1.4). When we contemplate Egyptian or Mesopotamian works of art, we

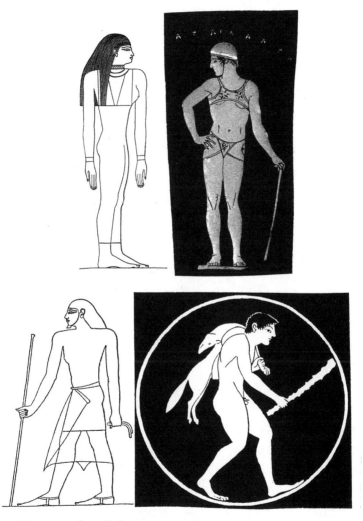

*Fig. 1.4. Above left: Princess Sedet, Fourth Dynasty, Egypt.*
*Above right: Atalanta from a fifth-century Greek cup painting.*
*Notice her foreshortened feet.*
*Below left: The nomarch Khnumhotep. Middle Kingdom, Egypt.*
*Below right: A hunter from a fifth-century cup painting, Greece.*

have the feeling that the mentality that underlies them is quite foreign to our own, for they have not yet attained a spectatorial view of the world, a view from the single standpoint of the detached observer. If we are inclined to say that the ancient Egyptian way of portraying a person is not realistic, we betray the fact that our own reality-standpoint is totally dominated by the visual sense and the spectator-consciousness that leans so heavily upon it. From our standpoint, the Greeks introduced a new "realism" in their portrayal of the human form. But the truth is rather that the Greeks inaugurated a new kind of *consciousness,* which we share, and which in its functioning was allied to the sense of sight. The cultural history of Europe suggests that this alliance, at first tentative, was progressively strengthened.

Despite the initial, "spectacular" shift in perception in Greek times, neither the primacy of the visual sense nor of the visual consciousness, was clinched until the time of the scientific revolution in the early modern period. The Greeks themselves still upheld a participative view of knowledge in which an inward dimension to all phenomena was recognized. Both Plato and Aristotle maintained that true knowledge could not be gained by a detached, noninvolved attitude of mind: the spectatorial metaphor, which had insinuated itself into the language of knowledge, did not prevent the continuation of an aural epistemology among the great thinkers of Greece. Knowledge was by *participation*— the participation of that which is inward in the human being (i.e., the intellective faculty) with that which is inward in the phenomenon, namely its essence or spiritual core. Accordingly, careful distinctions were made to express different kinds of knowing, depending on the degree to which in each, the mind was directed toward the spiritual interior of the phenomenal world. Thus, in Plato's *Republic,* four states of mind are distinguished: illusion, opinion, reason, and intelligence (or insight). These degrees of knowing correspond not only to the degree of participative knowledge attained but also to the degree of knowability that an object has, some objects being intrinsically deeper, in a spiritual sense, than others. As Plato says,

You may arrange them (the four states of mind) in a scale, and assume that they have degrees of clarity corresponding to the degree of truth and reality possessed by their subject-matter.[8]

Platonic epistemology thus contains an implicit admonition that we turn our minds toward the depths rather than the surfaces of reality.

This view was echoed by Aristotle in the *Physics* (and elsewhere) where we read:

The path of investigation must lie from that which is more immediately knowable to us, to what is clearer and more intimately knowable in its own nature; for it is not the same thing to be directly accessible to our cognition and to be intrinsically intelligible.

That which is "intrinsically more luminous" in the object—i.e., its spiritual essence—is "by its nature accessible to deeper knowledge."[9]

In medieval times the distinction between different faculties of knowing continued. Thomas Aquinas, for example, in asserting the priority of the *intellectus* (the intuitive intellect) over the *ratio* (the reasoning, planning intellect) pointed out that the word *intellectus* derives etymologically from *inter* and *legere*—"to read inwardly."[10] The contemplative intellect was capable of "reading" that which is concealed from external vision; and so it was, by rights, superior to the linear process of logical reasoning. At the same time, the functioning of the senses in medieval times was less dominated by the sense of sight than it was in ancient Greece, or came to be in the period following the Renaissance. Psychologically oriented historians like Lucien Febvre have shown that taste, smell, touch, and hearing were all better developed than they are now, and that people in the Middle Ages were motivated more often by these senses than by sight.[11] Just because the nonvisual senses open us to a more emotionally and symbolically resonant world, their comparative dominance in the total perceptual experience had its effect on the visual arts. Medieval art, like pre-Greek art (but nevertheless very different from it) was essentially contemplative art. Again, it may seem to us to

*Fig. 1.5. The dove of the Holy Spirit inspires St. Gregory.*
*Detail of a painting by the Master*
*of the Registrum Gregorii, tenth century AD.*

have failed in terms of visual realism, but in its symbolic and devotional quality it was art for the listening mind (fig. 1.5).

## VISUAL TOTALITARIANISM

Only in the Renaissance did the spectatorial metaphor really come into its own. With the new feeling of distance from nature, there was a corresponding awareness of the human individual as a subject over against an objective world "out there."[12] The world was accordingly portrayed as it appeared to the single observer from his or her particular angle of vision. The discovery of perspective in the visual arts was as much an affirmation of individual selfhood as it was a discovery of the laws of

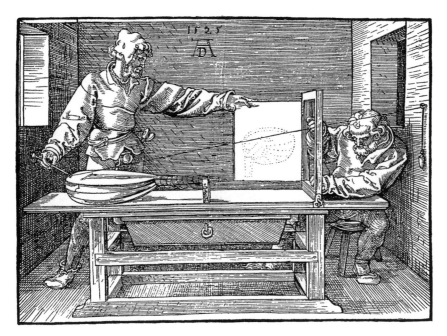

*Fig. 1.6. Albrecht Dürer's demonstration of the perspective drawing
of a lute, showing the apparatus required to produce scientifically correct
foreshortening on a purely mechanical basis.*

portraying the third dimension. Essential to this process was the new emphasis placed on the eye's view of the world, for the eye separates observer from observed where the ear unites them. The irony of Dürer's portrayal of two artists producing scientifically accurate foreshortened views of a lute by means of a grid apparatus is not lost on us (fig. 1.6). That Dürer should have chosen to illustrate his textbook on perspective and proportion with a woodcut of draftsmen gaining visual mastery over a musical instrument symbolizes the triumph of the eye over the ear in the new scientific approach to the world. It also symbolizes the triumph of the detached, onlooker consciousness. The hook in the wall (with some string dangling from it) marks the position from which the lute is viewed by the artist as onlooker.

Needless to say, the sound of the lute when played could be listened to in any part of the room. And in the act of listening, there is a sense of participation in the quality of sound that the lute characteristically produces. In the medieval portrayal of the world, the symbolic and religious dimension of the visual arts beckoned a similar type of participation. The gradual freeing of art from this dimension, during and after the Renaissance, shows that a quite different kind of relationship between human beings and nature was coming about.

The changing relationship is most evident in the scientific revolution, which was a revolution in perception, and whose leading protagonists systematically denigrated all senses other than the eye. The eye alone was trusted to reveal the world as it really is. The "New Science" of Galileo, founded on the application of mathematics and geometry to the study of nature, was specifically visual in its orientation: one cannot touch, taste, smell, or hear quantities of things with the same degree of precision as one can see them. The demand of the spectatorial mentality for exactitude in the observation of natural phenomena led to the exclusion of the nonvisual senses from the new scientific epistemology. This was based on the notorious distinction between those unquantifiable aspects of an object, which are apprehended by touch, taste, smell, and hearing, which were now thought of as subjective qualities arising *in the observer* and hence not truly belonging to the world, and those quantifiable aspects, which we become aware of through sight, and which now were regarded as objective qualities of the world. There is a disconcerting passage in Galileo's *Il Saggiatore* in which this extraordinary prejudice is stated:

> I do not believe that external bodies, in order to excite in us tastes, odors, and sounds, need anything other than size, figure, number, or slow or rapid movements; and I judge that if the ears, the tongue, and the nostrils were taken away, the figure, the numbers, and the motion would indeed remain, but not the odors nor the tastes nor the sounds, which, without the living animal, I do not believe are anything else than names, just as tickling is precisely nothing but a name if the armpit and the nasal membrane be removed . . .[13]

It is remarkable that the question of the status of the "objective" qualities of things, were the *eyes* to be removed, never arose for Galileo.

In due course the unquantifiable, nonvisual aspects of our experience became known as "secondary" qualities, for they were regarded as our subjective interpretation of intrinsically nonsensory stimuli. In contrast, the "primary" qualities comprised such measurable and hence "objectively real" aspects of our experience as a body's extension in space, position, and motion.[14] Ironically, while the affect of this distinction was to give precedence to the visual world, it sadly impoverished it at the same time, for our perception of color was also considered suspect, and its status relegated to that of a secondary quality. In the new scientific worldview, real reality would reveal itself only to the single, color-blind, quantifying eye (see fig.1.7).[15]

Fig. 1.7. Portrait of Anthony van Leeuwenhoek (1680), the Dutch merchant who developed the single-lens microscope.

To this day, the primary-secondary quality distinction underpins the scientific way of coming to know the world. Quantification is the key to exact, objective knowledge. The apotheosis of the color-blind eye has had its repercussions deep into our culture as a whole. We are in bondage to the visual interpretation of reality. It has become a modern need that our experience of the world, from when we wake up in the morning to when we go to sleep at night, be illumined either by natural or by artificial light. Waking consciousness has become equated in our minds with seeing, for sight is the guarantor of the nonsymbolic, surface-reality that our secular culture assumes to be all there is. If we wake in the middle of the night, disturbed by a dream or a strange noise, our first action is to turn on the light, for we know that ghosts and the creatures of the imagination cannot survive in well-lit rooms. But it is not possible in well-lit rooms for conversations to attain the depth of mood they attain by twilight, candlelight, or darkness. Stories, fantasy, drama, music, and dance all shun "good" lighting conditions. There are, indeed a vast range of human activities that flourish only when the light is positively bad! When the light is dimmed, when the surfaces of things lose their sharp definitions, then the imagination awakens.

But we have all become, in our rigorously illumined world, the victims of Descartes' reduction of real reality to that which is "clear and distinct." The depth-dimension has been displaced—we have come to accept that it is, after all, only subjective, only a projection, an illusion, which *we* conjure up but which has no objective status. It has become the privilege of the single-eyed mentality, itself "enlarged" by the vari-

Fig. 1.8. Not a telescope but a compound microscope developed
by Descartes. The scientist is observing the object Z, which is illumined
by light collected by the large parabolic mirror C.

ous instruments, which magnify or augment the faculty of sight, to arbitrate between what is real and what is—to use the modern visual metaphor—but illusory (see fig. 1.8).

## REHABILITATING THE EAR

My intention, though, is not to challenge sight as such; it is rather to question the exclusively visual model of reality. This model of reality has its source not in the eye as a sense organ, but in the *mind* that—because the exercise of the sense of sight corresponds most nearly to the inner functioning of the modern spectatorial consciousness—has raised this organ into the arbiter and judge of how the world really is. As spectators, we have come to relate to the world, in the phrase of Martin Buber, as to an "it" rather than a "thou." The world is comprised of things "out there," and between it and us there is a fundamental alienation. The reinstatement of listening rather than looking as the primary metaphor of our mental functions is, I believe, intimate to the recovery of the "I-Thou" relationship to the world.

The listening metaphor suggests stillness and a quiet attentiveness. Whereas the eye is constantly active and mobile, at the heart of the inner ear is the still spiral of the cochlea, which takes the sound waves into itself in order to convert them into meaningful impulses (fig. 1.9). If the seeing mind is incessantly busy, the listening mind is still; it is quietly attentive. It "attunes" itself to its objects in order to receive into itself what is most inward in them.

I suggest that the cultivation of the art of listening is one of the surest

*Fig. 1.9. Diagram of the eardrum (left) and cochlea (right). Vibrations from the eardrum are transmitted to the fluid within the cochlea, from which they are converted into nerve impulses.*

ways of developing a more open, responsive, and contemplative mode of relating to the world. But I am aware that the reader may well be thinking: "What about the other neglected senses? By concentrating on listening aren't you simply repeating the previous error of concentrating on the eye to the detriment of taste, smell, and touch?" My answer is that whereas the sense of sight tends to exclude the other senses, the sense of hearing is far more inclusive. The nonvisual encounter with the world naturally involves the faculties of touching, smelling, and tasting, even though the primary orientation is through listening. Listening welcomes the engagement of the other senses, whereas looking tends to thrust them to the periphery. The cultivation of the art of listening accordingly brings in its train a general reawakening of all the senses, including—ultimately—the eye. To the contemplative, listening mind, a new intensiveness is brought to the exercise of each of the senses, finally transforming the eye itself into the means of intensive "vision." To look "in the mode of listening" is to look beyond the surfaces of things into that which is expressed through them. In place of merely noting the external appearances, the listening mind's eye attunes itself to the interior dimensions of reality, "inwardly reading" that which is concealed from the viewpoint of the detached onlooker. From being a spectator of the world, even the eye is at last transformed into an organ of participation.

*Fig. 1.10. All the senses are engaged by the "listening mind."* Fool and Flower *by Cecil Collins, 1947.*

# 2

## THE HEART OF THE LILY

I question not my corporeal or vegetative eye any more
than I would question a window concerning sight. I
look through it and not with it.

WILLIAM BLAKE, "A VISION OF THE LAST JUDGMENT"

*This, and the next, essay arose out of a lecture given for the Friends of the Centre, at the London Ecology Centre on February 17, 1993.[1] Both trace critical changes in the perception of the natural world from the cultures of antiquity to the present time. "The Heart of the Lily" focuses on our changing perception of the plant world, contrasting the ancient awareness of the lily as bearer of symbolic meaning with the modern scientific awareness of the lily as no more than the physical organism whose structure is determined by its specific DNA. It asks the question: Which of these two modes of perception reaches the lily's true nature?*

## THE DEPICTION OF PLANTS
## IN THE MIDDLE AGES

This essay is concerned with our perceptions: with our modern perceptions, as compared with the perceptions of people who lived in medieval and ancient times. And as much with what we *don't* perceive that they did perceive, as it is with what we do perceive that they did not perceive.

Human perceptions have shifted over the ages, and it is virtually inevitable that any discussion of the subject will involve the consideration of nonperceptions as much as perceptions. For what is not perceived is not necessarily imperceptible. One mode of perceiving may simply fail to notice a certain type of reality, which is perceptible to another, different mode of perceiving. I have chosen to focus on the perception of the lily in cultures separated from each other by long intervals of time, in order to clarify the questions and challenges that the whole subject of human perception raises. There are many other examples of plants, animals, or landscape features, which could be focused on in a similar way.

I will begin by making some preliminary observations about the portrayal of plants in herbals from the late medieval period, when botanical illustration became more common. They show, I think, something of the relationship to nature that existed at that time—both how plants were represented and, by implication, how the perceiving mind saw them.

One of the interesting things about medieval herbals is that where one finds illustrations, usually augmenting a verbal description, they are for the most part rather vague and not very accurate. In fig. 2.1, for instance,

*Fig. 2.1. Late fifteenth-century woodcut of ivy.*

we see a late fifteenth-century woodcut of some ivy. It consists of the simplest outline of the leaves, whose size is much too small when compared with the thick squat stems, which in turn bear little resemblance to actual ivy stems. Nevertheless, owing to the characteristic leaf-shape, we can just about recognize the plant depicted as being an ivy.

Fig. 2.2 shows a double page from an early sixteenth-century herbal. On the left *Eruca sativa* (rocket) is shown, and on the right an opium poppy. While the opium poppy is recognizable, mostly from its seedpod, the *Eruca sativa* does not look faintly like an *Eruca sativa*. It is hard to avoid the impression that the artist had never seen an *Eruca sativa* before and was simply creating a plant form from his imagination. In these medieval herbals, it seems it was not a priority to make accurate representations.

Often one finds in herbals of this period, depictions of plants that are half-fanciful. The mandrake shown in fig. 2.3 is, through force of

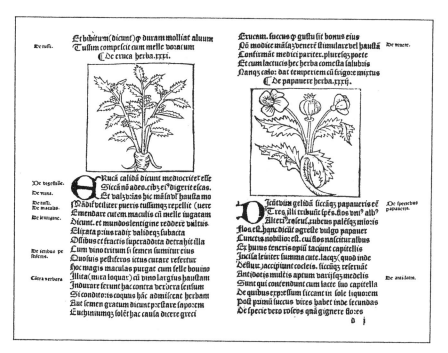

*Fig. 2.2. Early sixteenth-century herbal showing rocket (left) and opium poppy (right).*

convention and mental habit, always portrayed in a manner similar to this one, with anthropomorphic roots. So strong was this "perception" of the anthropomorphic roots of the mandrake that it continued through to the eighteenth century as the standard way of portraying the mandrake. It is as if people simply had come to see the mandrake in this way—so much so that it would have been unrecognizable in an herbal if its roots were depicted as normal roots. The other plants in this illustration consist of a vine to the right of the mandrake, a clover beneath the vine, and to the left of the clover an as yet unidentified plant that, we may presume, was the creation of the artist.

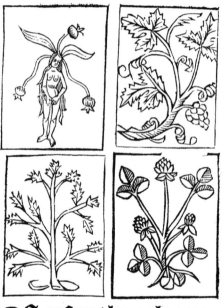

*Fig. 2.3. Mandrake (top left) and other plants. From a sixteenth-century herbal.*

The early sixteenth-century woodcut of a lime tree (fig. 2.4) comes from a botanical work entitled *De Stirpium* ("Of Plants"), which includes descriptions of plants and where to find them. Here the artist evidently feels that in order to really show the lime tree, one has to show what goes on underneath it and around it. A lime tree on its own, isolated from its social context, would only be half the tree it really is, for its reality extends beyond its physical form into the social sphere.

Throughout this period of the fifteenth and early sixteenth centuries, a quite different intention from that of a modern botanical illustrator lies behind these portrayals of plants. The intention is not to show the plant in all its physical details. It is as if its actual physical form was not the most important thing about it. In each case one senses that the depiction of the physical form was but a secondary consideration, and everyone concerned was content with an approximation, which in many cases bore virtually no resemblance to the actual plant. Or else its portrayal was overwhelmed by human associations—the mandrake's roots remolded into a human guise, or the lime tree set firmly into a human context.

If we ask why it is that botanical illustrators of this period paid so little attention to accuracy, the answer must be that not only they, but also those who wrote and those who used the books, regarded other aspects of the plant as more important than its precise physical details. Indeed, in medieval writings on plants, what was invariably the focus of attention was a plant's specific "virtue"—its healing power, which derived

*Fig. 2.4. Early sixteenth-century woodcut of a lime tree.*

from, or was an expression of, its spiritual essence. At this period in time, before the scientific mentality had taken root, the outward form of the plant served only to direct one's gaze toward its inner virtue. The whole focus of the medieval mind was less on precise observation of the physical form as such, than on what the physical form signified—namely a realm of inner qualities, essences, and spiritual principles, which often linked a plant with a certain heavenly body and also a specific human organ or bodily function, through a system of qualitative correspondences.

The degree of importance placed on these suprasensible qualities meant that, paradoxically, by far the most accurate depictions of plants are to be found not in the herbals or botanical textbooks, but in religious pictures, whose main subject was not actually the plant at all. In *The Garden Of Paradise* (fig. 2.5)—an early fifteenth-century work by an anonymous Master of the Middle Rhine—one finds accurate representations of plants, but the reason why they are portrayed is to illustrate the spiritual qualities or virtues of the Virgin, who dominates the

*Fig. 2.5.* The Garden of Paradise *by an unknown Master of the Middle Rhine, ca. 1420.*

paradisiacal garden. The plants, that is, are not shown for themselves but as metaphors carrying a transcendent meaning. The red rose on the left symbolizes divine love; the cherry tree near to it evokes the joys of heaven, for which the Virgin is the intercessor. The tripartite leaves of the strawberries in the center of the picture were thought of in the Middle Ages as echoing the Holy Trinity, and its fruits were the reward of the righteous. The blue iris and, above all, the white Madonna lily, were plants deeply associated with the Virgin Mary.[2] Precisely where we find plants accurately depicted, we encounter the paradox that they are only depicted with such care because they were seen as pointing beyond themselves to specific spiritual qualities. The environment in which they grow is thus one frequented by angels and saints (fig. 2.6).

*Fig. 2.6.* The Garden of Paradise *(detail).*

## THE SCIENTIFIC PERCEPTION OF THE LILY

It is only in the Renaissance that it becomes legitimate to make accurate studies of plants completely separated from their religious and symbolic context. The ideal of representing a plant simply as it is, stripped of all human and symbolic associations and, as it were, laid bare before the objective eye of the detached observer, is essentially that of the scientific spirit introduced into art. With it comes a new intensity of vision that

*Fig. 2.7. Leonardo da Vinci's study of a lily.*

injects the plant with life, as never before. One can see this in the work of Dürer, and one can experience it especially vividly in Leonardo's study of a lily (fig. 2.7). Here the lily speaks out at last with its own voice. It is neither merely a sketch gesturing toward the actual form the lily has, nor is the relative full-bodiedness with which it is represented overlaid with symbolic connotations. The artist has succeeded in simply revealing the plant as it is, in all its resplendent natural beauty.

Leonardo's lily was executed in about 1505, at the turn of the century. The scientific and artistic revolution soon began to affect the herbals and medical and botanical works. By the mid-sixteenth century, artists were employed specifically to depict plants for purposes of identification. For the rising medical establishment, increasingly brought up and trained in the city, accurate representations of plants, freed from the mesh of associated imagery, were essential.[3] The new scientific spirit coincided with the new spirit of Renaissance art. The artists of the time were as eager to portray the natural world according to the ideal of objectivity as the scientists were to investigate it.[4]

Fig. 2.8 shows Renaissance artist's drawing flowers in a vase. As much as the plants have been pulled out of the physical soil, they have

*Fig. 2.8. Artists prepare an illustration for a
medical textbook, mid-sixteenth century.*

also been pulled out of the psychological and conceptual soil of the
Middle Ages. The artists are in fact illustrating Fuch's *De Historia
Stirpium* (1542). Here the artist is essentially a scientific observer. The
work has been commissioned by the medical establishment, desirous of
accurate representations for the new herbals. It is just one of a whole
spate of botanical works and herbals that appeared toward the middle
of the sixteenth century, employing artists trained in the "scientific"
style of drawing.

This coincidence of the artistic and scientific projects was, however,
to prove short lived. The scientific spirit was soon to grow dissatisfied
with the limitations of the unaided human senses. In order to see what
is really there, it was felt that one must supplement the senses—especially the eye—with special instruments. One must look more closely;
one must perceive details, which are too fine for the unaided eye to
pick up. In the early seventeenth century Descartes was to develop the
rather cumbersome compound microscope (chapter one, fig. 1.8), which
was later succeeded by the much more compact single-lens microscope
shown in fig. 2.9. This was able to magnify up to 300 times and was
used to great effect by van Leeuwenhoek in Holland toward the end of
the seventeenth century.

The portrait of van Leeuwenhoek in fig. 2.10 shows him reclining
in his chair, facing a window, and peering through the microscope that

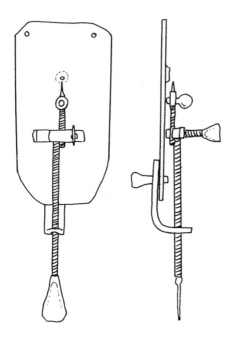

Fig. 2.9. The compact single-
lens microscope. Replica of
van Leeuwenhoek's single-lens
microscope.

he holds to his eye. The object, placed on top of a screw in front of the
lens, is now not even in a vase, but is totally displaced from any sup-
portive environment. It has been torn out of its natural context—save,
of course, for the sunlight necessary to illumine it for the benefit of the
eye of the scientific observer.

Fig. 2.10. Van Leeuwenhoek
looks through a single-lens
microscope.

Through the use of this new instrument, it was not only the senses that were augmented—especially the sense of sight—but human thought processes also took a new turn. Scientific thinking had already been turning in this new direction for some time, but here there was— or at least there *seemed* to be—confirmation that the new direction was right. The development of the microscope gave real weight to the idea that the more minutely one looks at things, the closer one gets to their real nature. Is it not evident that the magnified section through a plant stem, shown in fig. 2.11, reveals more of its true nature than simple, unaided observation could ever discover? Francis Bacon had given expression to this thought a century earlier when he wrote: "Without dissecting and anatomizing the world, we cannot find a real model of the world in our understanding."[5]

The emphasis of this sentence is on the word "real." In the medieval worldview, the real model of any object or creature was thought of as a spiritual archetype, which existed within the physical form as the latter's indwelling essence. No amount of dissecting and anatomizing, let alone magnifying, would reveal it, for the essence was apprehended by a spiritual faculty in the human soul, which the philosophers and theologians referred to as the higher intellect (*intellectus*). The *intellectus* was able to see into the inner nature of things, whereas the pragmatic, analyzing mind (*ratio*) remained tied to externalities.[6] But now the suprasensible world of spiritual essences was overshadowed by the discovery of a hitherto subsensible world of microscopic structures, cells, and organisms suddenly brought within the range of sense-perception.

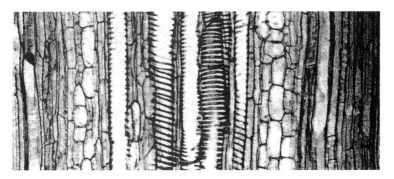

*Fig. 2.11. Magnified longitudinal section through a plant stem.*

Was not this the underlying reality that determines the structure of the forms that we meet in daily life? Could one not *see* that the basis of life was cellular, not spiritual? It was as if the idea of "intellectual insight" was rendered obsolete by the microscope. The vision of the *intellectus* was superseded by the vision of the instrument-aided eye.

As much as Leeuwenhoek's microscope revolutionized the perception of objects near at hand, so the telescope revolutionized the perception of distant objects. More than one hundred years before Leeuwenhoek, Galileo, in directing his telescope toward the heavens, had similarly introduced a different model of the real into human thinking about the planets and stars. The argument that this instrument was not appropriate for perceiving the real nature of the heavenly bodies—which in the old conception were thought of primarily in terms of their spiritual rather than their physical qualities—could not maintain itself in the face of what was being revealed to the "improved" vision of the telescope-wielding astronomer.[7] Because of its relationship to the light, the eye had been regarded by Greek philosophers as the sense organ most akin to the interior spiritual faculty of "intellectual" insight. But now it became inextricably linked to the analytical mind investigating the material substrata of the world.

This investigative pursuit led to the development of ever more refined and powerful instruments. It would be unjust to suggest that this development was not still intimately connected with a desire to see into the "real nature" of things. The driving force behind it was that such a vision was thought to be literally possible with the instrument-aided eye, because the real nature of things had been metaphysically relocated from the suprasensible to the sub—or potentially—sensible realm.

Interestingly, the more this realm was penetrated, the further one actually traveled from the realm of light. Hence, by the twentieth century, the electron microscope (fig. 2.12) would use an electron beam where an ordinary microscope used light to illumine an object, with electromagnets in place of glass lenses. The result was an ability to magnify things (necessarily colorless) to the order of nearly half a million times their actual size. The electron microscope, however, requires its

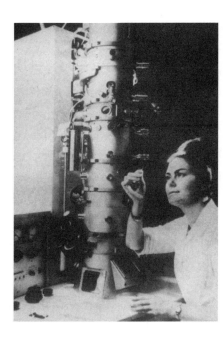

*Fig. 2.12. Electron microscope and its operator, ca. 1970.*

material to be examined in a vacuum, and hence has the singular draw-back of only being able to magnify organisms whose life is extinguished in the very process of their magnification.

## THE FALLACY OF MISPLACED CONCRETENESS

Let us return now to the lily of which, as we have seen, Leonardo produced such a vivid study. I have suggested that Leonardo's intention was to allow the lily to reveal itself in such a way that its essence would speak in and through his portrait of it. If we try to express the thought that was guiding Leonardo, we might put it like this: it is possible for the artist, through an accurate and loving observation of the physical form of the plant, to represent its unique quality, to portray not only what it is but also *that which makes it* what it is. Leonardo was still medieval enough to want to focus on spiritual qualities, but he was sufficiently modern to want to locate these nowhere other than in the physical plant in front of his eyes.

Now according to the modern scientific way of thinking, what makes a plant have the qualities that it does have is not some inwardly abiding spiritual essence, but a physically isolable substance within the cell: namely its DNA. In fig. 2.13, we see the chromosomes that contain the DNA of a lily. The lily's DNA carries the genetic information that underpins its cellular structure. The illustration shows lily chromosomes magnified one thousand times.

From the modern scientific viewpoint, we are here looking in the direction of the "physical essence" of the lily—toward the genes that make it have the recognizable form that it has. Were the genetic information contained in these chromosomes to be altered, the observable characteristics of the lily would also be altered.

We are looking, then, at a lily—and from the scientific viewpoint we are looking toward that which determines the outwardly visible form, which the artist portrays. And yet the lily has vanished before our eyes. Nevertheless, were we to magnify yet further—beyond even the range of electron microscopes into the atomic structure of the DNA molecules—we would then reach the genetic code, which, according to the scientific view, *determines* whether the lily be a tiger lily or a Madonna lily: or even a different species of plant altogether.

But what we see is colorless and scentless. It does not resemble a plant, let alone any specific type of plant. How can we regard this as a perception that brings us closer to the essential nature of the lily than Leonardo's drawing? Indeed, isn't to do so but to fall into the trap, which the British philosopher A. N. Whitehead termed "the fallacy of misplaced concreteness"? Namely, to describe an abstracted fragment of

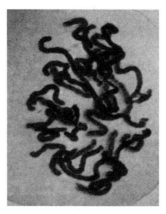

*Fig. 2.13. Lily chromosomes in the first stage of mitosis, magnified approximately one thousand times.*

the whole organism as if it were more concrete, more real, more "ultimate" than the whole of which it is a part?[8]

If it was a weakness of the medieval mentality to pay too little attention to the world of physical forms, projecting their minds beyond them toward the transcendent world of spiritual archetypes, then has it not been a weakness of the scientific mentality to place so much importance on the physical that it completely misses any perception of the spiritual? What can be perceived through a microscope is—though it be ever so minute—but an exterior aspect of an object, for the very means by which it is approached ensures that perceiver and perceived are mutually external to each other. For such a mentality, to speak of the "inner qualities" of a lily would be meaningless, unless this "inner" were conceived only in terms of the very small, which is accessible to microscopic examination. But evidently certain nonmicroscopic "inner" qualities radiate out from Leonardo's lily. Did he not perceive something imperceptible to the microscopic observer? And do we not catch a glimpse of this again as we look at his picture?

But then, perhaps we should ask: did Leonardo go far enough toward a perception of the spiritual qualities of the lily? The medieval awareness was, after all, far more self-consciously directed toward this inner realm. Perhaps they would have seen Leonardo's lily as being as much the product of a *reduced* perception of the lily's essence as the microscopic image of the lily's chromosomes appears in comparison with Leonardo's drawing. For Leonardo deliberately stripped away all the symbolic, religious, and ethical associations, which, in the Middle Ages, were interwoven with people's perception of lilies.

## THE LILY AS EPIPHANY

Fig. 2.14 shows St. Catherine of Siena holding the Madonna lily. Throughout the medieval period, the Madonna lily was inseparably linked in people's minds to the Virgin Mary. So much so that there was no need to represent the Virgin Mary with the lily—the lily alone acted as her representative. In this picture the lily therefore conveys the Virgin's presence, and the fact that the saint carries it indicates her deep affinity with the

*Fig. 2.14. St. Catherine of Siena holding a Madonna lily.*

Virgin. Perhaps the lily in this picture tells us that the saint has become an image of all the qualities that it symbolizes, each one an aspect of the Virgin. Its straight stalk, her godly mind; its slightly pendulous leaves, her humility; its white petals, her virginal purity; its golden anthers, her radiant soul; its fragrance, the fragrance of divine love, and so on.[9]

Whence come all these associations? Are they totally arbitrary or could it be that, after all, the lily is a rather special plant that really does suggest, or even expresses, certain spiritual qualities? And if they are not immediately suggested to us, could that be a result of *our insensitivity* rather than our superior objectivity? Where, in fact, does a plant begin and end? Where should we place its boundaries? Doesn't each plant have qualities of soul that its outward form does indeed reflect? And isn't the onus on us to attend to these qualities with no less diligence than we, in our scientific age, have attended to its physical attributes? Suppose that the plant does not simply *symbolize* the Virgin, but actually *is* the Virgin. Suppose that in each lily we meet, there is the opportunity to experience the *presence* of the Virgin Mary. The thought is no more difficult than the identification of the sacramental bread and wine with Christ's body and blood.

Now this mode of thinking is by no means restricted to the medi-

*Fig. 2.15. Lily design from the "Villa of the Lilies," Amnissos, Crete.*

eval mind. Its origins go much further back in time. And in the case of the Madonna lily, which was so significant for the medieval mind, we discover that the lily had a comparable significance in a culture three thousand years prior to that of the Middle Ages.

In ancient Crete, one finds that the Madonna lily was often portrayed. It was evidently a much-venerated plant. In fig. 2.15 we see a fresco of the lily, shown here with three stalks—a common way of representing it. In the Minoan culture, the lily was considered sacred to the goddess Britomartis, the "sweet virgin." She was the chaste huntress whom the Greeks called Artemis, and whom the Romans would identify with Diana.[10]

It is likely that part of the celebration of the cult of Britomartis involved an ecstatic dance among lilies, a dance that also included the handling of snakes.[11] This can be seen in fig. 2.16, which is an enlarged image originally engraved on a gold ring, found near Knossos. Looking more closely, one can see how the dance brings about a visionary experience of the virgin goddess, who appears out of the sky, top right. There is something, then, about lilies that may indeed point to a deeper level of human experience of the divine. In ancient Minoan culture, anyway, the ecstatic vision of the goddess would seem to be linked to

*Fig. 2.16. Women and lilies dancing. Engraved gold ring, Crete.*

the lily. And we should be clear that this is less a question of symbolic connotation than one involving a definite experience.

In Crete, lilies were very often associated with griffins—animals that have never existed physically, since they are half lion and half eagle (fig. 2.17). Nevertheless, it was possible to encounter a griffin in certain states of consciousness. This is why they featured in ancient Minoan art. They were beings that could be experienced and thus represented, but one did not experience them in the ordinary, sense-based state of consciousness. The griffin combines in itself the strength and courage

*Fig. 2.17. Griffin and lilies. Wall painting, Knossos.*

of the lion with the vision and capacity for ascent that characterizes the eagle. It appeared to people either as a frightening, demonic monster, or as a benevolent ally, depending on their own preparedness to undergo the transformation of consciousness implicit in the mystical ascent.

Fig. 2.18 shows this ascent. A woman devotee of the goddess flies up with a griffin. No separate lily is present here, but could it be that the woman herself has been transformed into a lily, the flower, stem, and leaves of which apparently compose most of her body? While it is difficult to tell exactly what is being represented on this small gold ring, it is unlikely that in the Minoan mind such ecstatic flights were *not* associated with lilies. For alongside the griffin, the lily was instrumental in the triggering of this experience. It facilitated it in some way. And so—whether represented or not—it forms the background context of the mystical flight.

*Fig. 2.18. Woman flies with griffin. Gold ring, Crete.*

But it is not unrepresented in the same sense as the microscopist's vision of the lily's abstracted chromosomes renders the lily itself as an unrepresented context of his narrowed perception. Here, in the Minoan illustration, we recognize a different order of experience; it is an order of experience that belongs entirely to the "soul-side" of the lily, into which the devotee flies. Here is an experience that transcends all reference to the outwardly perceptible lily, as the woman travels into spiritual depths that constitute or are constituted by the aura of the great virgin goddess. If we say that in Minoan Crete the lily was sacred to the goddess, we merely use a formula. We come nearer to the truth if we say that the lily was a gateway through which the devotee might pass in order to enter the divine energy-field of the goddess.

## THE HEART OF THE LILY

The perception of lilies is no simple matter. Not only are there a variety of different ways in which a lily can be perceived, but there are also different *degrees* of perception, defined by the extent to which one participates in the spiritual qualities of which the external form of the lily is an expression. To speak in terms of participation is to imply the possibility of the lily (and by no means only the lily) constituting a threshold that, once crossed, carries one into an interior spiritual world.

It may be objected, of course, that such an interior world is simply internal to the perceiver, and hence is purely subjective. But in fact the relationship could as well be the reverse. For in order that the perceiving consciousness genuinely experience the spiritual qualities of the object perceived, it is necessary that it—the perceiving consciousness— *be interior to the object perceived,* not the other way around. Such an "entering into" objects, in the spiritual sense of a participative or unitive experience, represents the other pole to the exteriorizing and objectifying mode of perception practiced by the analytical scientist.

Ultimately, the perception of lilies is a question concerning our relationship to our own cognitive and experiential powers. In recent centuries, these powers have been developed in the direction of ever more minute and exact perceptions of the physical aspect of nature. Such perceptions produce a cognitive relationship that is rich in facts, but poor in meaning. This poverty of meaning, intrinsic to modern science, is due to its methodological exclusion of any form of participation in the inner, spiritual qualities that lie beyond the self-imposed boundaries of strictly "scientific" cognition. But these boundaries do not need to confine us. We have the freedom to cross them, and in so doing to arrive at a very different kind of knowing, in which the perceiver travels into the interior of the perceived. This interior realm is ultimately transcendent of an individual's subjectivity—and indeed of the relative predispositions of a given culture. It is rather the divine ground where subject and object meet. And surely it is here, if anywhere, that we reach the heart of the lily.

3

## THE SOUL OF
## THE WEATHER

*This essay, like the previous one, traces critical changes in the perception of the natural world from the cultures of antiquity to the present time. The Soul of the Weather[1] focuses on our changing relationship to the weather, contrasting the ancient awareness of the weather as animated and expressive of divine energies, with the modern scientific approach to the weather through meteorology. Once again, we are presented with the question: Which of the two consciousnesses of the weather brings us closer to its true nature?*

### AN EPISTEMOLOGICAL PRELUDE

In mythologies from all parts of the world, the weather has always held an important place. The winds invariably are regarded as daemonic beings with distinctive personalities and attributes. Rain and storm, thunder, lightning, drought, and sunshine are all seen as manifestations of spiritual agencies. Despite cultural variations of conception and representation, there is a remarkable extent of agreement in principle that the atmosphere as a whole, as well as specific atmospheric phenomena, are to be understood as animated or ensouled. The spirits of the atmosphere are divine beings, some greater, some lesser, in dignity and power.

Some enjoy spheres of authority extending over many other domains than simply the weather (such, for instance, as the great "thunder gods" of antiquity—Baal, Zeus, Jupiter, Thor) while others are restricted in the scope of their activity to meteorological phenomena alone (for example, the wind deities of ancient Greece). But in every case, the primary subject of interest is the deity or animating spirit of which the meteorological phenomenon is a manifestation, rather than simply the phenomenon considered in isolation from its animating cause.

At a certain stage in the historical process, the consciousness of Europe began to carve for itself a trajectory that would eventually lead to the almost total deanimation of nature and the denial of any notion of spirit connected with weather phenomena. But of all aspects of nature to succumb to the interpretative hegemony of anti-animistic science, the weather has proved to be one of the most resistant. Not only has it defied any attempts to control its course, but it has also displayed a mischievous relish in retaining a considerable degree of unpredictability. Furthermore, it continues to hold a place in people's imaginations as in some way personifiable, so that we still talk of the weather as being "good" or "bad," "fine" or "miserable"; just as we describe winds as "fierce," "biting," "soothing," or "refreshing," as if these too are as much conveyers of qualities of soul as they are merely external meteorological events.

Here, then, in our relationship to the weather, we are in our everyday discourse and in our spontaneous perceptions perhaps closer to our animistic ancestors than many of us would readily admit. Here is a potential meeting point, a potential area of mutual understanding and rapport, where the greater sensibility of people in ancient times toward the spiritual forces at work in nature may still find a certain responsiveness in us, even a sigh of recognition.

My intention, however, is not to belittle or disparage the methods of investigation employed by modern meteorology, nor the extraordinary results achieved by their means. It is, rather, to point out that there may also be other methods that lead to modes of perception no less valid. It is these other modes of perception that are the particular concern of this essay, and which I believe will increasingly demand our attention in the future. The act of perception is not simply a matter for the senses: it also involves the mind. The ancient perception of nature as animated with spiritual life can neither be verified nor falsified by a naive appeal to the senses. If what is regarded today as "factual" or "scientifically established" leaves out everything that to the ancient consciousness was important, even essential, to the phenomena under consideration, then are we to assert all the more vehemently that we are perceiving what is *really* there, and that the ancients simply filled their world with phantoms projected from their own unconscious? Or should we at least entertain the possibility that their perceptions were not only as valid, but perhaps deeper, more profound, than our own?

Aristotle defined the act of perception as involving the realization of two potentialities: on the one hand the potential of the perceiver, to perceive; on the other hand the potential of the perceived object, to be perceived.[2] Such a perspective suggests that there is a certain responsibility that accompanies the act of perception. Not only a responsibility to ourselves, to live and act from our fullest potential; but also a responsibility toward the world, that it be fully recognized by us and not, as it were, shortchanged by a reduced awareness of its complete reality. From our own experience as human beings in various situations, we know what it feels like "not to be perceived"—not to be heard, not to be understood, and so on—just as we know the sense of affirmation when we *are* heard and understood. Could it be that the world of the gods and nature spirits, for so long spurned and denied, might be similarly affected?

## THE WIND SPIRITS OF ANTIQUITY

Of all weather phenomena, the wind has been universally perceived as living closest to the boundary between the physical and the spiritual worlds. We need think only of the Greek word *pneuma* to at once encounter the ambiguity inherent in the ancient consciousness of the wind. *Pneuma* means "breath" or "breath of life" as much as it means "wind." The popular conception of the breath in ancient Greece was that it was the medium not only of life but also of soul. The *pneuma* was thought of as having psychic, or psychospiritual qualities, and hence there was an immediate sense of continuum between the psychospiritual "breath-soul" within the human being and the wind, similarly conceived as psychospiritually endowed. Hence the adjective *pneumatikos* can be translated equally as "of the wind" and as "of the spirit" while the adverb *pneumatikos* is translated quite unambiguously as "spiritually."

An almost identical set of associations can be discerned in the ancient Egyptian hieroglyph of the sail (fig. 3.1), which translates both as "sail" and also as that which fills the sail, namely "wind" or "breath." In The Book of the Dead, the sail is used explicitly to denote the "breath of life"—a nonphysical "breath" that underworld travelers sought to draw into themselves in order to live in the spiritual state. In chapter 56, the underworld traveler addresses a prayer to the high god Atum:

O Atum, give me the sweet breath, which is in your nostril.[3]

Such divine breath is the spiritual sustenance of the soul as it traverses the regions of the underworld. It is significant that wind deities were often imagined in the form of a ram, the hieroglyphic animal symbolizing the soul (*ba*). All four winds could take the form of rams or ram-headed human beings, though as we shall see, they also had other characteristic forms.[4]

*Fig. 3.1. Ani holds a sail, enabling him to breathe in the underworld.*

*Fig. 3.2. The south wind as a lioness-headed goddess.*

And here we can begin to appreciate the subtlety of the Egyptian apprehension of the distinctive qualities of the winds that blew across their land. These four winds conveyed the four cardinal qualities of spiritual influence that emanated from the gods, each wind bearing that emanation into the psychophysical organism of the human being. The east wind had the aspect of Ra-Horakhty, the young sun god who rises in the eastern sky each morning. It was his breath that was felt in the east wind. Hence this wind was portrayed as hawk-headed. From the west, there came the dry and burning wind from the Libyan desert, imaged as a cobra, perhaps after the goddess Renenutet. The south wind, fierce and at times pestilential, was perceived to be the daemonic manifestation of the goddess Sekhmet, and hence was depicted as a lioness or lioness-headed (fig. 3.2). By contrast, the northern wind, cool, refreshing, and life bringing, emanated from "the throat of Amon" and thus was depicted as a ram, or ram-headed, the ram being his symbolic animal (fig. 3.3). The winds, then, were each perceived as soul-laden, and these soul qualities in turn derived from specific deities. People breathed into themselves these soul qualities, and thus were their lives interwoven with the gods.

Whereas in ancient Egypt the gods were experienced as acting in and through the winds, in other ancient cultures the winds were perceived as more independent daemonic beings. The Mesopotamian demon of the southwest wind (fig. 3.4) is not depicted in the likeness of any god, but is clearly an entity in his own right, named Pazuzu.[5]

*Fig. 3.3. The north wind, depicted as a four-headed ram, or ram god.*

With legs ending in the talons of an eagle, and arms ending in lion's paws, we are reminded of the griffin archetype. But this daemon has the head of a human skeleton with staring eyes, and goat's horns. He also has four large wings and a scorpion's tail. The southwest wind comes from the deserts of Arabia, burning and ravaging everything in

*Fig. 3.4. Daemon of the southwest wind. Akkadian statuette.*

its path. Representations such as this were made to be hung in trees or in the windows of houses as a protection against the malevolent force of the wind. The idea was that, should any daemon be confronted by the horrific ugliness of its own form, it would turn in terror from it. For this reason, many images of daemons have come down to us from ancient Mesopotamia. By contrast with the daemonic southwest wind, the northerly storm-wind was considered for the most part benevolent, for the revitalizing showers that he brought.[6]

In ancient Greece, a host of different winds are identified by name, some beneficent, some malevolent. The two primary winds are from the south and from the north. The southern wind was associated with destruction and pestilence, as it was for both the Egyptians and the Mesopotamians. It could thus be pictured in the form of a Harpy, a feminine daemon always hungry for death and destruction.[7] In fig. 3.5, the Harpy drives before it various destructive creatures—a locust (a pest from the south), two birds of prey attacking a hare, and a vulture.

The north wind, cool and health giving, was brought to Greece by wind spirits called the *Boreadae*. These were pictured as winged men with rough beards (fig. 3.6). It is interesting that there is agreement between the Greeks and the Egyptians as to the gender of the north and south winds. In the imaging of the invisible, gender is one of the first attributes that leads to a characterization of the type of energy that one is dealing with.

*Fig. 3.5. Harpy, from a vase in the British Museum.*

*Fig. 3.6. Boreas, from the Tower of Winds, Athens.*

Forming images of the winds was an essential step toward engaging with them through prayer, sacrifice, or magical rite. In ancient Greece, the normal sacrifice to avert a malevolent wind was a black sheep, while a white sheep was considered appropriate to incur the favor of a beneficent wind.[8] Pausanias, writing in the second century AD, gives a vivid description of a ceremony in which a cock was sacrificed at Methana, in Troezen, to avert the evil influences of a wind called the Lips, which would otherwise dry up the young vine shoots.[9] But whatever the sacrificial animal, it is clear that in ancient times relationship to the wind was primarily a relationship to the powers within the winds. The winds were experienced as soul-beings, their "breath" evidence enough that they were animate. It was the different qualities of breath of the various winds that indicated their soul-qualities, and hence determined both the manner of their depiction and the type of action felt to be appropriate in dealing with them. Beyond this, there was a sense, especially acute in ancient Egypt, that the winds made tangible, or were the tangible expression of, qualities ultimately attributable to far higher divine agencies.

## ESOTERIC METEOROLOGY OF THE RENAISSANCE

Now this latter tradition of the winds as the relatively coarse manifestation of more sublime spiritual agencies, survived to some extent into the Middle Ages, Renaissance, and Early Modern periods. From the Middle Ages on, the winds were integrated into the system or correspondences between zodiacal signs, planets, seasons, elements, humors, and temperaments. With regard to the latter, the south wind corresponded to the sanguine temperament, the north wind to the melancholic, the west to the phlegmatic, and the east to the choleric.[10] These temperaments correspond, of course, to the winds of northern Europe, which have very different characters from the winds of southern Europe, the Middle East, and northern Africa.

Beyond this system of correspondences lay a more esoteric teaching concerning the governance of the winds by daemonic and archangelic beings. This teaching is most comprehensively formulated in Robert Fludd's *Medicina Catholica* and *Philosophia Sacra* in the early seventeenth century. Fig. 3.7 is from the *Medicina Catholica* (1629) and shows the four archangels Uriel, Gabriel, Raphael, and Michael standing at the four cardinal points—south, north, west, and east respectively—directing the four main winds, each one of which is held on a leash by its presiding daemon (depicted like an angel).

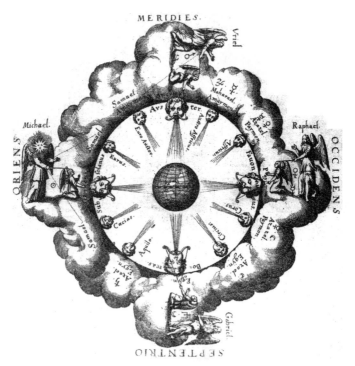

*Fig. 3.7. The four archangels and the twelve winds,*
*according to Robert Fludd.*

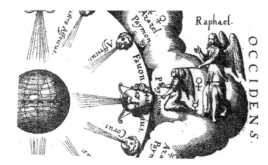

*Fig. 3.8. Detail of
Raphael, the west
wind, and its daemon.*

It can also be seen that each wind is under the influence of one or more planets. The detail (fig. 3.8) shows Raphael as the spiritual authority governing the west wind, which operates under the planetary influences of Venus and Mercury. The west wind is a daemonic being named Paymon, who blows from the southwest and northwest as Azazel.[11] The wind itself issues from a lesser spirit portrayed simply as a head whose mouth is tightly controlled by Paymon. It is given the name Favonius, the Latin equivalent of the Greek Zephyr.

This teaching belongs to the esoteric Rosicrucian tradition, and should be distinguished from the popular view of the winds in the mainstream culture of the period. We can form an idea of the latter from the fact that throughout the Middle Ages and Renaissance, through to the Early Modern period, wind spirits were usually depicted as simply bodiless heads, as if to suggest at one and the same time both the notion that the winds were animated "breaths" issuing from a veritable being, and that this being was nevertheless in itself without any intrinsic or substantial attributes. There was, in other words, a certain ambivalence in Christian Europe within the generally accepted animistic view of the winds. Very often, the idea of higher angelic agencies controlling and directing the winds was lost sight of altogether, and then the winds were regarded as daemonic and essentially chaotic powers, which had no place in the cosmic order. The fifteenth-century diagram of the universe shown in fig. 3.9 is not atypical in its location of the winds outside the cosmos, beyond even the sphere of God and the Elect. They fill the dark spaces of the unknown, their heads alarmingly big compared to that of God the Father.

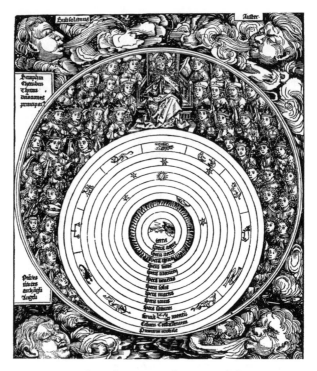

*Fig. 3.9. Fifteenth-century diagram of the universe
showing the winds in the four corners*

In fig. 3.10, the same truncated heads reappear juxtaposed with three of the four seasons. Here they blow within the earth's atmosphere, but their only distinctive qualities are the directions from which they blow. This sixteenth-century woodcut clearly illustrates the degree to which the animistic sensibility, which still existed at that time, could nevertheless become virtually emptied of any real spiritual insight. It is but a short step from this view of the winds to their being deprived of any claim to be treated as ensouled at all.

## MEASURING THE GODS

So long as the winds were regarded as ensouled, the most appropriate way of relating to them was with the respect and reverence due to a spiritual power. In ancient times, there was a profound sense that one was dealing with an entity, which has its own type of intelligence—

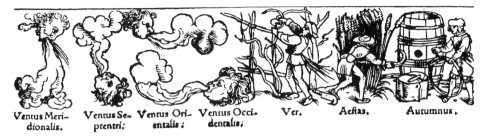

Ventus Meri-    Ventus Se-   Ventus Ori-   Ventus Occi-        Ver.        Aeftas.        Autumnus.
  dionalis.      ptentri:     entalis:      dentalis;

*Fig. 3.10. Sixteenth-century woodcut depicting the*
*four winds and three seasons.*

no doubt different from human intelligence, but nevertheless an entity
with a certain consciousness. This was the presupposition on the basis
of which supplications and offerings to the winds were made. It was
also the basis of magical rituals to divert or control them. The winds
were studied as much for their psychology as for their behavioral characteristics: the latter pointed toward the former, as indeed the former
pointed toward the higher divine agency to which each wind gave limited expression.

By the seventeenth century, such animistic presuppositions were
under attack in Europe, as the new mechanistic philosophy slowly but
surely began to grip the Western mind. It was in the seventeenth century that the new science of meteorology, very different from the con-
temporaneous flowering of "esoteric meteorology" in the writings of
Robert Fludd, was founded. The new science based itself upon instruments that could provide mathematical equivalents of uncalibrated
human sense-perceptions, thereby bringing into the arena of human
knowledge a hitherto unobtainable exactitude. It was an exactitude of
a quite specific type, which was restricted to precisely those qualities in
atmospheric phenomena that could be measured, leaving out of account
those that could not.

Robert Hooke's anemometer (after the Greek *anemos*—wind) was
just such an instrument. It was designed to translate the force with
which a wind blows, into a number. The anemometer is pictured in fig.
3.11. It consisted of a metal plate, fixed by an arm to the top of a pole,
but free to swing alongside a curved, graduated scale. The stronger the

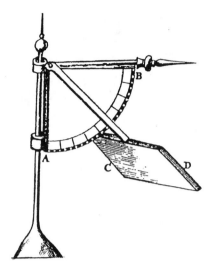

*Fig. 3.11. Robert Hooke's anemometer, ca. 1665.*

wind, the higher the plate traveled. As the plate was also free to swing around the pole, this instrument could also gauge the direction of the wind.

The simplicity of the anemometer should not lead us to overlook its deeper significance. It represents a totally different attitude toward the wind from that which prevailed in ancient times. The wind is here being approached as an object rather than a subject. The human subject must therefore distance himself from the wind, refuse to engage in a relationship in which the wind is regarded as a consciousness, and restrict himself to recording its measurable behavior alone.

Robert Hooke was responsible for designing another meteorological instrument in the 1660s: the wheel barometer (fig. 3.12). During the seventeenth century, there was intense interest in the atmosphere, and the idea that the atmosphere exerted differing degrees of pressure at different places, and at different times in the same place, was actually the result of the use of various measuring devices. Changes in atmospheric pressure are directly related to wind speed and direction, since the tendency is for air to flow from high-pressure to low-pressure masses. With the barometer, added to the anemometer, another key tool in the non-animistic understanding of the winds came into being. Hooke's wheel barometer was not the first, but its design illustrates well the mentality that was being brought to bear on the forging of the new relationship to the atmosphere. This new relationship was centered on the pointer reading, which was determined by the rising and falling levels of mercury in the tube. The fact that mercury is more sensitive to changes in atmospheric pressure than most human beings, posed a challenge to people's confidence in their normal sensations. The instrument seemed more reliable, more accurate, even more "knowing" than the instrumentless human observer. And yet, paradoxically, the information conveyed by the instrument amounted merely to the movement of a pointer. Could it be that the more human cognition limited itself to pointer readings, the more could actually be known?

Of all the numerous experiments conducted at the time, none symbolizes more aptly the new approach to the atmosphere than those conducted by von Guericke in Sweden. Fascinated by the idea of creating a vacuum, von Guericke went to considerable expense and effort to achieve this.[12] Having done so, it was then possible to weigh the air. Fig. 3.13 shows a small bronze sphere, from which the air has been systematically

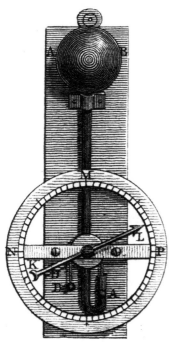

*Fig. 3.12. Robert Hooke's Wheel Barometer, 1665.*

*Fig. 3.13. The
experimental weighing
of air.*

pumped out, balanced by a weight. When the stopcock is turned, the
sphere suddenly fills with air and goes down. By adding weights on the
other side of the balance to restore equilibrium, the weight of the air
can be ascertained. This experimental weighing of the air epitomizes a
mentality for which nature has become devoid of spiritual content. The
air is regarded simply as a physical body that, like any other physical
body, has weight. In due course it would be decomposed into its chemical constituents like any other physical substance.

But we know that for the consciousness that characterized the
ancient world, the air was regarded as a spiritual being. I am referring
here not so much to the winds, as to the atmosphere as such. In ancient
Egypt the very atmosphere was a deity, whose name was Shu. This was
less a matter of religious dogma than a living perception of the nature
of the light-filled, life-giving region between the heavens and the earth.
There are few ancient cosmologies that do not give an important place
to this spiritual power. It is not here a question of the atmosphere being
"personified" as the air god, but rather a question of the atmosphere
being in a sense transparent, so that the indwelling deity becomes perceptible in and through it. By comparison, the modern, instrument-
dependent mentality was proceeding under the assumption that the

atmosphere is intrinsically opaque. Only on the basis of this assumption could such experiments as the weighing of the air be undertaken.

## THE DEMISE OF THE VISIONARY FACULTY

It is worth dwelling on the ancient perception of the atmosphere a little further. In most ancient cosmologies the atmosphere was regarded as having a supremely important function. It was regarded as holding apart heaven and earth. Most ancient creation myths posit a time "before" time—as we know it—when heaven and earth were united. There was no separation between the two. Conditions on earth were entirely assimilated into heavenly conditions. The creation, then, was really a separation, or splitting apart, of earth and heaven. As a result of this separation, a space was created into which plants could grow, birds could fly, and through which animals and humans could move. The stars appeared for the first time in the heavens above, and the earth came into existence as a separate entity below. The cosmos, in the sense of a hierarchically ordered whole, came into being. The god of the atmosphere was thus regarded as a creator god, the god who brought the cosmos into being.

In different cultures this role of the atmosphere-god as creative and ordering is pictured in different ways. In ancient Mesopotamia, the creation of the cosmos is the result of a tremendous battle between the Babylonian god Marduk (or Bel-Marduk) and the precosmic feminine deity Tiamat (fig. 3.14). Marduk goes to battle with various nature forces

*Fig. 3.14. Marduk and Tiamat, from the Temple of Ninurta, Numrud, Iraq.*

at his command—notably thunder, lightning, and the four winds. He defeats Tiamat by sending one of the winds into her mouth when she opens it to swallow him. The wind rages inside her belly and the cavity of her mouth so she cannot close it. It remains simply for Marduk to release a well-aimed arrow into Tiamat's open mouth to secure her defeat.[13]

Marduk was the Babylonian successor of an earlier Sumerian deity, Enlil, whose name means literally "Wind-Lord." Enlil was the prototype of many similar gods throughout the Middle East. He was primarily the deity apprehended in the atmosphere, responsible for life, fertility, and the growth of crops. His most striking manifestation, however, was in the thunderstorm. Here the atmosphere is convulsed into an awesome admixture of destructive rage and fecundating downpour. But it is the electric charge, seizing hold of the air, which brings the vision of the god. The tangible charge of electricity emanated directly from the divine presence, which threatens with each thunderclap and lightning bolt to break through the veil that protects human beings from too direct an encounter with divinity.

The atmosphere god, in the form of Adad, was pictured sometimes as riding upon a mighty chariot across the upper surface of the thunderclouds. Or more vividly, as riding on the back of a great bull—for the energy of the bull has the same elemental power that can be experienced in the storm. Adad, the storm god, continued to be recognized through both Babylonian periods. In Syria and Canaan he was known as Hadad, and usually syncretized with Baal, and hence referred to as Baal-Hadad. Fig. 3.15 shows Baal-Hadad riding on the back of his bull, squeezing lightning bolts in his clenched fists.

The bull, of course, is common to other gods of the atmosphere and fertility. In Greece, Zeus has a very similar status to Baal-Hadad as the god who fills the atmosphere, who manifests in fertilizing rain and electric storm, and who can also take the form of a bull. Farther north still, we meet a comparable figure in the god Thor, whose thunder chariot is pulled by wild goats.

Such visionary perceptions were married to the sense-perceptible phenomena, which we today experience, only we no longer have the

*Fig. 3.15. Baal-Hadad riding on his bull.*

visions. The phenomena have, as it were, fallen into the grip of the abstract mind. They have fallen from being the medium of the divine, to becoming locked into sheer physicality. The activity of divine agencies is not detectable by the instruments that furnish our highly sophisticated meteorological research stations. No matter how hard one looks into a computer screen, Baal-Hadad will not appear there. The meteorologist in fig. 3.16 is examining a mathematical model of the atmosphere in the

*Fig. 3.16. Meteorologist at his computer, at the Meteorological Office, Bracknell, ca. 1981.*

Meteorological Office at Bracknell in the early 1980s. The technologically advanced equipment upon which modern meteorology depends, requires for its successful utilization a mentality that functions in an entirely different mode from that of the visionary faculty. If our meteorologist did catch a glimpse of Baal-Hadad, he would swiftly find himself out of a job. But the fact is that he is not looking for Baal-Hadad on his screen, he is aiming for a very different kind of perception.

## THE WEATHER ABSTRACTED

The kind of perception that the modern meteorologist is aiming for has at its basis the presupposition that the weather is an object to be observed, examined, and analyzed, not a subject to be encountered with a tremor of awe. The weather is not a being, power, or divine agency, it is a system of physical processes, which can be measured and quantified. And hence its various elements can be isolated out from the whole and translated into a series of lines on graphs. In fig. 3.17, the top graph records the temperature, the second the relative humidity, the third the pressure, the fourth

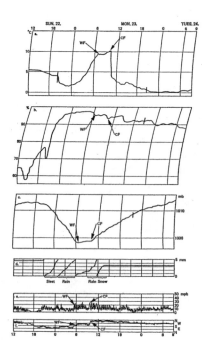

*Fig. 3.17. A frontal depression recorded on six graphs passes over Abingdon, Berkshire.*

the rainfall, the fifth the wind force, and at the bottom the wind direction. All these graphs relate to the single event of the passage of a frontal depression over Abingdon in Berkshire in 1956. But the language of the graph is such that it could as well be referring to a hospital patient's blood pressure, breathing, and pulse rate, a company's monthly sales and expense accounts, or the fluctuations of the population of haddock in the North Sea. The elements of the weather have been abstracted, quantified, and cast into a form that makes them amenable to a mentality, which demands, in the name of scientific rigor, that every subject be reduced to a similar set of statistics. These statistics can be universally transposed into the very simplest of images—the single black line linking numerical coordinates. The weather is thus rendered more intelligible. One might even argue that it is perceived more clearly. And yet, what sort of a perception is this? There the weather is, spread out before the analyst's gaze, and yet we could as well be looking at haddock.

Perhaps we see it better in fig. 3.18. The frontal depression can be observed in the center of the picture, with its familiar spiral shape. Surely now, from the vantage point of the satellite five hundred miles above it, our perception of the depression is not only restored but augmented.

Indeed, we can take an even more spectacular vantage point from twenty-three thousand miles above the earth, and see in a single glance

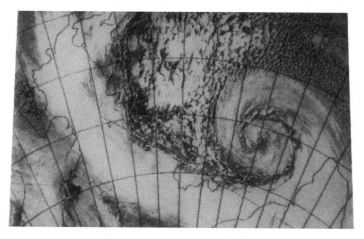

*Fig. 3.18. Satellite photograph of a frontal depression*
*approaching the west of England.*

a host of weather systems (fig. 3.19). Not only that, but we can cor-
relate the photographic image with an accurate map, such as the one
in fig. 3.20, in which the contours of high and low pressure zones are
charted. Or, if we are so inclined, we can select from a range of computerized images, which offer us, for example, infrared pictures of weather
systems, colored so as to highlight their temperature structure; radar
echoes of rainfall to which false color can be added, so as to give a visual

*Fig. 3.19. Satellite image of
global weather conditions.*

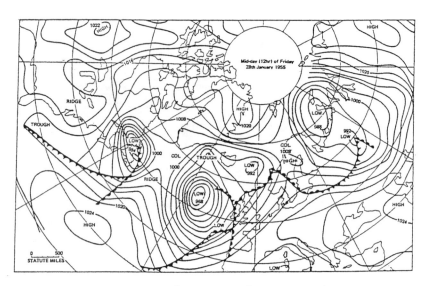

*Fig. 3.20. Northern Hemisphere synoptic chart.*

impression of differing rainfall intensities; or a computer rendering of cloud systems as viewed from a satellite and mathematically resolved into zonal sections (fig. 3.21).

One cannot but marvel. And it would be churlish to deny that there is something impressive and brilliant in these renditions of the weather into satellite images or computer displays. It is, nevertheless, important to pose a question. This question arises from the fact that not one of the last five illustrations could be described as truly corresponding to our lived experience of the weather. The key factor—what human beings actually experience—is regarded by modern scientific meteorology as of far less value and significance than the information produced by the wonderful array of scientific instruments presently serving the thought processes of meteorologists. It has to be asked: how do we assess the relative cognitive value of the experience of a man or woman walking through a wood at dusk in a rainstorm, brushed by wet leaves, smelling the wet earth, and hearing the sound of thunder rumbling in the distance, sensing with some excitement the almost tangible thrill of electricity in the air, and knowing that at any moment they might be dazzled by a lightning

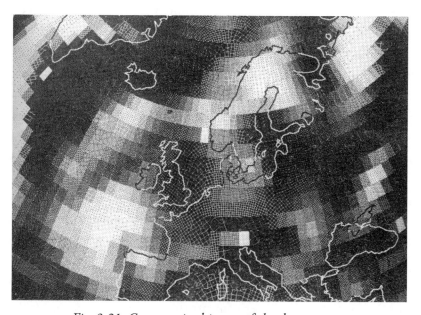

*Fig. 3.21. Computerized image of cloud systems over the Atlantic and Europe.*

flash—how do we assess the cognitive value of this, as compared to, for example (and I choose the least abstract) a satellite picture of the same event viewed from five hundred miles above it?

The satellite image may move us emotionally, and it may also provide us with a means of understanding the behavior of weather systems on a global scale. But it does not arise from the experience of being *in* the weather. It is, by definition, a view from the outside. And for that reason it lacks the quality of "encounter," which the human beings down below are experiencing. The same thing applies even more to a computerized image of rainfall intensity derived from radar echo, or an infrared image of temperature variations, or an isobar map, and so on. In each case the lived experience of human beings is not the basis of meteorological knowledge, and for that reason the latter is condemned to operate within certain self-prescribed limitations to which actual human experience is not, in fact, subject.

## RETURN TO EXPERIENCE

Marvelous as modern scientific meteorology is, it nevertheless seems that this science has become so divorced from living experience that the latter has been virtually excluded from the possibility of contributing anything valid to meteorological knowledge. And if scientific knowledge and living experience are thus divided, is there not a danger that on the one hand the science becomes a slave to the cognitive limitations built into the apparatus on which it depends, and on the other hand that human experience—excluded from the possibility of making any valid contribution to science—becomes steadily impoverished rather than enriched?

From a certain point of view, of course, our understanding of the weather is vastly enhanced by modern techniques. But it is only a certain type of understanding that, despite its undeniable breadth of scope, nevertheless precludes *experiential* depth. And this is precisely its weakness. For the more refinements that are made to meteorological equipment and instrumental aids, the more the perception of the meteorologist is circumscribed and delimited by the technology that intervenes between his or her awareness of the meteorological phenomenon and the phenomenon itself. Indeed, the primary phenomenon increasingly becomes the computer image, the statistic, the radar echo, rather than the weather to which they refer.

One of the things that can be said about the ancients' perception of the numinous activity of gods and spirits interpenetrating weather phenomena, is that this was integral to their experience, not added to it, nor abstracted from it, but absolutely integral to it. The ancient literature provides more than adequate testimony to this fact. The weather is time and again described as a numinous event involving these spiritual agencies. Such perceptions arose out of a heightened awareness of the sense-perceptible phenomena, and the heights or depths of this awareness depended on the degree to which a person was able to "enter into" the weather phenomena and apprehend their spiritual source.

The Aristotelian description of the act of knowing as a realization of two potentialities—one on the part of the knower to know, and one on the part of the thing known, to be known—gives us an open-ended framework in which it is assumed that there are differing degrees of knowledge. These degrees of knowledge arise in relation to the degree to which we realize our own latent experiential capacities. There is an implication here that there are different depths of experience possible to a human being, and these relative depths bear directly on the extent to which *what* is experienced reveals the fullness of its nature. It hardly need be said that this has little to do with the progressive refinement of our information technologies. What it has to do with is a fundamental recall to ourselves. Such recall to ourselves ultimately affects not only ourselves, but also the gods, angels, and nature spirits awaiting our recognition.

# 4

## THE REALITY THAT IS NOT THERE

*We all tend to subscribe to the common sense view of reality that for something to be real it has to be "somewhere." This, however, is a distinctively modern assumption, and in past times people thought very differently about the nature of what is real. In fact what is essentially "nowhere" was considered to be just as—if not more—real than what is "somewhere." This essay explores why it is important for us today to understand the reality that is "nowhere," and how we can begin to become aware of it.*

*The essay is based on a talk given for the Jupiter Trust in Oxford, on March 19, 2004, as a contribution to a lecture series on "The Presence of Other Worlds."*[1]

### LOCATIONAL SPACE

My aim is to question the "common sense" view of reality that we all tend to subscribe to, more as a collective reflex than as a considered standpoint: that for something to be real it has to be *somewhere*. That is to say, it has to be locatable. If we cannot say where a thing is, if we cannot locate it, then our culture tells us that we are quite justified in doubting whether it exists at all. Being locatable, of course includes not only being "out there" in space but also being locatable in a time framework: for a thing to exist, it must exist both in space and in time. This is perhaps one of the defining assumptions of modern culture: that if something cannot be located within the coordinates of space and time, we are entitled to doubt whether it has any existence whatsoever.

The assumption is, however, a distinctively modern one. People have not always felt like this regarding the nature of what is real. In previous times, symbolic, imaginative, moral, and spiritual factors were seen as equally, if not more, real than what is simply "out there." Today, however, these qualities tend to be regarded as subjective, while what is "really real" is what is physically locatable. This modern attitude is also the characteristically scientific attitude toward the world, which has led to the denial of metaphysical causes, agencies, and entities that people used to incorporate in their world picture. I am thinking here of spiritual archetypes, the Platonic Ideas or the Aristotelian "formal cause"— the *causa formalis* of medieval Scholastic philosophy. I am thinking also of gods, angels, nature-spirits, and so on that populated the premodern world. Modern science has set out not simply to restrict the parameters of its inquiry to physically locatable reality, it has also adopted the philosophical stance that what is physically locatable is the *only* reality there is. And this has now become a kind of collective reflex embedded in our predominately scientific culture.

This is not to deny that within certain areas of science—notably the spheres of subatomic physics and astrophysics—the boundaries of "locational" knowledge have been reached. And in these areas of the supremely small and the supremely large, the limitations of the purely locational way of thinking have had to be acknowledged. But in most other areas of mainstream science these limitations are scarcely questioned, and there has been a largely successful assault on any and every kind of reality that cannot be contained within the coordinates of space and time. In particular, the idea that human beings have a soul has come to be seen as the final stronghold of the out-dated, "premodern" mentality, to be relentlessly attacked, along with the idea that human consciousness is something different from physically locatable brain processes. Similarly, the idea that a person's character traits could be due to anything other than their genetic makeup or the influence of environmental factors is likewise seen as unscientific, and hence the target of repeated attack. It is important that we understand that within mainstream science there is a tremendous drive to apply the locational reality-principle to everything—to all phenomena of life, including consciousness and the human soul. And this reality-principle, with its assumption that something only exists when it has external location, does to a very large extent determine attitudes within contemporary culture.

I believe this assumption to be wrong. There are many areas of our experience in which it clearly fails to do justice to the fullness of what we are experiencing, which often—indeed normally—includes factors that are entirely "nonlocational." If we restrict ourselves to the view that in order for something to exist it has to be "out there" in locational space and time, then we will actually have to ignore a significant portion of reality taken as a whole. For reality as a whole includes both what is externally locatable and what is not locatable. There are aspects of reality that simply cannot be pinned down in external space or measurable time. Some things can exist and be real without having any physical location, without being "somewhere." Or, to put it more strongly, some things can exist and be real *despite the fact that they are nowhere.*

## THE KINGDOM WE DO NOT SEE

We don't realize that we live in the presence of mystery, and we don't realize it because we are so distracted, so fascinated, by the apparent "out-thereness" of everything. In the Gospel of Thomas, Jesus is reported as saying:

> The Kingdom of the Father is everywhere spread upon the earth,
> but people don't see it.[2]

The "Kingdom of the Father" that he refers to is the spiritual world that exists in a different dimension from the physical world and yet interpenetrates it at every point. There are three examples of this invisible but omnipresent "kingdom" that we meet in our everyday lives that I would like to consider.

My first example is something that we all experience every year in the cycle of the seasons. This is the disappearance of the plants from our gardens in the autumn. Where do they go? Where does the phlox go, the peony, the delphinium . . . ? Where does the poppy go, the lily, the nasturtium . . . ? In the case of the perennials, all that is left in winter are a few muddy roots or tubers, in the case of the annuals some tiny seeds. That is all that remains in physical, external space. The rest is gone—it is actually *nowhere.* But it is from this "nowhere" that the plants return in the spring, once more unfolding into locational space, once more taking on externally perceptible form. One of the reasons why it is such a joy to greet the plants again when they reappear in the spring or summer is precisely because they reappear miraculously from "nowhere."

The plants are nature's shamans, constantly passing out of "locational" space and then back into it again. They are travelers between worlds, repeatedly going through death and rebirth. They live as much in the invisible world as in the visible—in fact they spend a great deal more of the year unmanifest than manifest. In the overall cycle of their existence, they are more "nowhere" than they are "somewhere," and this is a very remarkable thing to contemplate!

My second example is again taken from our everyday experience—our experience of living within the diurnal cycle of day succeeding night, and night succeeding day. Every time someone goes to sleep, they pass out of locational space. Of course we see their body, just as we can see the tubers of the peony in winter, but their *soul* is no longer present to us. Despite the fact that their body is physically observable, the person who is asleep is essentially absent. For all we know, they may be dreaming that they are in the Sahara desert or trudging through the icy tundra of Greenland. When they wake, they may tell us exactly where they have been. Meanwhile, they were entirely unaware of what was occurring in the room where they were sleeping. They themselves were not present in any external location. They may have been doing extraordinary things in their inner world of dreams, things that seemed completely real to them, but these deeds and experiences of the dreamer are not real in the sense of occurring outwardly: the reality in which they occur is not the reality of external time or space.

Most of us remember only a tiny fraction of our dreams. Even those of us who make a point of trying to recall our dreams still only recall one or two each night. But then we do not spend the whole time that we are asleep dreaming. A good proportion of sleep is dreamless. Dreamless sleep, like dreaming, is something we all of us experience every night. If we ask where we are when we are in the state of dreamless sleep, the most accurate answer would be to say that we are not anywhere—we are, in other words, "nowhere." Here, then, is another remarkable fact to contemplate: we all of us, whether we remember it or not, have direct experience every night of being "nowhere."

My third example is something we will have direct experience of at the end of our lives, and during the course of our lives we will have indirect experience of it: this is the experience of dying. When someone dies we can feel that the person who was "there" has, like the sleeper, passed out of locational space and no longer has any existence in the external world of space and time. If we ask the question, "Where have they gone?" the answer that seems most appropriate is "inward"—inward to a kind of space that has no external location. Most of the great religious traditions regard the environment in which the dead find themselves as an inner environment. This environment is vividly described in Christian tradition in the literature and imagery of the three realms of Hell, Purgatory, and Heaven. In *Dante's Divine Comedy,* it is made clear that these after-life realms correspond to states of consciousness. As Rudolf Steiner has said, the environment of the dead is a soul environment in which one's inner world becomes one's "outer" world.[3] According to Jung, the only conceivable form of existence that the dead have is a psychic existence, because "the life of the psyche requires no space and time."[4]

If this is the case, and our existence is not simply snuffed out at the moment we exhale our last breath, then we can conceive of another truly remarkable fact. And that is that human beings actually have two very different modes of existence: one is incarnate in the physical body, living in external space; the other is discarnate, living in an interior and invisible "space." Whether or not we accept the idea of reincarnation, we are I think obliged to seriously consider the following implication: just as we spend a relatively large amount of our lives asleep, so we may spend a considerable proportion of our total existence *discarnate* and *invisible*.

## NONLOCATIONAL SPACE

In each of these three examples, we glimpse a hidden matrix to existence, which we could call "nonlocational" space. "Nonlocational" space seems an appropriate phrase because when things are "in" it, they no longer have an external, perceptible location, but they are nevertheless still real. They have being but they have no location. They are "nowhere." And insofar as things in nonlocational space are "nowhere"—in other words, insofar as they occupy no specific place, no specific point in space or time—the way in which we become aware of them has to be quite different from the way in which we become aware of external objects. Whereas external objects become present to us through their sheer physical mass (we will knock into them if we don't notice them, or we will tread on them—or they may tread on us) objects in nonlocational space only become present to us *from within our own consciousness*. They approach us, and we approach them, from "within" and because of this our knowledge of them is necessarily participative. We have to "make space" for them if they are going to become meaningfully present to us.

We all of us stand between two worlds: an outer world of objects in locational space, and an inner world that we become aware of within our own consciousness, in nonlocational space. This language of "inner" and "outer" is not really adequate, however, because the chief characteristic of nonlocational space is that it has no location. It is not *literally* within us. If anything, it surrounds us, it encompasses us on all sides— for it is the great "sea of soul" that Plotinus describes as follows:

> The universe lies in soul, which bears it up . . . like a net thrown into the sea . . . The sea is already spread out and the net spreads with it

... The universe extends as far as the soul goes, but no further. The boundaries of its extension are determined by the degree to which in going forth it has the soul to keep it in being.[5]

Henry Corbin has elaborated further the relationship of nonlocational space (which he calls "the imaginal world" or *mundus imaginalis*) to exterior or locational space. Speaking of the former, he writes:

This reality, previously hidden, is revealed to be enveloping, surrounding, containing what was first of all external and visible, since by means of interiorization, one has departed from that external reality. Henceforth it is spiritual reality that envelopes, surrounds, contains the reality called material. That is why spiritual reality is not "in the where." It is the "where" that is in it.[6]

## SPACE IN PREMODERN COSMOLOGIES

This was well understood in ancient times, right through the Middle Ages and to the beginning of the modern era. Up until the seventeenth century, the idea of nonlocational space was an essential part of cosmology. In fig. 4.1, a sixteenth-century cosmological diagram, we see the so-called geocentric worldview with the earth at the center of the universe. One of the great injustices done to this premodern cosmology is that it is so often literally interpreted by modern commentators. But the geocentric worldview was largely symbolic. As soon as one moves away from the center point of the earth, one is venturing into spheres that are only partially physical. The planetary spheres represent soul-qualities and the planets themselves are by no means simply physical objects—they are spiritual subjects, that is to say they are *beings,* they are gods. Once beyond the planetary spheres, one comes to the outermost boundary of the physically observable universe, the sphere of the fixed stars. Beyond this, one approaches a different kind of reality altogether from physical reality. It is an all-encompassing "sphere" that doesn't belong within space. It has no location "in" space. Rather it envelopes space. As Corbin said, it is not "in

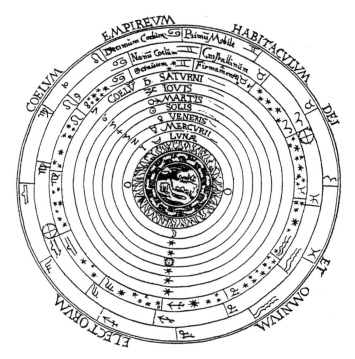

*Fig. 4.1. The premodern geocentric worldview was never intended literally to represent the externally visible universe: it also included symbolic and entirely invisible realms of being, belonging to the spheres of soul and spirit.*

the where," the "where" is "in" it. Here is the habitation of God and all the Elect (*Habitaculum Dei et Omnium Electorum*) including both the angels and the dead, and we may also assume that here, too, may be found the archetypal forms of all creatures on earth.

In fig. 4.2, while the planetary gods are on the "inside" of the universe, because they are visible, the angels and the Elect are on the "outside" beyond the stars. Although shown "outside," the point is that they are really beyond external space. The physical universe of the old cosmology thus borders on, or rather is bound within, a spiritual universe beyond space and time. The boundaries of the physical universe are not and cannot be physical, as Plotinus made clear, for the physical order of being cannot set its own boundaries: the only kind of reality that could mark the boundary of physical existence must be a nonphysical order. And the nature of this nonphysical order is that it envelopes, surrounds,

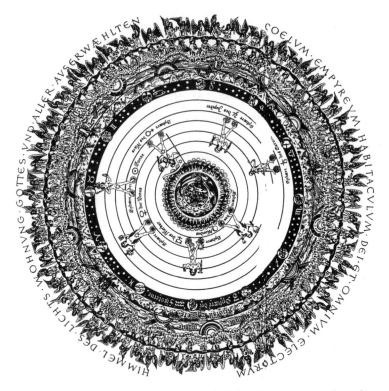

*Fig. 4.2. The angels and the sanctified dead are portrayed in this fifteenth-century cosmological diagram "outside" the externally perceptible spatio-temporal world because the spiritual world contains rather than is contained within the universe.*

and contains the physical. That this metaphysical order exists beyond the category of place, beyond the category of location, is beautifully expressed in the twelfth-century Hermetic dictum that "God is a sphere whose circumference is nowhere, whose center is everywhere."[7] From this perspective, those who call the premodern cosmology "geocentric" miss the crucial point that its true center is beyond location.

This was well understood within the medieval Islamic Shi'ite tradition, in which the planetary spheres were visualized as part of a great cosmic mountain, known as the Mountain of Qāf. This mountain was said to have been thrust up from the earth over a period of eight hundred years because the earth could not bear to be separated from heaven. The mountain is a wonderful blue color, and we see it encompassing us on all sides when we look up to the sky.[8] The Mountain of Qāf both links earth with heaven and also marks the boundary between them. That is to say, it marks the boundary between the visible and the invisible worlds or locational and nonlocational space. In the Shi'ite mystical tradition, the name for the region beyond the Mountain of Qāf is "The Land of Nowhere" (*Nā-kojā-Ābād*). It begins on the convex surface of the ninth heavenly sphere, i.e. the sphere beyond the sphere of the constellations.[9]

Journeys to this "Land of Nowhere" abound in the mystical literature of the Shi'ites, but are by no means restricted to this tradition alone. The prototype of such mystical journeys goes at least as far back as Plato, who in his famous dialogue *Phaedrus* describes the ascent of the soul through the planetary spheres to the heavenly constellations where it has a vision of the gods and then finally comes to "stand on the back of the universe" and "contemplate what lies outside the heavens." This, he says, is "a reality without color or shape, intangible but utterly real, apprehensible only by intellect (*nous*), which is the pilot of the soul."[10] Because this reality is spiritual, it is only the spiritual faculty that we inadequately translate as "intellect" (the original Greek word *nous* has the connotation of direct and immediate spiritual insight) that is capable of apprehending it.

A parallel but more ancient, more archaic, tradition is illustrated in fig. 4.3, which shows the eastern Siberian Chuckchi shaman's journey to the stars. In many different shamanic cultures, we encounter again and again the idea that the Pole Star marks a tiny hole—a gap, window, or entrance—that leads out of the physically perceptible world of space and time to the invisible spirit-world. Through this hole the gods pass to-and-fro. So also do the souls of the dead.[11] Perhaps the archetypal forms of the plants, the peonies and delphiniums, the poppies and nasturtiums, also make use of this passageway between locational and nonlocational space. In fig. 4.3, the main pathway from left to right shows the path from dawn to dusk taken by the sun. This is intersected by the flight path taken by the shaman to the heavens. And where the two paths meet is where the Pole Star, the passage between worlds, is to be found. The double lines represent the Milky Way.

*Fig. 4.3. A Chuckchi (eastern Siberian) map of the heavenly ways, showing the Pole Star at the vital intersection of the diurnal journey of the sun and the night journey of the shaman to the stars.*

The idea that the passage between worlds is a tiny point serves to remind us that we are not considering here an additional fourth or fifth physical dimension. Rather we are *taking dimensions away,* we are removing them one after another until we reach a point that vanishes into "nowhere," a kind of "negative space" in which matter is replaced by spirit.[12] The great Sufi mystic Ibn 'Arabi tells the following story: After God had created Adam, there was still a little clay left over, and with this clay He made the palm tree. And having made the palm tree, there was just a tiny amount of clay remaining, no bigger than a sesame seed. With this tiny amount of clay, God created all the worlds beyond the stars: the heavens and hells, super-celestial paradises, purgatories and underworlds, the angels and archangels, and all the spiritual hierarchies from the highest seraphim and cherubim to the lowliest of the genies and nature spirits.[13]

## SPACE IN MODERN COSMOLOGY

These nonlocational worlds and their denizens, which formed such an important part of the old cosmologies, are excluded from modern cosmology, which is concerned only to chart that which can be physically perceived. With the advances of astronomy in the twentieth century, we now know that the physical universe is of vast extent, so vast that our measurement of it entails distances more or less unimaginable to us. Of the many thousands of galaxies in our universe, ours has a total diameter of roughly a hundred thousand light-years. A light-year is the distance traveled by a ray of light in one year, a little under six trillion miles. So the scale we have to use when conceiving of the dimensions of the physical galaxy of which our solar system is a tiny part, is so immense as to be almost beyond our comprehension.

Our sun is one of not merely a few hundred or a few thousand similar solar masses, but one of an estimated one hundred and forty billion in our galaxy alone. Such statistics, hard as they are to conceive, nevertheless demonstrate the "uncontainability" of the physical universe if we restrict ourselves to a purely physical cosmology. While it could be said that the great achievement of modern astronomy is that it has successfully "located" us in the physical universe, this is an achievement that has been gained at the cost of dislocating us from the spiritual universe that was the all-enveloping "container" of the premodern cosmologies.

In fig. 4.4, we gain little insight, and even less reassurance, from seeing the exact location of our solar system within the galaxy. Instead of it being contained by the encompassing spiritual world, it is set within a physical system that is wholly exteriorized. Something vital has been left out that needs to be there if we are to orientate ourselves as human beings, as beings of soul and spirit, to the universe as a whole. The picture of our galaxy and—beyond that—other galaxies, in an unimaginably vast universe spread out in external space is the product of a literalizing mentality that views only the physical as real. The premodern mind knew that the universe as a whole is not simply physical, but includes— or rather should be thought of as *included within*—nonphysical levels of reality. To leave out these nonphysical levels is to give a very partial picture from which all that is most important and most meaningful has been expurgated.

If we should ask: Where in this worldview are we to find soul, or any quality of interiority, the only possible answer would seem to be—*it*

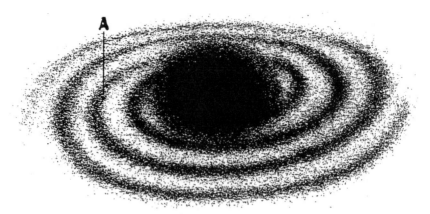

*Fig. 4.4. While modern astronomy has enabled us to know the exact physical location of our solar system (A) within the galaxy, we are left grappling with immensities of time and space so great as to be virtually inconceivable. Meanwhile, the nonlocatable reality of spirit is excluded from this picture.*

*is within us.* Human beings are the only bearers of soul in the wholly exteriorized modern universe of space and time. For we have taken the soul of the universe captive and imprisoned it within our own consciousness. And even there it is under siege by those who would like to convince us that consciousness is just a "neural computer" or the by-product of chemical processes occurring in the brain, thereby casting consciousness itself out into locational space.

We have, then, a certain responsibility today, if soul and spirit are once more to be rehabilitated in our universe. For they can only be rehabilitated through our understanding and treasuring the nonlocational reality to which consciousness alone can give us access. But for this to happen, we need to be less distracted by everything that draws us away from attending to our inner life. And in our modern exteriorized world, it is no coincidence that we are lured away from inwardness by a thousand distractions: for the cultivation of inwardness threatens the locational reality-principle. Inwardness is consequently one of the most difficult things to sustain in the climate of our extroverted culture. It is, however, only by attending to and intensifying our inner life that we can begin to develop a true picture of reality that includes both the visible and the invisible, both the physical and the nonphysical aspects of existence.

# PATHWAYS INTO
# NONLOCATIONAL SPACE

At the beginning of this chapter I referred to three areas of our experience that are enveloped by mystery. Let us return to them again in order to answer the question: What can we do to reconnect once more with the reality that is not "there."

The first thing we can do is to cultivate an inner stillness in relation to our life of thought, quietening the discursive, chattering mind and anchoring our thought-processes in this precious stillness. It is precious because it provides the basis from which it is possible to intensify consciousness so that the latter becomes inwardly receptive, like an inner listening, as if it were a big ear turned inward. We can then become aware that there are certain thoughts that *present themselves to us,* coming into our consciousness from a depth that is *not our own.*

To have this experience is at the same time to become aware of an inner threshold where specific insights are given to us. It is less that we win them through our own effort of will, than that they are given to us by our becoming receptive to this delicate threshold where our consciousness meets a reality that lies beyond our own striving. This is not to say that we must become inactive. It requires, on the contrary, an intensification of attentiveness, directing it toward what lives at the edge of our inner awareness. Through such intensification of attentiveness, we rediscover the nonlocational space that in premodern cosmologies marked the outer boundaries of the cosmos, only now it can be experienced as an inner boundary. As we have seen, in previous times the other side of this threshold was described as the habitation of God, the angels, and the blessed dead. Today we can rediscover at this inner threshold of consciousness a potential bridge to that same spiritual reality.[14]

It is therefore important that we nurture this experience, and through nurturing it come to know that as well as the threshold of the senses by which we become aware of the outer world, there is another threshold within human consciousness. At this inner threshold we can have experiences to which we may attribute the same unquestionable reality-status as we do to experiences that are mediated by the senses. Only what we experience is not the same kind of reality as sense-perceptible reality. It is the reality of that which has no location; it is precisely a "nonlocational" reality.

The second thing we can do to reconnect with the reality that is not "there" is to practice what Jung called "living the symbolic life."[15] This requires especially that we attend to our dreams. In order to attend properly to our dreams, we need to create an "inner space" in our waking consciousness in which we allow the dreams themselves to come alive within us and to speak to us, a space where we can work with them. If we are able to do this, then it is possible to find that we are led beyond the personal dream images to a symbolic language that is bigger than ourselves. We find that we are dealing with a universal language of one or more of the world's mythologies or spiritual traditions. This was Jung's great insight, that through attending to our dream-life we find that we are having to engage not simply with our own dream imagery but with a more universal source to which that imagery belongs.

When this becomes a matter of actual experience, then we may realize two things. First of all, that the inner world of myth and symbolic imagery, of which our dreams are composed, is not so much within us as that *we are within it*. Our individual dream-life is immersed in a much bigger "container"—it belongs to a soul-world that is larger than our own individual soul. And not only our dreams, but also much of the way we think and act when we are awake may equally be contained within a myth that we are, without being fully conscious of the fact, "living out." The second thing we may realize is that not only is our dream imagery the clothing of powerful psychic energies, but that these energies are more than simply *objects* we become aware of: they should also be regarded as *subjects*. The archetypal figures that frequent our dream-life have a certain autonomy, a certain independent life of their own, and in this respect they resemble the gods of ancient times. Just as the intensification of our life of thought can lead to an experience of an inner threshold with a world of spirit, so paying attention to our dream-life can lead to an experience of an inner threshold with a transpersonal soul-world, a coherent and autonomous inner world of mythic and symbolic imagery in which archetypal figures or beings move and—from semiconscious depths—have a profound influence upon our lives.

The third thing we can do to reconnect with the reality of what is not "there" is to practice what William Blake called "looking through" rather than simply "with" the eye when we turn our gaze outward toward the natural world.[16] This is to practice a different kind of seeing, a seeing into nonlocational space by activating the imagination. Normally when we look at a developing plant, for instance, we simply see what is physically present to the eyes. It is, however, also possible to see imaginatively what is *not* there, but is nevertheless in the process of becoming present.

In fig. 4.5, different stages of the development of the groundsel (*Senecio vulgaris*) are shown from seedling to full-grown plant. In contemplating this process of growth, we can imagine two boundaries to the plant as it develops. One boundary is the edge of the physical form of the developing seedling, as it is presented to us in external space at different phases of its life; the other boundary is the edge of the initially entirely invisible form of the fully developed plant as it gradually

*Fig. 4.5. Development of a groundsel (*Senecio vulgaris*) as it grows from seedling to full-grown plant.*

unfolds into manifestation. From a spiritual perspective, what is physically present at the end of the process of growth, namely the fully developed plant, is spiritually present from the very beginning, acting upon the plant from nonlocational space.

It is a question of training ourselves to look for the movement from the apparently "empty" periphery around the developing plant to the center, rather than from the center to the periphery. One has to imagine that the periphery is a fullness—a spiritual fullness—and it is pouring itself out into materiality.[17] From this perspective, the young seedling—rather than being a material fullness—can be seen as a spiritual emptiness that is gradually "filling out." If one practices focusing on the movement from invisibility to visibility in this way, then the whole process of growth can reveal itself to be guided and directed by the spiritual form or archetype of the plant that seeks to achieve material embodiment in space and time.

Here, then, we may become attuned to a third threshold between the sense-perceptible world located in external space and its nonsensory or inner aspect. But awareness of this threshold is necessarily mediated by our consciousness. It is a threshold that we may or may not become aware of, and whether we do or do not depends on the degree to which we are able to heighten our awareness at the liminal edge where nonlocational or spiritual form turns itself outward into external manifestation.

I believe it is one of the great tasks of our time, and of the future, to rediscover and live in conscious connection with the nonphysical, invisible worlds. Otherwise we simply live in one half of reality rather than the whole of reality. In these three practices of, first, stilling our thoughts so that awareness is intensified at the inner threshold where thoughts arise; second, attending to our dreams and "living the symbolic life"; and, third, practicing an "imaginative seeing" of the natural world, it is possible to become aware once more of the reality of what is not "there"—a reality that can become present to us in the three spheres of spirit, psyche, and nature. The reality that is "nowhere" will then be experienced by us as it should be—a reality that is after all "everywhere."

**PART TWO**

*Deepening Our Foundations:*
*The Gods*
*and Ancient Egypt*

# 5

## ANCIENT EGYPT AND
## THE SOUL OF THE WEST

*We live in times of tremendous spiritual ferment. Despite the seculariza-*
*tion of society, there is intense and persistent spiritual questing in individu-*
*als discontent with the established secular paradigm. Many people feel that*
*our Judaeo-Greek cultural heritage does not have the resources to meet the*
*longing that exists for spiritual renewal. This essay explores the relevance*
*of ancient Egypt in the contemporary struggle for our cultural identity.*

*The essay originated in a talk given at the launch of* Temple of the
Cosmos: The Ancient Egyptian Experience of the Sacred *in Oxford, on*
*May 18, 1996.*[1]

### THE INWARD MIGRATION TO ANCIENT EGYPT

Despite the threat of terrorist attack, hundreds of thousands of tourists continue to visit Egypt each year. They come from every country
in Europe, from all over the United States, as well as from many other
countries the world over. What is it that attracts them? Is it simply the
desire to look at old ruins, or is there a deeper, though perhaps semiconscious, motive that draws them to this ancient culture? Having long
felt the lure of ancient Egypt myself, I have come to believe that the
widespread interest in ancient Egypt is symptomatic of a profound shift

in our own culture. Ancient Egypt does not only belong to the past, it speaks directly to our contemporary situation, and even points the way toward our own future.

The culture that created the temples and pyramids that enthrall the modern tourist was steeped in esoteric learning. It could hardly have been further from the Hollywood image of self-glorifying warrior pharaohs exercising power through brute force, with gangs of slaves in tow. The Egyptian king was divine not in virtue of an honor bestowed on his personality by an obsequious Senate as in Rome, but because his consciousness had been raised, through rites of initiation, to a divine level. The ancient Egyptian social and political order reflected a spiritual hierarchy, and the country was ruled from a profound awareness of the spiritual principles operating at all levels of society and in nature (see chapter 8).

It is a little-known, but interesting fact that the Egyptians bear the credit for having produced the first maps roughly four thousand years ago. But what is really fascinating is that these maps were not of the physical world, but of the otherworld. Islands, swamps, and different regions were charted in minute detail, even though they did not have any physical existence (fig. 5.1). Why? Because these were regions that the soul traveled, and it was considered vitally important that the soul be equipped with the means of negotiating them. Despite their extraordinary technological skill, which enabled the Egyptians to construct monumental buildings that would last for millennia, the main focus of Egyptian civilization was on the invisible world. This applies not only to their mapmaking but to their literature as well. The most famous piece of Egyptian literature—The Book of the Dead—is entirely concerned with the transformative journey of the soul in the otherworld, and The Book of the Dead describes the course of this journey with both psychological subtlety and symbolic sophistication. Some of The Book of the Dead papyri are beautifully illustrated with archetypal episodes from this journey. Here we find a deep wisdom expressed in symbolic images that still have the capacity to profoundly touch the modern soul.

Today, Western culture is in crisis, but the danger is that we sleep through it. Something is occurring within us, and there are critical moments, all too easily passed by, when we find ourselves coming up against the boundaries of the modern secular worldview, and we know that it cannot meet what is moving within us. It is then that we may feel the real questions that face us in our current crisis today are on a different level from economics, politics, or anything that technology can fix. There are deeper questions, deeper longings. We are engaged in a battle for soul. There is a battle being waged for the soul of the West, and what is at stake is our whole cultural identity, our whole "Western mentality."

My own experience of coming up against the old parameters of the "Western mentality" came about through studying philosophy in various universities in England. Like many people who are drawn to philosophy, I wanted to absorb the wisdom of the great philosophers through the ages. But after fourteen years of study, I felt that something

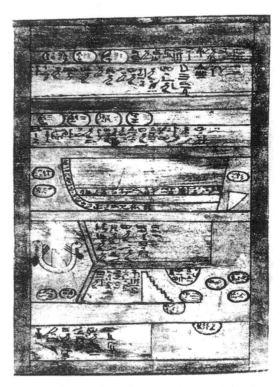

*Fig. 5.1. One of a number of very early maps, showing a region of the underworld known as the Fields of Peace. From El Bersha, Middle Kingdom, ca. 1850 BC.*

inside me was not being, and could not be, nourished by philosophy alone. It was as if whole areas of human experience were untouched by the philosophical mentality, which pursues wisdom with the abstract concept and the rules of logic. The mind is disciplined to reason with an undeniable conceptual clarity but at the cost of the imagination.

Having trained my mind to think in abstract concepts, I found myself drawn toward the symbolic image. Plotinus once wrote that the gods and the blessed do not contemplate philosophical propositions but beautiful images, for it is images that convey the substance of true wisdom.[2] It is a thought echoed more recently by Jung, who stated: "Wisdom . . . is neither a question of belief nor of knowledge, but of the agreement of our thinking with the primordial images of the unconscious."[3]

In my longing for the image, I found that I was in fact drawn to the prephilosophical mentality that weaves together symbolic images to create myth, the language of the soul. It became increasingly apparent to me that some other content can come through the image that otherwise is driven away by the spotlight of pure thought. Images have a fluidity, a luminescence, an aliveness, which makes them permeable to transcendent content in a way that concepts are not. And so I found myself inwardly migrating to ancient Egypt. Here was a culture that possessed a wisdom that was expressed in the language of living images and symbols. Here was deep wisdom, but hardly an abstract concept anywhere to be discovered. Even Truth was a goddess (fig. 5.2).

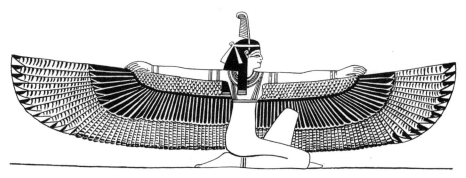

*Fig. 5.2. Truth as the Egyptian goddess Maat.*
*Tomb of Nefertari, Nineteenth Dynasty.*

## THE DRIVE TO SOLIDIFY THE WORLD

The modern Western mind has its roots in ancient Greece. Greece is really the soil from which "the West" has sprung. It was the Greeks who gave us science, as well as philosophy, and the habit of thinking logically. They also laid the foundations of naturalism in art. To the Greeks we owe such ideals as democracy, and the freedom of the individual to make their own choices and to take responsibility for them. But underlying all these gifts of the Greeks, to whom we are so indebted, there is another less obvious gift that we owe to them. Above all else, the Greeks gave us a solid world. The belief in a solid world, understood as hard, dense physical substance is what really defines the Western mentality. We are reassured by the world of things visibly, tangibly, *there* outside us, distinct from us and hence observable by us, allowing us to know ourselves as separate from it. Such an "external" world is by its very nature lacking in interiority. It has no inner life, no soul. Hence it poses no threat to us, but is relegated to the neutral "objective" backdrop of *our* interior life.

The drive to solidify the world could be regarded as the peculiar project of the West. Along with the Greeks, this project was given a great impetus from the Judaic tradition. The Israelites waged a long and often bloody campaign against the consciousness that perceived physical things as being "inwardly open"—as being endowed with soul or spirit. They called this type of awareness "idolatry," and the prophets and psalmists raged against those who worshipped "idols" castigating them as godless unbelievers. In Psalm 115, verses 3–7, we read that idols have eyes but never see, ears but never hear, noses but never smell. Not a sound issues from their throats. They are just hollow pretenses of life. While this may have been true for the Israelites, it was not, however, true for the other ancient cultures—including Egypt—for whom the "idols" *were* able to see, hear, smell, and speak, and indeed continued to do so throughout ancient history. The Colossus of Memnon at Thebes in Egypt (fig. 5.3) is one example: it was speaking well into the Roman period.[4]

It took a very long time to accomplish the project of solidifying

*Fig. 5.3. The Colossus of Memnon, still speaking in Roman times.*

the world, but to the extent that this project has been definitive of the Western mentality, Western culture could be said to be essentially Greek or Judaeo-Greek. The solidification of the world was only finally achieved in the seventh and eighteenth centuries, with the establishment of the materialistic and mechanistic view of nature as matter in motion, and the successful marginalization of all modes of consciousness that resisted this way of regarding nature.[5] For Descartes, the requirement that nature be perceived as *res extensa*, as the "extended substance" of unyielding matter, demanded that the conscious mind be disciplined to think nonanimistically, in the most abstract way possible. The new science had to embrace the language of mathematics as the only way of ensuring that the world was thoroughly objectified.

## A NEW ALIGNMENT

Today, it is disturbingly evident that our solid, "literal" world is dissolving all around us, just as is Descartes' counterpart to it—the "thinking substance" (*res cogitans*) or ego. In the twentieth century, not only did we see the principle of uncertainty take its place within the New Physics as the basis on which the whole discipline uneasily rests, but in archetypal psychology the gods came back to reclaim the soul from its monotheistic ego entrenchment. The end of the world is upon us, the end of that solid old world that used to be so reassuring, for it is becoming increasingly permeable, increasingly transparent. Subtle energies surface in the landscape, just as meridians reveal themselves flowing through the human body. We are living through a second Exodus, an Exodus from the Judaeo-Greek paradigm, because that paradigm is no longer able to nourish the growing shoots of the new consciousness.

As the old edifice crumbles, a range of possibilities open up. One is that we turn completely away from our Western heritage, and embrace the traditions of other more spiritually mature cultures such as India or China. Another possibility is that we work on our own foundations, in order to recover a wisdom that lies at a deeper historical and spiritual substratum. If we do this, then the direction that we take is toward the culture that lies blazing on the other side of the Greek horizon, the same culture that the Israelites turned away from in that fateful first Exodus.

I do not say that we should "go back" to ancient Egypt in the sense of trying to relive something that is in the past, but rather that we should take cognizance of that past, and realize the extent to which the spiritual foundations of the West are sunk in Egypt. This was a culture for which the world was still permeable, into which a spiritual light shone, illuminating it with a divine radiance. The gods were still present in the land of Egypt, for nature was still transparent, not yet solid and opaque. Nature mediated divine energies that people became aware of by "seeing through" the phenomenal world to the numinous presences beyond.

When the Greek sage Solon visited the Egyptian city of Sais, the cult center of the goddess Neith, he was questioned at length by the Egyptian priests who wanted to ascertain just how learned he was. Solon did his best to impress the priests with the great extent of his knowledge, but when he finished speaking, one very old priest looked at him and shook his head. "O Solon, Solon," he said, "you Greeks are just children. You have no really old and deep knowledge." The priest then instructed Solon concerning many mysteries.[6] The Egyptians were wise about things that the Greeks did not understand. They were wise about the invisible worlds that interpenetrate the physical, for they perceived the powers that move behind the facade of sense-existence. Above all they understood that the real world is not solid, and that if one is seeking spiritual foundations for one's life, then it is necessary to develop a consciousness that is able to travel through the literal world to the symbolic world, to the world of the sacred imagination.

Could it be that a half-conscious recognition of this quality of awareness that used to live in ancient Egypt is what attracts so many tourists there today? Like thirsty travelers, who have wandered in the parched desert, they are drawn to Egypt as to an oasis that still sparkles with the water of life. As we come to the end of the Judaeo-Greek era, perhaps it may prove possible to resecure ourselves spiritually by aligning our Western culture with that other, deeper axis whose source is in ancient Egypt, and which lies behind so many of our Western esoteric traditions such as Alchemy, Gnosticism, Rosicrucianism, and Freemasonry. Egypt calls to us like a lost part of ourselves, and I believe that as we strive to achieve a new sensitivity toward the spiritual powers that pervade our lives, Egypt will come increasingly into focus for us. For although the Egyptian era flourished long ago, we may nevertheless discover that, as we venture toward our own future, we feel our deeper affinities to be less and less Judaeo-Greek and more and more Egyptian.

# 6

## ON THE DIVINITY
## OF THE GODS

*Modern depth psychology may have enabled us to rediscover the ancient gods as psychic energies, or archetypes of the unconscious. But should we consider them divine simply because they are powerful factors in our soul-life, or because they really are autonomous spiritual realities? What, exactly, is it that makes a god divine? By considering the ancient Egyptian understanding of the nature of the gods, we may find some clues as to how to approach their essential divinity.*

*The essay is based on a talk entitled "De-psychologizing the Gods: Reflections on what it means for a god to be divine." The talk was given at a workshop on "God and the Gods" at the Abbey, Sutton Courtenay, on December 11, 1993.[1]*

### THE NEW DAWN OF POLYTHEISM

Contemporary culture is in a position comparable to that of the ancient world on the eve of its spiritual collapse. During the Greco-Roman period, the presence of the gods, worshipped for thousands of years, was no longer so keenly felt. Doubts and uncertainties concerning the nature of the gods assailed the minds of sensitive thinkers. Philosophers like Chrysippus, Posidonius, and Cicero all wrote searching treatises that bore the same title "On the Nature of the Gods."² The gods had become problematic. The old order was fading away before their eyes, and there was nothing that they could do to stop it.

Today, we may look back to the Greco-Roman period as comparable to our own. The monotheistic religious sensibility that succeeded the ancient polytheism no longer enjoys the confidence that it used to enjoy. Things are on the move again. The ancient gods are once more appearing in our midst. And they are appearing where we can least afford to ignore them—in our own souls. We discover them, embedded in the old myths, under the guise of the archetypes of the unconscious. But this reappearance of the gods as psychic factors is, I suspect, but the first flush of a new dawn of a regenerate polytheism.

If in Greek and Roman times, the gods were retreating from people's awareness, they are now advancing into ours. And we should be ready for them. It is necessary, therefore, to reflect once more on the nature of the gods. I believe that by referring back to an epoch before the Greco-Roman—an epoch far wiser and more knowledgeable about spiritual matters than the Greeks and Romans ever were—it may prove possible to find guidance for our own future. But if we look back to the past for our spiritual education, let us not do it from nostalgia, neither with any misplaced desire to revive ancient religion. Rather, let us do it so as to go forward into our own future with as much wisdom and clarity as we are presently capable.

## GOD AND THE GODS

There is a mystical text that begins to appear on the walls of the tombs of certain ancient Egyptian kings from the fifteenth century BC onward. Evidently, it was considered to be an important and powerful text because it continued to appear for over three hundred years, and in the tombs of some of the most famed kings of New Kingdom Egypt: Thutmose III, Seti I, and Ramesses III.

Like most New Kingdom mystical texts, it has illustrations, but these are very simple, and they accompany only one part of the text.

The illustrations consist entirely of representations of gods—a parade of seventy-four (sometimes seventy-five) gods—who, although the style varies a little from tomb to tomb, are recognizable as being the same seventy-four gods in each case. In fact great care is taken to ensure that each deity retains his or her characteristic form and position, relative to the other gods depicted.

Fig. 6.1 shows part of this parade of the gods as portrayed in the tomb of Thutmose III. Some of the gods shown here have rather unfamiliar titles. On the bottom row on the far left—"Flaming One." Next to him is "Resting Soul," then "He Who Causes to Breathe." The feminine deity who comes next is called "The Ejector." The god at the end on the right is "The Decomposed One." But on the top row, the names are more familiar. Here are some of the major gods and goddesses of ancient Egypt: on the left is Nun, the Primordial Ocean, which precedes all the gods, and from which they all emerge at the beginning of creation. Then comes Nephthys, the sister of Isis, and then her mother

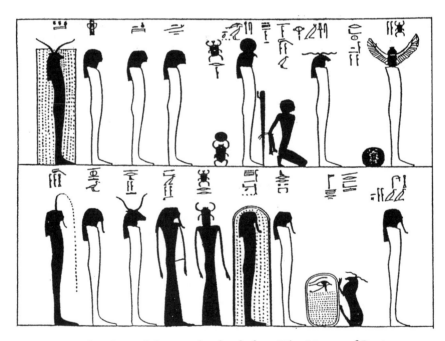

*Fig. 6.1. Part of the parade of gods from* The Litany of Ra *in the Tomb of Thutmose III, Valley of the Kings.*

Nut, the goddess of the heavens. Next we see Tefnut and the scarab beetle Kheprer. To the right are various forms of Ra. In fact the text as a whole contains the names of most of the main deities in the Egyptian pantheon—Atum, Shu, Geb, Isis, and Horus are all explicitly mentioned, and represented. Other gods such as Ptah, Osiris, Thoth, and Amon are clearly alluded to.

What is significant about this text is that all these gods—all seventy-four of them—are affirmed to be but aspects of Ra. The whole text is known to us as *The Litany of Ra,* and the section that concerns us here, has the form of a great hymn of praise to the sun god. Each stanza begins:

> *Praise to you, O Ra, Supreme Power!*

And each stanza ends with an affirmation that Ra is to be identified with the "bodies" now of this god and now of that god. Concerning the use of the word "body" (*khat*) Alexandre Piankoff explains:

> It might be understood as a kind of divine personality, a hypostasis, which the supreme deity may assume at a certain moment. Thus, when speaking of Ra, the text says: "Thou art the bodies of Isis." This implies that Ra, the creative energy whose main manifestation is the sun, appears also in the different aspects of the goddess Isis.[3]

And so we read that Ra, the Supreme Power, is the "bodies" of Atum, the "bodies" of Kheprer, of Shu and Tefnut, of Geb and Nut, of Isis, Nephthys, and Horus.

> *Praise to you, O Ra, Supreme Power,*
> *who approaches the caverns of He at the West,*
> *You are the bodies of Atum.*
> *Praise to you, O Ra, Supreme Power,*
> *who comes to what Anubis hides,*
> *You are the bodies of Kheprer.*

> *Praise to you, O Ra, Supreme Power,*
> *whose existence is longer than that*
> *of She Who Hides Her Images,*
> *You are the bodies of Shu . . .*[4]

And so it goes on. Ra, we are told, is the "Lord of Manifestations." The text expresses very clearly the attitude of ancient polytheism toward the multiplicity of gods. They are all but manifestations of the one Supreme Power. We meet this attitude throughout the ancient world—not just in Egypt. But I want to stay with Egypt, because it is simpler to pursue the implications of this attitude if we remain within the one culture.

One of the main implications of The Litany of Ra is that every god provides a point of entry to the "Supreme Power." Just because each god is a specific and limited manifestation of the Absolute, each god provides a recognizable doorway through which one can pass, and travel toward the Godhead. The Supreme Power, the Absolute, the Godhead—call it what we will—is at the source of that particular god or goddess. Each god and goddess, precisely because they are an aspect of the Absolute, also provides a means of access to the Absolute.

It is for this reason that in ancient Egypt one finds relatively insignificant deities addressed in hymns as if they were the Absolute. For in a sense, every deity—no matter how insignificant—*is* that Supreme Power. There is a hymn, for instance, to the local god of the region called Thinis (the area around Abydos). This god is named Anhur (or Onuris), and he was primarily a warrior god. Nevertheless, we find him addressed in this hymn as

> *Lord of All, omnipresent,*
> *Great God, who creates himself,*
> *Accomplished Power, who comes out of Nun,*
> *He who gives light to mankind.*[5]

Anhur can be seen in fig. 6.2 with his lioness consort Mekhit. Despite the brave pose, we do not feel convinced that we are face-to-face with

*Fig. 6.2. Anhur, the local god of Thinis, with his consort Mekhit.*

the omnipresent Lord of All. And yet such hymns are by no means uncommon. Many gods whom one does not immediately think of as creator gods were in fact regarded as being so.

The god Ptah is one example. Ptah is known chiefly as the local god of Memphis, and as the patron of craftsmen and artisans. Ptah's name probably means "the sculptor." He guided people engaged in the transformation of matter for spiritual purposes—people, for instance, who were working with wood, stone, or metal and who worked with the intention of causing these substances to become the receptacle of specific energies. The making of sacred statues, for example, would have been conducted under the auspices of Ptah.

Ptah is normally shown mummiform, like Osiris, wearing the close fitting skullcap of the craftsman, and grasping a *was* scepter, signifying his dominion over the material world (fig. 6.3). But we also meet Ptah as the creator-god, Ptah Tatenen (literally "Exalted Earth"). In this other role, it is said of him that he is

*. . . father of the gods,*
*Tatenen, the oldest of them all.*
*He gave birth to himself by himself,*
*before any becoming became.*
*And when his becoming became,*
*he made the world*
*from the thoughts in his heart.*[6]

Practically every major god of ancient Egypt had this capacity to, as it were, jump into the skin of the creator-god, the Supreme Power. Shu, Thoth, Hathor, Neith, Khnum, even the Nile god Hapi, are all examples. Now I think that the reason why they had this capacity takes us to the kernel of the Egyptian understanding of divinity as such. It was regarded as essential to the very nature of divinity that whatever or whoever was described as divine was so described not by virtue of their limited and quite specific qualities as god of this or god of that—god of craftsmen, god of learning, goddess of love, god of the Nile, and so forth—but because of their relationship to the *unlimited*. What made them gods was the fact that their home and their place of origin was—to put it in mythological terms—the Primordial Land that, at the very beginning of existence, emerged from the great Ocean of Nun. This ocean, or "Watery Abyss,"

*Fig. 6.3. The god Ptah.*

was for the ancient Egyptians, the image of the Unlimited. It is the image of the infinite, formless, and unmanifest source from which limit, finitude, form, and manifest being issue. The ocean itself is beyond any kind of definition. It is an ocean of nonbeing. Hence the creator-god must first of all create himself, must bring himself into being, bring himself into definition, from out of the Primordial Ocean.

Many are the images of how this occurs, but at Heliopolis, the center of the cult of Ra, it was taught that the creator-god emerged first as solid land, surging up from the abysmal waters. And then he set about creating the other gods. The crucial relationship between the creator-god and the unlimited waters of Nun is that the creator-god taps the hitherto untapped creative energy within Nun, and brings it into manifestation. The secret essence of divinity, then, is this mysterious identification with and magical ability to quicken the creative power by which existence is brought forth from nonexistence.

Every god and goddess, no matter how seemingly far removed from the creator-god they are, connects back into the creator-god, the Supreme Power, who is active on this metaphysical edge between nonbeing and being. Hence Anhur must be the "Great God, who creates himself," and Ptah must "give birth to himself by himself, before any becoming became." So we could say that at the heart of each god, the creator-god is present. And that is why each god must be both a manifestation of the creator-god, and allowed to speak as if he or she were the creator-god. For each god is identified ultimately with the cosmic creative power. What makes a god a god is that the source of the divine being of each is located in the seam of pure creative energy that runs between nonbeing and being.

## GODS AND HUMANS

But as well as having this direct connection with the cosmic creative source, the gods were involved in the natural world and in the human psyche. To refer to the natural world and the human psyche as if they were two different spheres of existence is to think in a modern way. In ancient times no such clear distinction was made. The natural world spoke to human beings of psychic realities, and human beings recognized their own psychic energies not as confined to themselves but as pervading all of nature. Thus, in focusing on the relationship of gods to human beings, it is necessary to remember that in ancient times, human experience of what we today would regard as constituting our inner life was in those days something from which nature, to a large extent, was not excluded. Psyche was a category within which both nature and humanity participated.

All ancient cultures, as much as they were aware of the intimate intertwining of the gods with forces in nature, were also aware of the gods in the soul-life of human beings. Fig. 6.4 shows the New Kingdom King Seti I clasping the hand of the goddess Hathor. Apart from the symbolic attributes characteristic of the goddess—the cow's horns with the sun disc between them, and the *menat* necklace—the goddess looks like a very beautiful woman. Gazing at this picture, we may feel a certain confusion. Is it possible that the king is really holding hands with a goddess? Can a human being come *this close* to a divine being? How

*Fig. 6.4. King Seti I joins hands with Hathor.*

are we to understand this apparently intimate consorting of the king with a deity?

I think the answer depends on our understanding of the experience of deities in ancient times. It was possible for the devotees of a goddess such as Hathor to feel themselves inwardly united with the goddess. Through the shaking of the sistrum, the chanting of hymns of praise to the goddess in celebration of her sacred rites, through dance and music, and through many other means of worshipping the goddess, her divine energy awakened within them. The goddess did not simply become present to them, but could actually manifest through them. Each female devotee of Hathor, to the extent that she (the devotee) became attuned to her, became the embodiment of the goddess. What we see in fig. 6.4, therefore, is Seti with a woman who has *become* the goddess. Hathor is made present to him through the woman (most probably his wife) who feels herself transfigured, inwardly identified with the deity.

Perhaps the classic example of human identification with divinity in ancient Egypt is the way in which people became united with the god Osiris. This was a pious wish in New Kingdom Egypt, for all who passed over to the otherworld. Osiris was the god who died in this life to be born anew in the otherworld. It was a pious wish, but it was also a necessity if one was to undergo the transformational experiences involved. And so we often see people portrayed as Osiris, and we read their names in The Book of the Dead conjoined to that of Osiris. This same Osiris, it should be said, governed the cycles of death and regeneration throughout the natural world. He was by no means simply a god operating in the human realm alone.

Fig. 6.5 may look as if it portrays a priest offering incense to the god Osiris. In fact it shows a god—Iuen-mut-ef, a manifestation of Horus—offering incense to the same King Seti that we saw with Hathor in fig. 6.4. But here Seti is totally assimilated to Osiris. Again, how are we to understand what we see? How is it that a god can offer incense to a human being? And how is it that a human being can be so completely fused with a god?

Clearly, the deity is here not beyond human reach. On the contrary,

*Fig. 6.5. King Seti I
as Osiris.*

Osiris is open to human participation. Osiris represents a state of soul
through which the human being passes. He presides over and facilitates
this rite of passage from one mode of existence or awareness to another.
As "an Osiris," a person is able to enter into and come out of the otherworld. Their consciousness is liberated from the limitations that normally restrict it in this life. So here we see the soul of Seti merged with
the divine energy of the god, and thus he accomplishes the metamorphosis to which the god holds the key. It is most likely that the god
Iuen-mut-ef is embodied here in a human priest. The priest, for the purposes of the ceremony has, like Seti, become one with a god.

Such mingling of human beings with gods, and gods with human
beings, occurred in a specific sacred context, for a specific purpose. But
it could also occur in other contexts in which, through extremes of pas-
sion—joy, desire, or hatred—a person contacted a suprahuman energy,
and became filled with divine fervor. It was as if, in the ancient world,
the gods stalked the perimeters of human consciousness. And these
perimeters were not so guarded as they later became, but were readily
breached from either side.

Fig. 6.6 shows Ramesses II at the Battle of Kadesh, charging into
the enemy hordes on his war chariot. The mighty warrior king is here

transformed into an invincible god. He has become the god of violent destruction, Seth, and is thus capable of superhuman feats. Indeed, it is recorded in the famous account of this battle inscribed on the walls of various New Kingdom temples, that he slays hundreds of thousands on the field, until the enemy chief is compelled to worship him saying: "You are Seth, Baal in person."[7] The literal truth is of course less important than the attitude of the protagonists, and the language used to describe the events that took place. A fierce and merciless warrior would be one whose soul was infused with the suprahuman energy of the god.

The ancient Egyptians believed that the gods not only interacted with the human world but also could be encountered in the depths of the psyche. And when those depths were plumbed, union with a divine being could become a lived experience. But they also understood that what makes the gods divine is not the fact that they are powerful transpersonal forces in the human psyche. The experience of being overwhelmed, uplifted, or transfigured by such a force was not regarded as in itself sufficient to warrant naming that force a god. Rather, what made a god divine was its relationship to a level of being, transcendent of the psychic—that edge or boundary between nonexistence and existence—where every deity eternally recreates itself in union with the Godhead, the source and Supreme Power. It is here, in the First Time, the time beyond time that the gods truly

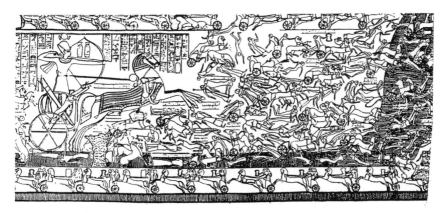

*Fig. 6.6. Ramesses II attacks the enemy hordes at the Battle of Kadesh.*

reside. This is their true home, their true place of origin. Not the psyche.

## SOUL AND SPIRIT

Today there is growing interest in and responsiveness toward the gods. By no means simply the gods of Egypt, but the gods of ancient Greece and of Mesopotamia, Hindu gods, Buddhist Bodhisattvas, Roman, Celtic, and Teutonic gods. The late twentieth century is awash with gods from every corner of the earth. By and large, this reawakening to the gods occurs within the framework of an understanding that sees them in terms of personified archetypal energies, as deep psychic energies.

This framework of understanding we owe in large part to C. G. Jung. It was he who really opened the way toward a rehabilitation of the gods for the modern consciousness. But it is worth repeating here one of the things that he said concerning this modern rapprochement with the gods: "All ages before us have believed in gods in some form or other. Only an unparalleled impoverishment of symbolism could enable us to rediscover the gods as psychic factors, that is, as archetypes of the unconscious."[8]

For Jung, there is little doubt that the gods are to be understood as archetypes, as psychic energies. But he also recognizes that this modern rediscovery of the gods as psychic factors is due to a decline in symbolic awareness. In various writings, Jung refers to the symbol as always pointing to a dimly recognized goal—a goal, as he puts it, "as yet unknown."[9] Perhaps we should take Jung's reference to "the unparalleled impoverishment of symbolism" as an acknowledgment that in previous ages symbolic awareness existed in the context of a theology and metaphysics that treated precisely of this transcendent goal.

More recently, James Hillman has argued passionately for the restoration of the gods as psychic realities. The psyche must be "dehumanized" so as to reveal more clearly the indwelling divinities that people the psychic domain. Hillman advocates a "polytheistic psychology" in which the archetypes are treated as utterly real "persons." But, like so many Jungians and post-Jungians, he draws back from following these psychic energies through to their trans-psychic source. Concerning his view of the gods as personified archetypes, he writes:

> Whereas this view of Gods does not infringe upon their reality for the theology-fantasy—which, like science, is a fantasy of the soul— this view does put in doubt their theological substantiality and literal existence, their absolute ultimacy beyond the reaches of the soul.[10]

This resistance to approaching the gods as spiritual realities is deep-seated in the modern psyche. After nearly two thousand years during which spiritual life has been gripped by a monotheistic understanding of the divine, it is hardly to be wondered at. Yet such resistance must be overcome if we are to relate to the gods in a manner appropriate to their divinity.

In ancient Egyptian religious literature, the process by which a person became aware of the gods as divine rather than as simply psychic factors, involved a spiritual journey through the psychic domain to a level of reality beyond it. This journey was essentially a traveling toward the source of the divine multiplicity—the "Supreme Power," Ra. It involved coming to know each of the gods in their psychic aspect, but it also required that a person apprehend how each was at the same time a form of Ra.

In The Litany of Ra, after the gods—the seventy-four or -five forms of Ra—have been described, the king is said to "know their names, he knows their forms completely." He "knows what is in their bodies, all their mysterious forms." He "calls them by their names, he convokes them in their forms." As a consequence of this intimate knowledge of the gods, "they throw open the gates of the Mysterious Region for his soul."[11] Each god, precisely because it is a manifestation of the Supreme Power is also a gateway to that power. The king is led beyond the gods toward the primordial landscape of the First Land arising from out of the waters of Nun. It is here that the gods originate. This is the source of the divine multiplicity. And the king here becomes immersed in the source. He experiences himself as mystically identified with the Watery

Abyss, from which the creator-god emerges in the First Time. And he experiences himself as one with the creative power through which being comes forth from nonbeing. He experiences himself as Ra. In *The Litany of Ra*, Ra is addressed with these words:

> *Hail Ra! he [the king] is the Watery Abyss.*
> *Hail Ra! he is yourself and you are he.*
> *Hail Ra! your soul is his soul,*
> *and your going is his going in the Dwat [the region*
> *of psychic energies].*
> *. . . Such as you are, such is he;*
> *your glory, O Ra, is the glory of the king.*[12]

The union of the king with Ra is so complete that the text states (still addressing Ra).

> *His soul is your soul,*
> *his body is your body.*
> *. . . You rejoice at his glory,*
> *he rejoices at your glory,*
> *as your second self.*
> *Ra says to the king:*
> *"You are like my second self."*[13]

The king, having reached the source of creation, has reached in himself the creative power of becoming and self-renewal: it is an experience of his own inmost essence as divine. This event is qualitatively different from becoming absorbed into the energy-field of one or other of the gods. For one contacts in one's own being, at the core of one's own identity, the power through which all the gods and creation unfold into manifestation. The epitome of this experience has to be *rebirth*—being spiritually reborn. For the capacity for self-regeneration is the hallmark of divinity, and this is what is here realized. United with Ra, the king is reborn through Ra and as Ra.

> *Truly, O Ra, you give birth to him,*
> *you create him like yourself...*[14]

This profound experience of union with the divine creative power that is
the source of the gods has clear consequences regarding the way in which
the king will now relate to them. Before his initiation, the gods were
apprehended as powerful vortices, each of which drew into their energy-
field the otherwise peripheral contents of normal conscious life. As we
have already seen, it was quite possible to become wholly absorbed into the
being of a god or goddess, literally putting on the guise of that deity, who
became the center of one's consciousness. But now, having been reborn as
Ra, the king has passed through to a deeper center, which transcends the
multiplicity of deities, and is—as it were—the vortex of all vortices, into
which they all pour and from which they all emerge.

The initiated king has experienced identification with, and rebirth
as, the very being of whom the divine multiplicity are but a manifestation. Therefore, instead of the old experience of being drawn into the
sphere of one or other of the gods, the gods are now themselves apprehended as absorbed into the cosmic-creative energy with which the king
has become united. It is from this ultimate source that they all originate. Thus the text, referring now to the king, explains:

> *His members are gods.*
> *He is a god completely.*
> *There is not a member in him without a god.*
> *The gods have become his members.*
> *He is the coming-into-being of forms,*
> *Lord of Spirits.*
> *... Indeed he gives them shape.*
> *It is indeed he who begets them.*
> *It is indeed he who creates them.*[15]

As a result of the mystical experience of union with the cosmic-creative
power, a new relationship to the gods arises. They are now perceived as

radiating out from this central point of divine generative activity, with which the king has become identified. They are therefore perceived in their divine rather than their psychic aspect. This perception occurs because the source of their power and their being is one's newborn self—one's own realized spiritual essence as "the second self of Ra." It is in this experience of the deepest root of one's own being that one also experiences the root and origin of the pantheon of gods. It is an experience of the very substance of divinity in which every god partakes. I return to this theme in chapter 11.

If today we are beginning to rediscover the gods as energies of the soul, then the ancient Egyptians can help to direct us toward the ultimate divinity of these energies. The direction in which the ancient wisdom encourages us to travel is—like that of contemporary depth psychology—toward deeper self-knowledge. But it is toward a depth that is, in the end, trans-psychic: the universal creative power that essentially precedes every god. It is upon the primordial ground of identity with this transcendent power that the recognition of the divinity of the gods depends. This is not to deny the profound implications of the modern rediscovery of the gods as psychic factors, but rather to take these implications to their conclusion—which is the apprehension of what it means for a god to be divine. Such apprehension does not entail denying that the gods can be understood as personified archetypes. But until we have experience of the divine presence—not of this god or that god but of divinity as such—at the core of our very existence as human beings, we cannot know the gods in their truly divine aspect. Neither can we relate to them in a way that does not compromise our own spiritual potential, unless we ourselves enter upon the long path toward union with the radiant source in whose praise *The Litany of Ra* was written.

# 7

# THE ARTIST AS PRIEST

## Reflections on the Sacred Art and Culture of Ancient Egypt

*In ancient Egypt, images were seen as potential receptacles for divine or archetypal energies. The gods and spirits could inhabit statues and paintings, and so the latter existed as interfaces between the physical and spiritual worlds. This gave them a magical power, for they could act as conduits for spirits to become present in the human world. The ancient Egyptian artist was thus positioned, like the priest, as the mediator between worlds. In this position, artists had a key role in sustaining the sacred culture of ancient Egypt.*

*This essay is based on a lecture given at the Temenos Academy, London, on January 24, 2007, entitled "Image, Archetype and Magic in Ancient Egyptian Art."[1]*

### ISFET AND MAAT

One of the most striking things about ancient Egyptian culture is the enormous amount of time, energy, and labor that was invested in fostering the relationship between the human and the spiritual realms. One sees this wherever one turns. It is evident in the painting and sculpture, in the literature, and in the temples, pyramids, and tombs. It is to be seen in practically everything that has survived of the culture, from the greatest monuments down to the smallest personal ornaments. The orientation of the Egyptians was always toward that other, invisible world of the gods, ancestors, and spirits. This was not simply something with which individuals alone were concerned, but it was also a major concern of the state. It was generally believed that Egyptian society could flourish only if it was in harmonious relationship with the world of the gods, ancestors, and spirits. If it fell out of harmonious relationship with the spirit-world, then social chaos, famine, and various disasters would ensue.

The Egyptians were strongly aware that there are two tendencies that can be observed in the world. The first is a tendency for things to fall away from connectedness with the spiritual order, and this is why natural organisms become sick and diseased and die. They become dislocated from their inner archetype, which governs and directs their life forces when they are healthy. In the social sphere, this falling away from the spiritual order can be seen in the unleashing of egotism, lying, and deceit, where each person looks out for himself or herself alone, and as a result social disintegration follows. Injustice displaces justice, and human relations fall prey to selfishness and immorality. This tendency toward loss of form, decomposition, and disorder in both nature and society the Egyptians called *isfet*. It is a universal tendency that operates in every sphere of life, but in the human social and moral sphere it needs to be actively countered by human beings.

The cosmic force or energy that opposes this tendency the Egyptians called *maat*. Often translated as "truth," "harmony," or "cosmic order," *maat* was greater than any of these concepts because she was a goddess. The goddess Maat presided over the world of the gods, which functioned in conformity with her nature. It was believed that the gods lived off Maat: she was their "food." And so in the temple hymns we read of how Maat is offered to the gods as the bread and beer that makes them strong and healthy.[2] In fig. 7.1, the king offers an image of the goddess Maat to Ptah, an important moment in the offering ritual to the gods on earth, who reside in their temple shrines. Since the gods in heaven

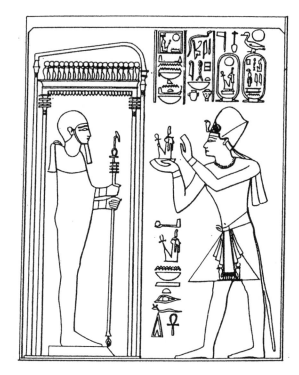

*Fig. 7.1. The king offers Maat to the god Ptah in a shrine.*

are accustomed to feed on Maat, spontaneously living in accordance with her being, so on earth it is necessary to make the offering of Maat to them on a regular basis.

The Egyptians saw the conditions of life on the material plane as disturbed by conflict: *maat* and *isfet* are constantly embattled with each other. Maat therefore has to be reconstituted actively and repeatedly on earth, and for this reason Maat has to be offered repeatedly to the gods in residence upon earth. The task of the pharaoh was to ensure that not only in the social and political spheres, but also in the realm of nature, *maat* was continuously reestablished. The pharaoh's role was "to put *maat* in the place of *isfet*," thereby restoring Egypt to its pristine state at the First Time when *maat* was originally introduced into the world by the creator god Atum.[3]

For Egypt to prosper and flourish, a good deal of effort had to be expended, for otherwise *isfet* would inevitably take over. Not only for the pharaoh, nor even simply for the higher echelons of society, but at all social levels there was an awareness of the ever-present danger of succumbing to the entropic tendency to fall into *isfet*. And so in the administration of justice, in the daily moral conduct of individuals, and equally in the productions of music, poetry, and art, the ideal was to bring human deeds into conformity with *maat*.[4] Insofar as the human world aligns itself with the goddess Maat, we align ourselves with the divine order, and with what is highest and best in ourselves. *Maat* can be likened to the concepts of *rita* and *dharma* in Hindu tradition, with the Tao of Chinese thought, with *Asha* in Zoroastrianism and with *Dike* in Greek thought: all these concepts express the idea that the cosmic order, the natural order, and the human moral order are interrelated and interdependent.[5]

One of the root meanings of *maat* is "straightness" both in the physical and in the moral sense. The earliest hieroglyph for *maat* was a long and narrow pedestal or plinth, one end of which sloped at an angle to the ground. On this pedestal statues would be placed.[6] Without the pedestal, the statue would wobble. On the pedestal, it was firm, stable, and sure. *Maat* was thus the precondition of a god's ability to be on earth, for as we see in fig. 7.1 the god in his shrine stands on a pedestal that represents *maat*. The pedestal ensures the stability of the god in the physical world. Ptah, the god of craftsmen and artisans, with whom the Greeks were later to identify their blacksmith god Hephaistos, was one of several creator gods. He was regarded as particularly responsible for the final stages of the divine creative outpouring of form into the physical world. Ptah was the god who channeled the spiritual into material embodiment.

## THE ART OF ANIMATING IMAGES

The shrine portrayed in fig. 7.1 was located in the temple of Seti I at Abydos, where the god was regarded as being tangibly present in the statue. He would have been washed and dressed in fresh linen each morning; he would have been censed with fine incense, sung to, and given food offerings. In this way the divine presence was maintained on earth. The statue was animated: it was not, as we might think today, "the statue of a god": it *was the god*. Just as we today would not regard the friend we meet in the street as "the body of a friend" unless they were lying dead on the ground, so the statue of the god was animated with the living presence, vitality, and power of the deity. And insofar as the god had become present within the statue, there would have been an alignment, a harmonization, and an interrelationship forged between heaven and earth, between the material world and the spirit-world.

Fig. 7.2 shows the same king, Seti I, offering vases of milk to Ptah's wife or consort, Sekhmet. She is a fiery lioness goddess, often portrayed with the solar disk on her head. Just as Ptah is creative, so Sekhmet can be destructive, and so she is a goddess to be treated with care. In one story that has come down to us in several versions, long ago when the sun god Ra still ruled the earth, Sekhmet indulged in an orgy of destruction, killing every human being she saw, and leaving them in pools of

*Fig. 7.2. The king offers milk to the goddess Sekhmet.*

blood, because Ra suspected that humankind was plotting against him. In this story Sekhmet was the avenging "eye" of Ra set loose upon the world. As such she was unstoppable and Ra (getting justifiably anxious about where it would all end) was only able to avert the total destruction of the human race by commanding his high priest in Heliopolis to mix together red ochre and beer and to pour this out over the land. When Sekhmet arose in the morning to continue the slaughter of the previous day, she drank it, thinking it to be human blood, and became so drunk her fury abated.[7]

Sekhmet is never represented in limestone, except when carved in relief. Statues in the round are always sculpted in hard igneous stone—usually granite or diorite. If one were to make a statue of Sekhmet in limestone, it would be difficult to entice the fiery goddess into the statue. She would not be interested. The hard firestones are much more attractive to her. There were therefore certain rules that had to be obeyed if the sculptor was to successfully produce a viable sculpture, a sculpture that would have had the capacity to draw down and embody the spiritual energy of a certain god or goddess.

The same applied to the painter. The god Amon, for example, was never painted with green or purple skin, but it was felt appropriate to paint him with red skin (the same as men), and during the New Kingdom he was increasingly portrayed with blue flesh. Blue, the color of the heavens, is the most cosmic of colors, and therefore was considered the most appropriate color for this deeply mysterious, cosmic god, whose name means "The Hidden One" or "The Invisible One."[8] Similarly Osiris was never portrayed with blue skin, but was often portrayed with black skin, black being the color of both putrefaction and death and also of fertility and the renewal of life, for the fertile mud left after the subsidence of the annual flood was black. As the god of the cycle of death and resurrection, it was considered appropriate that his flesh be not only colored black but also green—green being more obviously associated with the regeneration of life.[9]

One can see from these examples that the ancient Egyptian artist was bound by certain rules. Egyptian art had nothing to do with personal expression. The artist's function was to create a physical vessel capable of containing a transpersonal reality. The statues and pictures of the gods were specifically intended to provide the means by which invisible powers could become present on earth. They were receptacles of a divine energy, and in the case of the temple statues there would have been special rituals performed on them in order to "bring them to life." These rituals involved censing them with incense, sprinkling water over them, presenting them with a naturally occurring salt called "natron," sacrificing animals before them, and then ritually "opening" their mouths, ears, and eyes by touching them with special implements. Finally the statue was clothed, anointed, and given various ornaments before being presented with food offerings. Only at this point was the statue regarded as being completed, for then it was fully animated with the life of the god who now resided within it.[10]

In the making of images, and especially temple statues, the artist bore a heavy responsibility since every image had the potential to become the vehicle of a divine power. The making of images, however this was done—in stone, wood, or paint—was like opening a window between worlds. After a lot of chiseling, or careful work with the paintbrush, that window would open and something would come through. The rituals subsequently performed would seal this visitation of spirit, but unless the material basis was right, the rituals alone would not have been adequate to ensure the embodiment of the god. The ancient Egyptian artist, therefore, was positioned at the interface between the visible and invisible worlds, and in that position the artist's role was precisely to make the link between worlds: between the divine and the human, and between spirit and matter.

For the ancient Egyptians, then, every image was an invitation to a god, or archetypal energy, to inhabit our world. So, for example, the image of the baboon in fig. 7.3 was an invitation to a quite specific spiritual energy, associated with the god Thoth, to become present in the image. No creature was simply what it is to us today. Each creature was felt to have a certain openness toward a spiritual archetype: it pointed beyond itself to the world of spirit. In having this openness in a specific spiritual direction, it could become the carrier of that spiritual quality toward which its nature pointed. And just as the creature itself could become the manifestation of a god, so to make an image of the creature was to entice the god into the physical form that most suited the god's archetypal disposition.

*Fig. 7.3. Sculpture of a baboon.*

The ancient Egyptians understood that there is a world of gods, spiritual beings, and archetypes who are looking for ways into our world. In those days the natural world was still experienced as having a spiritual resonance, and so it was possible for a baboon in the wild to be the bearer of the sacred energy of the god Thoth. The world of nature was infused with spirits. Spirits were everywhere, and so nothing was simply what it appeared to be. Today we have a problem because our natural world has been made so literal, so prosaic, that it has lost its sacredness. It no longer has the kind of permeability in relation to the realm of spirit that was experienced by people in antiquity. Everything "is as it is," as the English philosopher G. E. Moore put it at the beginning of the twentieth century. In a phrase that epitomizes what many today feel to be the "common sense" approach to reality, he wrote, "The world is as it is and not another thing."[11] To the ancient Egyptian nothing "is as it is": it is always potentially another thing. When an ancient Egyptian saw a baboon, while there would be no denying that it was a baboon, it was also a great deal more than just a baboon, for every baboon was potentially the *ba* or "manifestation" of the god Thoth.

The baboon could, however, not only manifest the god Thoth. It could also manifest other spiritual beings. And so one had to take care when making images of baboons that one was indeed invoking Thoth and not some other spiritual entity. Every image was like a magnet to a spiritual power: it could become "charged" with an invisible energy that might not be as benevolent as one might wish. Fig. 7.4, for example, may look like Thoth in baboon form, but in fact it is a night demon called Babi who, if you get on the wrong side of him, will cut you into little pieces.[12] For the Egyptians, making images is dangerous. Every image is a potential entry point for a spirit. Ancient Egyptian art was therefore closely allied to magic, because it had to do with the provision of imaginative conduits between the invisible and the visible worlds, and the infusion of material objects with spiritual vitality.

*Fig. 7.4. Babi, Lord of the Night.*

## ART AND MAGIC

For the Egyptians, magic was less something that human beings practice than an energy that pervades the universe, which human beings may activate and direct. As such, magic was understood to be a god, named Heka. If *maat* is cosmic order, then *heka* is the primal cosmic energy that permeates all levels of existence, from the spiritual to the material levels.[13] *Heka* animates the bodies of gods and men, and is present in plants and stones as their vital essence. Thus the god Heka describes himself in Spell 261 of the Coffin Texts as "the Lord of *kas.*" *Heka* resides within the *ka* or vital essence of every god, creature or natural element, instilling it with spiritual power. It is thought that, etymologically, his name originally meant "He who consecrates the *ka.*"[14]

As the invisible current of life-energy that flows (like the Chinese *chi*) inside all creatures as an animating force, *heka* can also be understood as the means by which what is spiritual becomes physically manifest. *Heka* governs the circulation of energy between the inner and outer worlds, and so could be thought of as making the link between the spiritual and material levels. Equally, it is by means of *heka* that something that exists physically is enabled to participate in and become operative on the spiritual plane. In either case, the artist would have to have been aware that all creation of physical images, precisely because it was work at the boundary between worlds, was incipiently magical.

*Fig. 7.5. Heka and Maat either side of the sun god Ra-Herakhti.*

In fig. 7.5, Heka and Maat are shown together, either side of the sun god Ra, with whom both were closely associated. They are like brother and sister here, for just as Maat, the daughter of Ra, is the guiding principle by which true spiritual alignment is established throughout the universe, so Heka is the energizing principle by means of which such alignment is made possible. Everything is made alive and put in touch with its spiritual potency through *heka*. That is why in this picture an *ankh,* the symbol of life, hangs from the arms of the god Heka while in front of him is the *was* scepter symbolizing his power. On Heka's head is the hieroglyph *pehety* (meaning "strength"), which from the Twentieth Dynasty onward frequently replaced the phonetic spelling of the god's name.

We have seen that one of the ways of activating and channeling *heka* was through the creation of images. The image attracts to itself a certain spiritual charge. But not all Egyptian art was concerned with representing gods. Another major part of Egyptian art was concerned with portraying semimythical or archetypal situations, and this also had a magical function. Fig. 7.6 shows the "pylon" or entrance gateway to the

*Fig. 7.6. Approach to the pylon of Luxor Temple.*

temple of Amon at Luxor. This temple was the god's dwelling place on earth, and would have been approached from a long avenue of human-headed sphinxes. At the end of the avenue the visitor was confronted by the formidable barrier of the pylon, consisting of two massive towers, which supported four cedar-of-Lebanon flag masts, in front of which stood two gigantic obelisks and six colossal statues of the deified king Ramesses II.[15] To enter the temple one would have had to pass through the narrow gateway under the gaze of the statues of the king.

The pylon could be regarded as a statement in stone. It is stating that on the inside of this gateway is sacred space, for the temple is the dwelling place of the god Amon. Unless you are in atunement with *maat,* you should come no further than this. The pylon demarcates the sacred space within from the profane space without. One of the essential characteristics of sacred space is that throughout it *maat* prevails. The message of the pylon is incised on its outer walls, which are covered with reliefs depicting the king engaged in battle with the Hittites at Kadesh, who represent here the forces of chaos, or *isfet.*

The king portrayed on the pylon walls at Luxor temple is Ramesses II. In fig. 7.7, which is a drawing of the relief carving on the eastern

*Fig. 7.7. Ramesses II defeats the Hittites.*

side of the pylon, Ramesses is shown on his chariot at the Battle of Kadesh, defeating the enemies of Egypt single-handed. Viewed literally, the picture is recording an episode in the battle in which Ramesses was supposed to have become cut off from the main body of his army, and therefore had to fight numerous enemy soldiers virtually single-handed. But on a symbolic level what the picture is depicting is the triumph of *maat* over *isfet*. Attuned to *maat,* the king is in a completely clear and calm space. The sense of order and strength around him and his chariot contrasts with the chaotic rout of his enemies. The relief carving is therefore not just a celebration of a famous victory but is serving a magical function of keeping *isfet* at bay. Here on the eastern side of the pylon of Luxor temple, we see a magical invocation of the universal truth that *maat* is stronger than, and will inevitably defeat, *isfet*. This is why the image is placed precisely here, at the entrance to the temple: it protects the sacred space within by invoking this universal truth.[16]

Fig. 7.7 is one example of many depicting the Egyptian pharaoh in similar scenarios, defeating the enemies of Egypt. In fig. 7.8, we see Ramesses's father Seti I defeating the enemy (this time Libyans), again apparently without the aid of his army. This relief is one of a series of battle scenes carved on the exterior wall of the hypostyle hall of the temple of Amon at Karnak. The positioning of these reliefs on the exterior wall reiterates the point that they are not simply historical records of Seti's military campaigns but also serve the magical function of protecting the sacred interior space of the hypostyle hall.

## PORTRAYING THE IMAGINAL

For the Egyptians, such scenes are as much representing a mythical reality as a historical event. In portraying them, the artist is reaching into the mythical world in order to lay hold of a level of reality that transcends the historical circumstances of the day. He thereby gives expression to an archetypal situation, which will manifest historically again and again in various ways. In the language of Henry Corbin, one would say that the artist is portraying an "imaginal" reality—that is, a spiritual

*Fig. 7.8. Seti I defeats the Libyans.*

reality that has an objective but supersensible existence, that can only be accessed by imaginative perception.[17] Each pharaoh—insofar as he is "putting *maat* in the place of *isfet*"—aims to bring this imaginal reality into existence on the earthly plane.

It is unlikely that every depiction of the pharaoh engaged in this kind of single-handed rout of the enemy actually corresponds to a historical battle, as it does in the case of Ramesses II and Seti I. These images were primarily imaginal rather than literal. While each image is different, there is a degree of standardization in their design, which makes us feel that the location in which they are taking place is not recognizably geographical, but is rather transgeographical. While figs. 7.7 and 7.8 undoubtedly record the historical victory of Ramesses II at Kadesh and Seti I's defeat of the Libyans, similar scenes of Tutankhamun's supposed battles with the Nubians and Syrians, depicted on the famous painted chest found in his tomb, lack any known historical counterpart. It is in fact extremely unlikely that Tutankhamun actually participated in any such battles, assuming they took place at all.[18] Should we therefore conclude that they were fictitious or imaginary battles, invented for propaganda purposes? No. They were rather *imaginal:* their purpose was to affirm the transhistorical truth of the pharaoh's rout of *isfet*.

In fig. 7.9, Tutankhamun is shown hunting gazelles in the desert, and one can see that the picture invokes the same imaginal reality. The desert gazelle was believed by the Egyptians to be an animal of Seth, the god who opposed the Horus-principle that the pharaoh embodied. The gazelles are put to rout, with the aid of hunting dogs (symbolizing the Horus-principle), in much the same way as are the Nubians and Asiatics. Indeed, it is interesting to find that in the nearby scenes on the same painted chest depicting the defeat of the these enemies of Egypt, hunting dogs are shown helping the king in battle. It is as if in all these pictures there is the suggestion of some kind of cosmic, archetypal "hunt" enacted as much in battle as in the desert chase. And while in neither case, be it the battle scenes or the hunt, can we be certain that there is a correspondence to any physical occurrence, the one thing we can be sure of is that the king's triumph represents the eternal truth of *maat's* defeat of *isfet*.

So powerful was this imaginal motif for the Egyptians, that one can detect its presence informing the many scenes of ancient Egyptian (nonroyal) tomb owners hunting in the marshes. The remarkable

*Fig. 7.9. Tutankhamun hunting desert gazelles.*

*Fig. 7.10. Nebamun goes hunting in the marshes.*

consistency of design in these scenes, which first appear in tombs of the Old Kingdom and continue through the Middle Kingdom and into the New Kingdom, is an important pointer toward the fact that they should be seen as existing in a symbolic rather than a literal world. The marshes, which team with life both in the air and under the water, provide, however, a very different imaginal environment from that of the desert where Tutankhamun hunts gazelles. While the forces of nature tend toward barrenness and death in the desert, in the marshes one encounters an overabundance of life. These images are in fact less concerned with the establishment of order over the wild and chaotic energies of the marshes than with the tomb owner's appropriation of their vitality for his own benefit. They are less about defeating than drawing sustenance from these exuberant life forces. The pictures are full of extremely rich and diverse symbolism, much of it connected with motifs of fertility and rebirth.[19] Thus do they provide a point of entry to a realm in which layer on layer of symbolic meanings are revealed to one who approaches them with the contemplative imagination.

Fig. 7.10 shows part of a typical "hunting in the marshes" scene, in which the tomb owner, who was a "scribe and counter of grain" called Nebamun, accompanied by his wife and daughter, attacks the birdlife with the aid of his remarkably agile cat (shown leaping in the air just in front of him). The hieroglyphs explain that he is not simply hunting but is also "seeing what is good in the place of eternity (*neheh*)."[20] This scene, in other words, is not located in any physical or literal marsh, but provides us with a window into a trans-temporal reality. There his naked daughter picks lotus, a plant, which for the Egyptians had both sexual and solar connotations, while his wife stands fully dressed behind him carrying a bundle of lotus flowers and wearing her wig, which for the Egyptians had specific erotic associations.[21] With his throwstick in his hand, Nebamun is (by means of a visual pun) in the act not only of "throwing" but also of "begetting," for the Egyptian word *qema* has the double meaning of both "to throw" and also "to beget" or "to create."[22] Thus although at first glance the world in which this hunting expedition takes place might seem to be composed of frenzied birds and docile fish, it soon reveals itself to be the spiritual source of procreativity, generation, and regeneration.

Fig. 7.10 in fact shows just one half of a traditional scene that usually included the tomb owner portrayed a second time spearing fish with his harpoon, as in fig. 7.11. The assault on the birdlife is now complemented in the full scene by an assault on the fish under the water. The two fish

*Fig. 7.11. Fishing and fowling in the marshes.*

being speared here are *Tilapia nilotica,* which have a particularly unusual characteristic. Once their eggs have been laid, the parent takes them into her mouth and broods them there until they hatch. She then spits them out in much the same way as Atum originally spat out the first gods Shu and Tefnut. To catch these *Tilapia nilotica* is thus to have caught the life-giving power of the creator god. Since the word *seti,* which is used for the spearing of fish, resembles the word *seti* "to impregnate," yet another layer of meaning is visually present in this scene.[23] Indeed, one even has the feeling here, as in many other similar representations, that the fish are less being caught than are offering themselves to the hunter voluntarily. As with the throwstick motif, we find ourselves in a symbolically charged imaginal world that transports us to the origins of creation, and to the sources of the generation of life.

Every element of the picture is part of a symbolic language, from the papyrus and lotus plants to the omnipresent cat, the butterfly, and the different species of fish and birds. If we ask the question, "Where is this hunting scene taking place?" The answer is that it is located in a kind of collective dream that the artist reaches into and represents anew, so as to make it once again live on the plane of sense perception. The artist draws the imaginal reality into a certain physical space, in the upper chamber (or chambers) of a tomb, which would have been accessible to the living.

In this way *heka* is activated in the tomb, and its transforming energy is injected into the interweaving cycles of time and eternity, death and rebirth. This picture would have had as much of a magical function as had the depiction of the pharaoh slaying the enemies of Egypt: there is no question that these images were intended to invoke specific spiritual forces for specific purposes, first and foremost for the spiritual regeneration of the tomb owner.

## THE ARTIST AS PRIEST

Ancient Egyptian artists were expected to be able to mediate between worlds, expressing in sense-perceptible forms essentially nonperceptible realities. In this respect, their work took place at the threshold between worlds. It is therefore unlikely that the artist's training was solely in technique. A certain spiritual training, as well as technical expertise, would have been required of the artist, in order for the images created to have been capable of serving the purposes for which they were intended.

We know that in ancient Egypt artists worked in teams, some of which were surprisingly large.[24] These teams were hierarchically organized, from the humble assistants who mixed the pigments with glue or gum in preparation for their application, to the apprentices, the skilled draughtsmen and finally the senior artisans and workshop masters or "overseers" who would have supervised the work and borne ultimate responsibility for it. As an apprentice moved up the hierarchy, we may surmise that a spiritual training accompanied the technical training, for the underlying aim of the artist was in most cases to produce images capable of magical activation.[25] The stele of a Middle Kingdom artist, named Irtisen, supports this supposition for it not only lists his technical accomplishments but also ascribes to him the following claim:

> I know the mysteries of the divine word and the conducting of ritual.
> All prepared magic—it belongs to me, without (any) thereof passing
> me by. Moreover I am a craftsman, successful in his craft, "one who
> knows and comes out on top" through that which he knows.[26]

Irtisen is claiming the kind of knowledge that one would expect of a lector priest (*khery-heb*). We know that at the New Kingdom artists' village of Deir el Medina, draughtsmen acted as ritualists and one is specifically named as a "lector priest of Amon."[27] So, at a certain level of seniority, it would seem that artists were qualified to take on specific priestly functions.

Since ancient Egyptian art was for the most part sacred art, this should not be a cause for wonder. Just as the production of icons in the Christian orthodox tradition placed a requirement on the icon painter to undergo a definite inner discipline, so too we must assume something similar in ancient Egypt, where images were regarded with comparable awe as the potential medium of spiritual presences. In his study, *Icons and the Mystical Origins of Christianity*, Richard Temple has argued for the existence of esoteric schools in both antiquity and in the Byzantine era. In these schools artists would have developed knowledge of working with psychic and spiritual energies, which was then demonstrated in their art.[28]

The only institution that we know of in ancient Egypt that comes near to being an esoteric school is the so-called "House of Life" (*per ankh*) that probably existed in every important town and was loosely attached to a temple.[29] The House of Life was the source of rituals, medical potions, and religious writings and was also where "secret" or esoteric knowledge was preserved. Those connected with the House of Life were greatly concerned with magic, and many "scribes of the House of Life" were lector priests (essentially professional magicians).[30] Literacy was a key condition for belonging to a House of Life. It is worth remembering that apart from the king and priests it was only scribes who constituted the tiny elite of just one percent of the population who had the ability to read and write. It is therefore significant that in ancient Egypt the artist was regarded as a kind of scribe—the *sesh-qed* or *sesh-qedwt* translated variously as "outline scribe," "image scribe," or "draughtsman." A vital element in the training of the artist involved acquiring the ability to read and write, and this in itself is an indicator that higher ranking artists would have potentially had access to sacred texts, and so, by implication, to a House of Life.[31] They would have had to have had this access if they were meaningfully to incorporate sacred texts in their work, for example in the decoration of temples and royal tombs.

The large extent of the spiritual responsibilities of the artist is indicated by the fact that the planning of several royal tombs in the New Kingdom—from their overall dimensions, the size of each chamber, and the passages between chambers, to the subjects of the pictures and their composition in general—was apparently carried out not by priests but by the leading draughtsman (the *hery sesh-qedwt*) implying that a man in this position was expected to have just the kind of priestly credentials claimed by Irtisen.[32] This does not mean that priests were therefore excluded from decisions concerning the decoration of royal tombs, which seems inconceivable, but only that the leading draughtsman evidently bore a good deal of the responsibility. A connection between leading draughtsmen and the House of Life is therefore extremely likely.[33]

Ancient Egyptian art itself, with its intricate symbolism and its strict adherence to such formal requirements as the use of the canons of proportion and the various conventions of representing the human form, speaks of something far more than mere mechanical adherence to established norms and rules. These formal requirements were based on profound spiritual principles, as Schwaller de Lubicz has shown.[34] Furthermore, we cannot ignore the devotional quality that pervades Egyptian art, the source of which must have been not simply in an outward adherence to convention but also in an inward alignment of the artist with *maat*. Such inner alignment to *maat* implies that a spiritual discipline was integral to the training and ongoing development of the artist, as he progressed toward becoming a master.

## THE RESPONSIBILITY OF THE ARTIST

One of the main obstacles to understanding ancient Egyptian art today is that, in comparison with the world of the ancient Egyptians, our world has become extremely literalized. The scientific reality-principle that prevails in our culture is one that has no place for the symbolic image and no recognition of levels of existence that lie beyond the material. For those who subscribe to the dominant scientific outlook, what is real must be externally observable, or at the very least measurable. By contrast, the Egyptians lived with an awareness of levels of reality that exist in a dimension that is at once interior, collective, and immeasurably "imaginal." The meaning of ancient Egyptian art will therefore escape us unless we deliteralize our thinking and our mode of perception, and open ourselves to the reality of the powerful archetypal and spiritual energies that the Egyptians accessed through the realm of images. Despite the fact that in our own times the realm of images has been largely co-opted by "glamour" and the forces of commercialism, the image nevertheless remains one of the most important mediums by which we are able to become aware of interior worlds. Ancient Egyptian art was based on an understanding of this spiritual potential of the image to mediate interior realities.

We have seen that for the Egyptians there was a special responsibility borne by the artist working with images, whether these were two or three dimensional. This responsibility derived from the awareness that every image is potentially an invitation to the denizens of the spirit world to become visibly or tangibly present. One of the terms used by the ancient Egyptians to refer to artists—especially sculptors, but it was also used to refer to other artists as well—was "he who makes to live" or "he who brings to life" (*s-ankh*).[35] Precisely because images were seen as the medium through which spirits become manifest, the ancient Egyptian artists had a responsibility to know and understand the spiritual import of their creative work.

Today we fall short of the kind of awareness of the spirit world that pervaded ancient Egyptian culture. If there was then a recognition of the peculiar capacity of the image or object created by the human hand to provide a physical home for spirit, we, by contrast, have constructed for ourselves a world that rests upon the presupposition that what is material excludes spirit. We fail to see that the objects that we surround ourselves with, and which in some cases accompany us through the day, can mediate spiritual presences. We delude ourselves into thinking that they are simply inanimate. But in the world of the ancient Egyptians there were no "objects" as such: every object was at the same time potentially a subject. Thus paintings and sculptures could become alive, because they formed a living point of contact, a kind of magical juncture, between exterior and interior realities.

Under these circumstances, the artists of ancient Egypt were positioned, like the priest—and in some cases *as* the priest—between worlds: they were the mediators between worlds. Theirs was undoubtedly a key role in sustaining the sacred culture of Egypt. It goes almost without saying that they could only fulfill this role if they were able to work beyond their own personal desires, fantasies, and neuroses into the transpersonal. This required inner discipline and the moral rectitude associated with aligning the soul with the goddess Maat. The Egyptian artist needed to align inwardly with Maat in order to avoid the ever-present danger of falling under the spell of *isfet,* and thereby of giving an entry point to diabolical rather than benevolent spiritual powers.

Should we be so inclined, we could learn a great deal from the ancient Egyptians not only about the innate possibilities of art to connect us again to transcendent realities, but also about what it might mean to live in a sacred culture. For a sacred culture is one that cultivates and continually renews its relationship to the principle of truth or cosmic harmony (whether this is referred to as *rita, dharma, dike,* or as in Egypt, *maat*) and, basing itself upon this principle, establishes a conscious relationship with the spiritual dimension of existence. This, as we have seen, was what was fostered in ancient Egypt, not least through its art. I do not suggest that we should try to imitate or emulate Egyptian art or revamp the old rituals. But we can draw inspiration from ancient Egypt in our endeavors to rehabilitate the sacred in our own times, and in our own way. In these endeavors I believe the artist has a vital role to play.

# 8

## ANCIENT EGYPT AND MODERN ESOTERICISM

*What is it about ancient Egypt that people today find so fascinating? This essay suggests that what really draws people to Egypt is less the great monuments and works of art than the religious consciousness that produced them. This religious consciousness of the ancient Egyptians exposes a tension in our own culture between the worldview of modern scientific materialism on the one hand and a worldview that would connect us once again with the reality of the spiritual dimension. Looking back to the ancient Egyptians, we find that their awareness of the interior realms of gods, spirits, and archetypal images strikes a surprising chord with our own deepest longings.*

*The essay is based on a talk given at the Theosophical Society, London, on November 27, 2003.*[1]

### THE FASCINATION WITH ANCIENT EGYPT

Today, there seems to be an unprecedented fascination with ancient Egypt. We see evidence of this in the unceasing flow of books on ancient Egyptian history, culture, and art; in the seemingly inexhaustible TV coverage that ancient Egypt attracts; in the amount of journals and magazines, both scholarly and popular, dedicated to widening our understanding of the civilization; in the plethora of societies devoted to studying and celebrating it; in the numerous lecture courses being given in the adult education departments of our universities; and not least in the huge amount of tourists visiting Egypt each year. We might well ask: what lies behind this modern fascination with ancient Egypt?

Certainly, the Egyptians produced some monumental buildings and stunning works of art, the grandeur of which makes the achievements of contemporary civilization seem paltry by comparison. Were we to attempt to build a replica of the Great Pyramid, I doubt that we would succeed. We are good at mobile phones, washing machines, motorways, and aeroplanes, but I don't think we could manage to construct the Great Pyramid, nor for that matter the temple at Karnak, nor the tombs of the Valley of the Kings. It somehow isn't in us to do the sort of things the Egyptians did. We aren't motivated that way, and have neither the patience nor the skill. Could it therefore be due as much to our own deficiencies as to their genius that we feel attracted to the Egyptians? They did things that are to us extraordinary, almost superhumanly extravagant and at the same time deeply mysterious. While there are of course many things about the Egyptians that we can relate to, fundamentally they were *not like us.*

It seems to me, therefore, that in order to answer the question as to what lies behind our fascination with Egypt we need to go beyond our feelings of awe and wonder at the great monuments and works of art, to the less comfortable feeling of ancient Egypt's utter strangeness, its *otherness.* There is something about Egypt that can strike us as positively uncanny. This is especially the case when we encounter the religious world of the Egyptians, populated as it was by a multitude of gods and spirits. Despite the reassuring images of "daily life" Egypt, which are presented to us in the media and in popular books by Egyptologists, we can often feel that the ancient Egyptians inhabited a world that was disturbingly different from our own. In order to understand that world, and to understand the consciousness of the people whose world it was, we need to stretch our imaginations away from everything that is familiar to us today.

There was (in the autumn of 2003) a particularly lavish drama-documentary series on ancient Egypt on TV. It reconstructed famous episodes from ancient Egyptian history with the aid of large casts, including actors who were supposedly speaking ancient Egyptian (made to seem all the more authentic by adding English subtitles). One of the programs in the series was on Thutmose III's campaigns against the Syrians, his capture of the cities of Megiddo and Kadesh, and other spectacular military triumphs. It included an authoritative voice-over assuring us that the reconstructions were based on hieroglyphic inscriptions at Karnak. Needless to say it was all absolutely riveting, and viewers must have felt themselves to be witnessing virtually the real thing—Egypt as it truly was.

The approach that was taken followed that which has been taken time and again by Egyptologists, in which Thutmose is presented as a great warrior and empire builder, somewhat akin to Napoleon, conceiving of bold and daring plans, and leading his armies from one victory to another.[2] The "Napoleonic" image of the Egyptian king is given credence by the fact that Thutmose III was indeed a daring and shrewd military commander, who significantly extended the overseas territories of Egypt and added vastly to the wealth and power of his country. But if Thutmose III was a figure who we feel inclined to compare with Napoleon, then we must also take care to remember that there were important differences not just between the two personalities, but also between the two cultures in which they lived. In ancient Egypt the kingship was not simply a political office, but was also religious. Even for a warrior king such as Thutmose III, the relationship to the invisible world of gods and spirits was fundamental not only to his power and success, but also to what it meant to be the king of Egypt.

There is an interesting document that has come down to us that gives us some insight into what the kingship of Egypt actually entailed. It is a coronation text of Thutmose III in which he claims to have had a mystical encounter with the sun god Amon-Ra, which was, as it were, woven into the coronation ceremonies. The key features of this experience were that the king transformed himself into a falcon, flew up to heaven, and there had a vision of Amon-Ra. The king was infused with the god's spiritual power and assimilated into himself "the wisdom of the gods." This is how the text reads:

He [Amon-Ra] opened for me the doors of heaven and unfolded the gates of the *Akhet* [a place of spiritual transformation]. I rose to heaven as a divine falcon and saw his secret image in heaven. I worshipped his majesty . . . I was infused with all his *akh*-power [luminous spiritual power] and instructed in the wisdom of the gods.[3]

This text confronts us with a rather different image of Thutmose III from the favored Napoleonic stereotype. The text itself could go back to 1504 BC, but it is similar to much older Egyptian texts (the so-called Pyramid Texts) found on the inside of certain fifth- and sixth-dynasty pyramids, some eight hundred years earlier. There we find the same themes of the king of Egypt transforming into a falcon and flying up to the sky, where he has a vision of Ra, becomes inwardly infused with the solar light and the wisdom of the gods.

Anyone familiar with the literature of shamanism will recognize a shamanic undercurrent to this type of mystical experience. One might say that it has a shamanic "prototype" for in this literature we read of initiations in which the shaman transforms into a bird (often an eagle), flies up to the sky, and becomes inwardly illumined after encountering the Great God, and then returns to his tribe with a newly acquired spiritual knowledge.[4] Seen in this light, it would appear that during the coronation rites of the king, Thutmose III had an experience similar to a shamanic initiation, and was thus in touch with a dimension of reality that was beyond anything Napoleon knew. Because it does not fit our preconceptions of how we would like to see the great warrior Thutmose, it has been "screened out" of the mainstream portrayal of the king. It has indeed been screened out of the mainstream portrayal of Egyptian culture as such. Within Egyptology there is still a great reluctance to accept that either mysticism or shamanism existed in ancient Egypt: this is the line taken by most Egyptologists today, with just one or two exceptions. So it is hardly surprising that the media follow suit.[5]

Nevertheless, behind the fascination with ancient Egypt today I would suggest that there is a deep longing to reconnect with precisely the aspect of ancient Egyptian culture that is oriented toward spiritual realities. This longing may be more or less conscious in those people who feel drawn to ancient Egypt, and many may wish to deny any such longing. But as time goes on and it becomes increasingly difficult to ignore the spiritual foundations of ancient Egyptian culture, so it may also become harder to ignore what it is in the culture that works so mysteriously to draw people to it. It is as if ancient Egypt has a certain karmic role to play in our times, and that this role is to expose the tension in our own culture between, on the one hand, our allegiance to the worldview of modern science that seeks to account for everything in the world—past and present—in materialistic terms, and, on the other hand, a longing to escape from the confines of this worldview and reconnect with spiritual realities once again. Put in more general historical terms, this tension could be seen as living between our habitual deference to the worldview inaugurated by the religion of Judaism and the philosophy and scientific rationalism of the Greeks on the one side, and an underlying sense of dissatisfaction with the Judaeo-Christian and Greco-Roman foundations of Western culture on the other. Undoubtedly the latter have determined the way in which the consciousness of the West has developed over the last twenty-five hundred years. But if we look back to Egypt with a sensitivity toward the spiritual matrix within which the Egyptians lived, then we may find that the pre-Judaic and pre-Greek consciousness of the Egyptians was a consciousness that strikes a surprising chord with our own deepest longings.

## THE IMAGINARY VERSUS THE IMAGINAL

The tension that I have referred to in our own culture and sensibility has been noted by Erik Hornung, one of the most eminent contemporary Egyptologists who has specialized in the study of ancient Egyptian religious literature. He is also one of the foremost apologists for the non-mystical interpretation of ancient Egyptian religion. In his book, *The Secret Lore of Egypt,* he takes on the question of the relationship between ancient Egyptian religious life and those Western esoteric traditions that see Egypt as the source of an initiatory wisdom. To this end, Hornung makes a distinction between "Egyptosophy" and Egyptology proper.[6] For Hornung, "Egyptosophy" involves projecting onto ancient Egypt an ill-founded wish to see it as a repository of spiritual knowledge. Egyptology, by contrast, shows us that there were no mysteries, no esoteric or initiatory teachings or practices in ancient Egypt. Western esoteric streams like Alchemy, Gnosticism, the Hermetic Tradition, Rosicrucianism, which in their different ways see their roots as going back to ancient Egypt, are all dealt with by Hornung in a summary and deadpan manner. Chapter by chapter he sets out to demonstrate that their understanding of Egyptian religion has been tainted by illusory fantasies that fail to correspond with the facts as revealed to us by modern scholarship. Hornung's stance is that Egyptology studies real Egypt, whereas "Egyptosophy" constructs an "imaginary Egypt," which bears only a rather "loose relationship to historical reality."[7] Hornung's approach is very much that of the modern rationalist for whom what is real and what is imaginary form two sides of an irreconcilable opposition.

It is scarcely surprising to find that, as a modern rationalist, Hornung fails to refer to—let alone utilize—an important distinction that many modern esotericists, as well as depth psychologists, make. It is the distinction between what is merely "imaginary" and what is "imaginal." Whereas what is imaginary is the product of personal fantasy and may therefore be regarded as subjective, what is imaginal gives access to a transpersonal content that has an objective reality, even though it may not correspond to any historical fact or physical event.[8] The imaginal realm, or *mundus imaginalis* as it is often termed, has an existence that is independent of those individuals who become aware of it. It thus possesses an ontological status that has a universal validity that the products of a person's private fantasies do not achieve.

Even people with the most slender knowledge of ancient Egypt will be aware that their world was populated by a very large number of gods and goddesses. These were essentially invisible beings who were given imaginative forms, which were then represented in sculpture and painting. If the question arises as to whether the Egyptians would have regarded these beings as imaginary or imaginal, we hardly need pause for an answer. It is quite obvious that these deities were regarded as both real and powerful agencies by the Egyptians, and that it would have seemed to them most unwise to ignore their objective existence. Whereas the "Egyptosophist" would concur with the Egyptians in seeing the gods as real entities, most Egyptologists would be far less willing to do so. As one specialist put it, they are to be regarded rather as the product of "vivid speculation" that is likely to "disappoint the modern inquiring mind" than as pointing to any objective reality.[9] We are therefore entitled to ask where the problem of interpreting ancient Egyptian religion really lies. Is it with the so-called Egyptosophists projecting an imaginary Egypt onto real Egypt, or with the Egyptologists who are unable to recognize that for the Egyptians literal and historical reality was not the only reality: "imaginal" reality was just as real as hard and fast historical "facts."

So let us once more return to Thutmose III and his campaign against the Syrians. Undoubtedly, Thutmose III was a great warrior. But if we ask, "How did he learn to become such a great warrior?" the Egyptian answer would be that he was taught by the god Seth and encouraged by the goddess Neith. Fig. 8.1 shows the two deities instructing the young king. Both were renowned for their violent disposition—they were both warrior deities. If Thutmose III was a great warrior, then it was not, according to the Egyptians, by virtue of his human qualities as much as by virtue of his having been infused with the energy of these two deities.

For the Egyptians, there was a world of archetypal energies or powers that had to be called upon in order for the king to be a great warrior. Reality was for them twofold in this sense: it was both visible and invisible. What we see portrayed in fig. 8.1 is Thutmose III with two invisible beings. We could of course dismiss these beings as imaginary, but if we were to do so then we would no longer be seeing the world of the Egyptians as the Egyptians themselves saw it. For them, these invisible beings were imaginal in precisely the sense that they were objectively real.

*Fig. 8.1. Thutmose III, instructed by Seth and Neith. Neith is represented abstractly in front of the king, holding a was scepter.*

Let us stay with Thutmose III. A very different situation is portrayed in fig. 8.2. Here there are no invisible deities represented. We see a relief of Thutmose slaughtering the defeated enemy. The king is depicted as a veritable giant, grabbing the hair of forty-two paltry Syrians, who are shown in three ranks of fourteen, with their arms outstretched, begging for mercy. In his right hand (unfortunately missing from this damaged relief), the king holds a mace with which he is about to dispatch them with one blow. They are all on their knees, helpless before the superhuman power of the king. One might be tempted to say that this hardly represents a realistic picture of the pharaoh overpowering the enemies of Egypt, for, as we all know, it would be impossible for one man to grab hold of the hair of forty-two warriors and slay them all with one blow. The image, however, is evoking an *imaginal reality* that every pharaoh embodied, or sought to embody. This imaginal reality was portrayed from the very earliest dynastic period, and was represented consistently throughout Egyptian history as something far more than simply a picture celebrating a pharaoh's military victory.

To understand such an image we have to see its primary purpose as religious: it was not so much meant to record a historical event as to magically evoke an imaginal archetype. While the image may have been engraved upon stone after the event, it was—precisely insofar as it served a religious function—present at the imaginal level and was utilized at that level to determine the outcome of the pharaoh's campaign.[10] The magical efficacy of these images (for this is just one of a large number, from the very earliest dynasties, in the same genre) is due to the fact that they align the pharaoh with greater than human cosmic forces. What the pharaoh is shown as enacting is a cosmic battle between *maat* (cosmic order, truth, and justice) and *isfet* (cosmic disorder, untruth, and injustice). It is this archetypal reality that was made to supervene and, as it were, impress itself upon the historical events in order to make the pharaoh's power truly godlike and to assure him of victory.

*Fig. 8.2. Thutmose III about to slay forty-two Syrians. From a damaged relief at the temple of Karnak.*

Fig. 8.3 shows a relief carving in the same genre, made about three hundred years after the reign of Thutmose. It portrays the pharaoh Merenptah almost single-handedly defeating the invading Sea Peoples. Surrounding the king is an aura of calm, quiet confidence, while the invading Sea Peoples are in total chaos. Once again, what is portrayed here is the archetypal reality that each successive pharaoh actualizes. And in so doing, he manifests a spiritual energy-field on the physical plane. The kings of Egypt may have been great warriors, but their prowess did not rely solely on physical might. They also operated with magic, and it was as much through magic as through military skill that they defeated their enemies.[11]

*Fig. 8.3. King Merenptah defeats the Sea Peoples.*

The mythological source of these images of the king single-handedly defeating the enemies of Egypt is the defeat of the cosmic python Apophis every day at midday and every night in the middle of the night.[12] Apophis is the form taken by the cosmic forces of chaos, darkness, and disorder that would swallow up the light- and life-giving sun god Ra on the god's journey across the skies.

*Fig. 8.4. Seth, on the prow of the sun boat, defeats Apophis.*

Sometimes Apophis is attacked and defeated by Ra's son Horus, sometimes by Seth. In fig. 8.4, it is Seth who stands on the prow of the sun boat and strikes the opposing serpent. Seth is here the protector of the principle of light, personified in the falcon-headed sun god, just as he was the instructor of Thutmose in the arts of war. Thutmose III was both the defender of Amon-Ra and his protégé and representative in his campaigns against the enemies of Egypt in the East.

*Fig. 8.5. Amenhotep III is in the role of Ra as he sails with his wife in a ritual during his Sed festival.*

The association of the king of Egypt with the sun god Ra has a further significance. In the coronation text of Thutmose III, to which we have already referred, the king was infused with the luminous spiritual power (the *akh*-power) of the sun god in a mystical experience of union with the mysterious essence of the lord of light and life. This "solarization" of the king was an important initiatory event that was undergone not only at his initial coronation but also in subsequent coronation ceremonies, particularly those of the Sed festival. The king was therefore more than just Ra's representative on earth, for he also mystically embodied the solar principle. One of the purposes of the Sed festival was to renew the inner union of the king with the solar principle.[13] In a representation of the Sed festival of king Amenhotep III, the king is clearly fused with the sun god in a ceremony that involved his sailing in a replica of the sun boat with his wife, who is probably in the role of the goddess Hathor (fig. 8.5).

## THE HIDDEN REALM

On an inner level, this ritual sailing of the king occurs in the heavens. Just as in the coronation text of Thutmose III the king flies up to the sky in order to worship Ra and be filled with his *akh*-power, so the context of the ritual sailing is cosmic. The ancient Egyptians understood that to become enlightened one must become aware of that which is cosmic in one's own nature. One must realize that there is something deep within human nature that is essentially not of this earth, but is a cosmic principle.

The cosmic being who presided over Ra's diurnal voyage across the sky was the heavenly goddess Nut. It was she who gave birth to Ra each morning, and who received him into herself again in the evening. Each evening, when Ra entered her interior realm, he entered the secret and wholly invisible world that the Egyptians called the "Dwat." The Dwat was conceived as being on the other side of the stars that we see when we look up at the night sky. The stars were imagined as being on the flesh of the goddess Nut, and the Dwat was in some sense behind or within the world of which the stars demarcated the outermost boundary.[14] It was not just the sun god, however, that entered the Dwat at the end of the day. All creatures were believed to return to the Dwat at the end of their lives, pass into its dark interior, and were born from it again, just as the sun god was born from the Dwat each morning. There was thus a very important mystical threshold between the outwardly visible cosmos—the stars on Nut's body—and what exists invisibly in her interior. It is a threshold we all come to when we die, when everything becomes concentrated in a single point, and then disappears from view. Fig. 8.6 shows the stages of the sun god's night journey through Nut's body, as he travels from death to rebirth.

*Fig. 8.6. The sky goddess Nut conceals within her body the mysterious inner region known by the Egyptians as the Dwat.*

Knowledge of this interior world of the Dwat was considered by the Egyptians to be the most important, most profound knowledge, for people living on Earth to acquire. The Dwat was not only the realm of the dead, but also the realm of the gods and spirits and, furthermore, the realm from which all living things emerge.[15] All life issues from the Dwat. To know this mysterious interior world was to become truly wise, because then one knew both sides of existence—the invisible along with the visible. It is interesting that Thutmose III had the complete text and illustrations of the most comprehensive guide to the Dwat (The Book of What Is in the Underworld) painted on the inner walls of his tomb in the Valley of the Kings. As his coronation text reminds us, this was a king who was "instructed in the wisdom of the gods." Unlike

Napoleon, Thutmose III was initiated into a deep spiritual knowledge. It is not without significance that the name Thutmose means, "born of Thoth," the god whom the Greeks identified with Hermes, and from whom one of the most important of the Western esoteric traditions—the Hermetic Tradition—derives its name.

## THE THREE TASKS

I have tried to show that the Egyptians lived with an awareness of a dimension of reality that is best described by the term "imaginal"—a nonphysical yet objective reality that we become aware of through the human faculty of imagination. For the Egyptians, the agencies and powers that can be reached through contact with the imaginal world are far more potent than anything merely physical, because through them physical reality can be transformed. Thus we have seen how Thutmose III called upon Seth and Neith to infuse him with a superhuman martial energy that enabled him to go to war with an irresistible ferocity. In battle after battle, he and his accompanying priests could also magically invoke the imaginal reality of the defeat of the powers opposed to the sun god and Maat, both of whom the pharaoh represented, indeed embodied, on earth. It was this, according to his own account, which brought Thutmose his victories.[16]

I have also tried to show that the Egyptians lived with an understanding that we are not just terrestrial beings—we are also cosmic. As such, our spiritual fulfillment is only possible in a cosmic setting. This understanding is to be found from the earliest sacred literature (the Pyramid Texts) to the coronation text of Thutmose III and the Book of the Dead, where, for example, such mystical episodes as flying up to the sky, seeing the image of the sun god, boarding the sun boat, and/or becoming inwardly "solarized" are all recorded.[17]

Finally, I have suggested that the Egyptians had an orientation toward the world of the dead (the Dwat) that saw it as being the source of the most profound wisdom concerning the nature of reality. There is a remarkably rich metaphysical literature concerning the Dwat, knowledge of which was evidently regarded as relevant not only to the dead but also to the living.[18]

All of this was "mainstream" ancient Egyptian religious consciousness. At the end of the Egyptian era it went "underground," moving from the temple to the private household, and the small group meeting in secret, from whence it would pass into various esoteric traditions.[19] Thus in the alchemical tradition there is a particular focus on the imaginal realm of archetypes and the path of inner transformation; in the Hermetic tradition there is a concentration on the realization of our cosmic nature; while in Gnosticism we find a particular emphasis on the invisible hierarchies of the spirit world. These three Western esoteric streams could be understood as each preserving in their different ways the ancient Egyptian wisdom into the next cultural era. Meanwhile the emerging mainstream culture with its Judaeo-Christian and Greco-Roman basis increasingly rejected the old consciousness. The world became more and more impermeable to the divine, archetypal, and imaginal presences. In Judaism the notion of idolatry—which would have been incomprehensible to the ancient Egyptians—came to dominate the religious consciousness, while the Greeks and Romans saw the gods slowly fade away and become less and less easy to communicate with.[20] The new consciousness meant that people experienced the world going through a kind of solidification, so that it was no longer able to transmit the radiant energies of the divine.

At the same time there emerged an increasing sense that human beings were simply terrestrial beings, and consequently our happiness was conceived less in cosmic terms and more in terms of satisfying our physical needs, desires, and comforts. The material world had to be mastered to this end, and this in time became the great project of science and technology, which involved an almost complete forgetfulness of our cosmic origins. It also involved a forgetfulness of that part of human existence that belongs between death and rebirth. There was a growing identification of the human being solely with the life that we lead between birth and death. Already, both the Greek and Judaic conceptions of life after death expressed the conviction that the soul survived as a pale and ghostly reflection of its former self. As the ghost of Achilles says in Homer's *Odyssey,* "the senseless dead" are "mere shadows of men outworn."[21] This view, so very different from that of the Egyptians, culminated in the modern idea that there simply is no existence at all after death. Modern scientific materialism is founded upon a total ignorance of the spirit world.

At the beginning of this essay, I proposed that ancient Egypt exposes a tension in our own culture, and that in so doing we can see its karmic role today. The reason why it may be helpful to see Egypt in these terms is because we are now coming to the end of the Greco-Roman/Judaeo-Christian era. It has achieved its purpose, which was to make us more individuated, more self- rather than god-centered in our soul-life, and thus more free. But now there is a need to become aware again of inner, spiritual realities, but to become aware of them grounded in our own sense of self and with a clear and discriminating intelligence with which we can once more turn toward them. So I would suggest that it is here that the profound karmic relationship is working between ancient Egypt and the new era that is beginning to unfold before us. While our relationship to ancient Egypt is certainly based upon our acquiring a deeper and more accurate knowledge of its culture and religion, the relationship is by no means simply in the direction of the present to the past. It is also about how the past can support us in forging our own future by helping us to reengage with the spiritual dimensions, which were so intrinsic to people's experience in times of old.[22]

What ancient Egypt can do today is to provide both the impetus and the anchorage for a modern esotericism. By esotericism I mean knowledge of inner realities. There is no question of "going back" to ancient Egypt. It is rather the case that by wrestling with ancient Egyptian sacred texts we are drawn *down* to a deeper level of awareness that we need to make more conscious. And feeling this need, we are driven to find our own new relationship to the spiritual dimension.

As I see it, there are three tasks ahead for contemporary esotericism. The first is to grow into a fully felt and participative relationship with the imaginal worlds that stand behind the physical. We need constantly to work at dissolving the density of the physical and literal world. We need to loosen its solidity in order to see through to the luminous world of spirits, gods, and archetypes that are its invisible matrix. They are, in a sense, the "dream" of the world that our modern, all too wide-awake consciousness has destroyed. There is a need today to return our waking consciousness to this dream, by bringing it once more into a living relationship with the imaginal dimensions of the world.

Along with this comes the second task, which is to expand our conception of ourselves beyond the confines of the earth by developing a sense that the cosmos that surrounds us is not just dead matter, but full of soul. To do this, we need not so much to *work against* as to *work through* the materialistic conceptions that permeate modern cosmological thinking. We can develop once again a feeling for the soul qualities of the planets and constellations, for the whole world of the stars. And the more we are able to do this—the more we are able to connect with the "world soul" or *anima mundi* as it used to be called—the more will we be able to reconnect again with our own cosmic nature.

I see the third task as being once more to become aware of the realm of death as the other half of life, as much a part of our existence as sleep is a part of our life between birth and death. It requires that we see this realm of death not so much as a place that we go to after we die as a realm that we inhabit—or one might say *inhabits us*—alongside the world of the living. The world of death can be understood as a completely interior world, and yet despite the fact that it has no dimensions, it is not necessarily inaccessible to consciousness. For its interiority ultimately coincides with our own. The more we become aware of the source of what arises in our own consciousness, the more do we extend our consciousness toward this deeply interior realm of death. And in extending our consciousness toward it, we extend our consciousness toward that other half of existence without which we cannot fully participate in life.

PART THREE

*The Path of Consciousness*

# BEING ANCIENT IN
# A MODERN WAY

## Divination in the Light
## of the History of Consciousness

Today, the widespread interest in divinatory practices like astrology, the
I Ching, and tarot could be seen as expressing a yearning to reconnect
with realms of soul and spirit with which ancient cultures were all too
familiar. And yet the modern relationship to these realms must inevitably be different from that which pertained in antiquity. For thousands
of years the examination of the entrails of slaughtered animals (extispicy)
was regarded in the ancient world as the surest means of ascertaining the
will of the gods, but extispicy would be deemed quite unacceptable today.
How and why does modern divinatory consciousness differ from that of the
ancients? What does this tell us not only about our changed relationship
to the divine, but also our changed relationship to ourselves? As we turn
once more to embrace divinatory practices, how are we to do it in a way
that is distinctively modern, a way that belongs to the future rather than
to the past?

This essay is based on a talk given at a conference at the University of
Kent, Canterbury, on "The Imaginal Cosmos: Astrology, Divination and
the Sacred" on October 3, 2004.[1]

## THE YEARNING TO RECONNECT

For thousands of years the practice of divination held a central place in the ancient cultures that preceded modern Western culture. Among the ancient Mesopotamians, Hittites, Greeks, Etruscans, and Romans divination was regarded as one of the most important ways of acquiring knowledge. It was a science, not in the modern sense of a method of acquiring knowledge of the physical world, but rather as a method of observing the physical world in order to acquire knowledge of the world of spirit. Observation of physical phenomena was put at the service of attaining knowledge of the disposition of the spiritual beings that were believed to determine the unfolding of events on the physical level of existence. Behind the practice of divination there was an assumption that certain physical phenomena are, or can become, linked to the world of gods and spirits. Divination was therefore practiced in the context of an experience of nature that was quite different from that which prevails today. For the divinatory consciousness of antiquity, nature was still permeated, or at the very least permeable, by the spirit world.

The historical development of European consciousness has led away from this experience of nature toward a feeling of scepticism regarding the existence of a world of gods and spirits, and incredulity as to the possibility that natural phenomena could give us any kind of privileged access to it. Our modern scientific worldview rests upon a philosophy of materialism that sees nature as intrinsically meaningless and without value. The overriding purpose of scientific knowledge is to gain power and control over nature for human benefit. There is no question that the observation of natural phenomena might lead to insight into the world of the gods, for the world of the gods no longer exists as a reality for people who have come under the sway of contemporary Western culture, save perhaps for those few who are rediscovering it in the depths of their own psyches. Nature does not have that openness to the gods that it once had: most people today do not feel the natural world to be "full of gods" and "ensouled and full of spirits (*daimones*)" as it was for the Greek philosopher Thales at the beginning of the sixth century BC.[2]

The contemporary revival of interest in divination could be understood as expressing a yearning to reconnect with the realms of soul and spirit as immanent within the spatio-temporal sphere. Despite their marginality to mainstream culture, the popularity of such divinatory practices as astrology, the I Ching, and Tarot is due at least in part to their resacralization of the dimension of time, if not space, in the divinatory act. The "divinatory moment" is set aside from the flow of profane time in order to give the diviner access to the spirit world. For modern practitioners, the act of divination presupposes the experience of creating a *temenos*—a kind of temporal "sacred space"—that enables one to see what spiritual forces are active in the present situation, and how one can successfully interact with them.[3] And yet the modern relationship to this realm of spiritual forces must inevitably be different from that which pertained in antiquity. Not only would it not be advisable to return ourselves to the old divinatory consciousness, but even if it was our ardent wish to do so, it would not be realizable, as I hope to show. If we seek once more to embrace divination today, then we have to do so from a standpoint radically different from that which characterized diviners in antiquity. The path taken by this essay is therefore to examine one particularly important and widespread divinatory practice of antiquity, in order to exemplify the old divinatory consciousness; and then to consider in what ways our modern practice of divination must differ from that of the ancients.

## EXTISPICY IN ANCIENT MESOPOTAMIA

Mesopotamia is celebrated today as being the home of Western astrology, largely because the division of the zodiac into twelve signs is of Babylonian origin, having occurred around the middle of the sixth century BC.[4] Prior to this comparatively late development, divinatory astronomical observations were being made at least as far back as the early second millennium BC.[5] It comes as a surprise, therefore, to find that the most important form of divination in Mesopotamia was not the observation of the sun, moon, and stars but the observation of the entrails (*exta*) of sacrificed animals, especially the liver, but also heart, lung, and colon. From the third millennium BC, extispicy was regarded as being more reliable than the observation not only of celestial bodies but also of other ominous phenomena, and was generally considered more dependable than the visions of prophets and ecstatics.[6] This may largely have been due to the fact that specific questions could be put, and their answer read in the appearance of the liver and other internal organs. Judging by the omen reports that have come down to us, observation of the stars was not used to answer specific questions, whereas extispicy nearly always was. We have, furthermore, records from the reign of Hammurabi (1792–1750 BC), and later, which show that it was sometimes felt necessary to confirm an astrological omen by performing extispicy.[7] Of the many different forms of divination practiced, liver divination was one of the earliest and was regarded as the most authoritative. Later on, other organs were also included and it became standard practice in civil administration when decisions of state had to be made, on military campaigns and also at critical junctures in the lives of those individuals who could afford it, to consult a diviner who would examine entrails: such diviners were omnipresent in ancient Mesopotamian society.[8] For the sake of simplicity, the following account will focus on the interpretation of the liver, which was the central organ examined by diviners performing extispicy.

The earliest written records of liver divination come from the Sumerian period in the middle of the third millennium BC, during the reign of Ur-Nanshe, king of Lagash. We know that it was used to determine the choice of the *en* priest of the city god in Sumerian times.[9] Liver divination was carried out by a diviner known as a *barû* (literally "examiner"). The *barû* was not a priest attached to any particular cult, but was recognized as a scholar, who was an expert in the inspection and interpretation of livers; these were invariably the livers of sheep— normally a young ram.[10] A sacrificial ram without blemish was thought to serve best as the vehicle of communication between the divine and the human world.

Before the ram was killed, the *barû* would wash and anoint himself,

*Fig. 9.1. Barû extracts liver from a ram laid out on a table. Reign of Assurnasirpal, 883–859 BC.*

put on special garments, offer a prayer to the sun god Shamash and/or the thunder god Adad, who were both regarded as "lords of divination" and then state the question to be asked in very specific terms, whispering into the ram's ear: "Will the enemy attack in the next hundred days?" "Will the king's sick son recover?" "Should the treaty be made?" and so on.[11] A ritual text from the Neo-Assyrian period details a divination ritual that took place through the night, lasting from sunset to sunrise, in which probably more than one sheep was sacrificed. During the ritual the question was literally placed before the gods, inscribed on a clay tablet, and put in front of their images.[12]

Great care would be taken in the slaughtering of the ram, which was killed by slitting the arteries in its throat. Owing to the speed with which the blood runs out of the body, the muscles would often contract and shake, sometimes violently. These convulsions were regarded as a sign that the god had made the omen descend into the ram.[13] Now placed upon a table, it had its belly cut open and its intestines were inspected *in situ,* while both lung and liver were removed for closer examination, the liver being of foremost significance (fig. 9.1). The order of inspection was in general from above downward, from right to left, and from front to back, with the diviner standing at the tail end of the sheep.[14]

It was believed that when an animal was sacrificed, it was in its death assimilated to the god or gods to whom it was sacrificed. Subtle forces and energies of the spirit world were thus impressed upon the soul of the animal. According to Morris Jastrow,

The animal is sanctified by the sacrifice, acquiring the very attributes which were associated with the god to whom it was offered . . . it seems certain that in animal sacrifice an essential feature is the belief that the soul or spirit of the god becomes identical with the soul of the sacrificial animal. The two souls become attuned to one another . . . Through the soul of the animal, therefore, a visible means was obtained for studying the soul of the god . . .[15]

According to Jastrow, both in ancient Mesopotamia and in ancient Greece up until the Archaic period (mid-seventh century BC), it was believed that the seat of the soul was the liver. There are old Mesopotamian texts, which have phrases like "his liver rejoiced" or "his liver was at peace" just where we would expect the word "heart" or "soul" to be used.[16] Here, then, we have the reason why the liver was the organ preeminently used in divination: it was the physical base of the inner life of the soul.

The liver was evidently regarded as a particularly sensitive organ. Its smooth, glistening surfaces could register the slightest psychic disturbance in the soul, and thus by implication the soul of the god. It was like a moist clay tablet, which could receive the imprint of the god's writing. What for the modern consciousness appears simply to be a sheep's liver was for the ancient Mesopotamian a highly receptive mirror of spiritual and psychic energies, by means of which spiritual conditions beyond the range of normal human perception could be "seen" or "read." Whereas for us a liver is and can only be just the physical organ of an animal, for the ancient Mesopotamian engaged in the act of divination the liver existed between the physical and spiritual worlds. It provided a kind of bridge between what is and what is yet to unfold from the spiritual realm into the sphere of human destiny. It could catch the fleeting movement of becoming before what-is-to-be has actually become, and thereby could give to those practicing divination the possibility of acting in harmony with the spiritual forces emanating from the realm of the gods and spirits.

To function in this way, the liver had to be viewed from a specific angle. For divinatory purposes, it had to be laid out as in fig. 9.2, with the gallbladder lying on top of it. When viewed like this, it becomes an imaginal landscape, with its own topography. Every feature of this landscape will vary slightly with each liver, and so each liver will be capable of conveying a unique "reading." The Babylonians recognized two main hemispheres, the left lobe and the larger right lobe, to which three appendices are attached: (1) the pyramid-shaped caudate lobe (also referred to as the *processus pyramidalis*) or *ubanu* ("finger") on the top right, (2) the smaller papillary process (*processus papillaris*) or *sibtu* ("increase") to the left of it and (3) the gallbladder or *martu* ("shepherd"), covering the center of the right lobe.[17] As in so many cultures, the right was regarded as lucky, the left as unlucky. For divinatory purposes, the right as the *pars familiaris* would refer to "us" and the left as the *pars hostilis* to "them"—so a good sign on the right was favorable, a bad sign on the right unfavorable, and vice versa. This applied to the right and left sides of each "appendix" and to all other significant zones and markings on the liver too.[18] So if the right side of the gallbladder was discolored but the left was not, then this would be taken as a bad sign. But if the left side was discolored and the right was normal, then this would be taken as a good sign.

The three appendices each had specific connotations of meaning. The *ubanu* (caudate lobe) represented what was foreign, hostile, sinister, or secluded, whereas the *martu* (gallbladder) represented the king and the throne. Thus, according to one apodosis from an Old Babylonian compendium, "If the *martu* is turned around and surrounds the top of the *ubanu,* the king will seize a hostile country."[19] The shape of the *ubanu* was of critical importance. An *ubanu* that was crescent shaped was regarded as a bad omen, whereas if it was shaped "like a lion's ear," it was a good omen.[20] Other factors such as color, size, firmness, perforation, and atrophy were all significant. A large gallbladder that spread over the surface of the liver was regarded as a good omen, but a gallbladder, which was split from left to right, was a bad omen. If the split was from right to left, then it was a good omen.[21] The same principles of interpretation applied to the *sibtu* (papillary process), which represented crops and the economy.

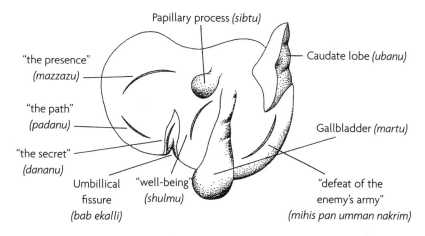

*Fig. 9.2. Diagram of a sheep's liver laid out for divinatory purposes.*

As well as these more obvious topographical features, more subtle ones were also recognized. The umbilical fissure where the left and right lobes meet at the bottom was known as the *bab ekalli* or *abullu* ("palace gate" or "city gate") and represented the palace, its administration, income, and personnel, and also the city gate. If this was long on the right side and short on the left side, it was a good omen, but if it was long on the left and short on the right, it was a bad omen.[22] In addition, there were five markings or creases that were expected to be present on the liver surface. These were (1) the *dananu,* a vertical fissure on the left side of the *bab ekalli,* which signified strength and a well-guarded secret.[23] (2) The *padanu* ("the path"), a horizontal groove on the left lobe, a little way from the *bab ekalli,* which had a range of meanings depending on the circumstances: it could indicate the military campaign, the journey to be undertaken, or the course of human life. (3) The *manzazu* or *mazzazu* ("the station" or "divine presence") or the *naplastu* ("the view"), a somewhat larger fissure above the *padanu,* which was regarded as particularly significant as it represented the presence of the god in the liver. (4) The *shulmu* ("well-being"), a vertical crease between the umbilical fissure and the gallbladder, which represented safety, health, and prosperity. (5) The *Padan shumel martim* ("path to the left of the gallbladder") or *mihis pan umman nakrim* ("defeat of the enemy's army"), a vertical crease to the right of the gallbladder, representing the enemy's campaign. The absence of any of these features, or any abnormality in their position or appearance would be carefully noted.

The liver was divided into zones, each of which was inspected in the same canonical order, beginning with the *mazzazu,* and proceeding counterclockwise to the *padanu,* the *dananu,* and the *shulmu;* then to the gallbladder and so on around, ending with the *sibtu* (papillary process or *processus papillaris*). The main markings, as well as various other fissures and grooves, were all assiduously observed, and each was assigned specific meanings. A large number of technical terms were used, which provide evidence of a minute knowledge of the liver—as an imaginal rather than a merely physiological organ. We learn of how, for example, small deposits of fat were called "the request" and interpreted as a demand made by a god or by an enemy; cavities or "holes" represented death or loss of eyesight; certain protrusions of flesh, called "weapons" if they were pointed, represented the army, but if such protrusions were mushroom shaped, the "weapons" were evidently blunted and thus signified defeat. "Crosses," "splits," "recesses," "branches," and "white patches"; "stings," "hollows," "rivers," and "pouches" were all features to be noted by the diviner. Each had their significance, which the diviner had to interpret.

The interpretation of livers was an elaborate science based on detailed empirical observation. It required expert training and the keeping of extensive records. While it was a means of entering a complex imaginal world, full of meanings and significances that escape us today, it was also a rigorous intellectual discipline antipathetic to any kind of ecstatic procedure for knowing the will of the gods.[24] That is to say, it involved the exercise of an informed and scholarly kind of thinking, utilizing careful analysis, consultation of records, and a deliberative rather than an inspired reading of the "god's writing" on the liver and other entrails. Fig. 9.3 shows one of many clay models of livers that have survived from Mari, Ugarit, Babylon, and other centers of Mesopotamian culture. Models like this were used for making reports in Old Babylonian times, and subsequently were used for

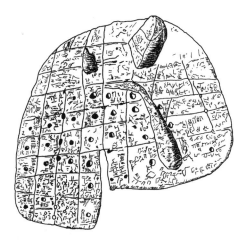

*Fig. 9.3. Babylonian clay model of a sheep's liver, ca. 2000 BC.*

teaching purposes. This particular Old Babylonian model is divided into fifty-five sections, covered with cuneiform texts, and pierced by holes. The three main appendices of the *ubanu, sibtu,* and *martu* are clearly visible.

It is important to understand the amount of care that was taken to build up a body of knowledge in the ancient science of extispicy. Over many hundreds of years, records were made of questions put to court diviners by the king or state officials concerning many varied topics, and to these were added the detailed results of the diviners' examinations of the appearance of the liver, and their judgment as to the meaning of these results. Finally, the outcome of the king's action would subsequently be appended to the records, and the tablet or clay model would then be filed as a precedent.[25] In this way a science was built up in which rules of association were formulated and expressed in omen tablets in the standard divinatory syllogism of "If . . ." followed by "then . . ." For example, "If the *mazzazu* is long and reaches the *padanu:* the prince will fulfill the campaign on which he is going." Here length is associated with fulfillment. In another example, we find protrusion associated with fame: "If the head of the *mazzazu* is protruding: success of the prince; my army will win fame." And, in another, thickness is associated with strength: "If the narrow part of the *martu* (gallbladder) is thick: the heir will become stronger than his father."[26]

In these and countless other examples, our impression is that in ancient Mesopotamia it was felt that the sure path to knowledge of how best to conduct oneself in harmony with the gods, was through the exercise of the intellectual faculties rather than through medium-ship or through visionary states of consciousness. And yet the object upon which all this intellectual effort was expended was the essentially imaginal liver and other exta of a sacrificed ram, believed to bear the impress of spiritual energies that emanated from the divine world. If we are inclined to fault the reasoning of the omen tablets, it is not because the syllogistic form was faulty (the middle term left out, for example), but only that most people today would disagree with its premise: that valid associations can be made between the appearance of a sheep's liver and human destiny. For us, the variations in the appearance of the liver are due either to chance or to diseases such as hydatid or liver fluke, which have no bearing at all on human destiny.[27] But then we have lost sight of the gods, who no longer reveal their intentions to us through the entrails of sheep. So on what grounds are we to dismiss the prem-ise of the Mesopotamians that for thousands of years supported the truth of the divinatory syllogism? We might say: "On the grounds of our knowledge." But the Mesopotamian *barû* would doubtless without hesitation reply: "No! It is on the grounds of your ignorance, for you have deprived the liver of its transcendental meaning."

The extent to which decision making at the highest levels of state was determined by divination can scarcely be overemphasized. It is important to remember that in ancient Mesopotamia, the official ruler of each city was the city god rather than the human king, who was appointed by the god to act as his servant.[28] The first duty of the king was to interpret the will of the god in the administration of the realm, and this required a reliable means of access to the divine will. Omens, dreams, and various forms of divination were all vital tools in the successful running of the state, but the most reliable was undoubt-edly extispicy. This, then, was the context of extispicy: the king was charged with interpreting the will of the god and the divine community to which the god belonged. His duty was perpetual observance of every form of communication from the spirit world.[29] He did not act from his own will or initiative: his actions were performed on behalf of the god and the divine community.

A particularly revealing story has come down to us from the later part of the third millennium BC, that tells of the great warrior king Naram-Sin, the grandson of Sargon of Agade, to whom the gods refused to grant favorable omens. This provoked the king to a rare sacrilegious outburst in which he angrily said:

> *Has a lion ever performed extispicy?*
> *Has a wolf ever asked advice from a dream interpreter?*
> *Like a robber I shall proceed according to my own*
>     *will!*[30]

The text makes it clear that to proceed according to his own will was, for Naram-Sin, to align himself with wild animals and outlaws. Needless to say the king soon repented, and was in due course granted the privilege of hearing Ishtar speak to him directly from the sky. In ancient Agade, the distinguishing mark of a civilized human being was the observance of signs, portents, and omens, for only thereby was it possible to act in harmony with the divine world. The text shows us that Naram-Sin, in his angry outburst against the gods, sank to a level that was to the ancient Mesopotamian mind to all intents and purposes subhuman.

## EXTISPICY IN
## ANCIENT GREECE AND ROME

Extispicy was practiced not only in ancient Mesopotamia but also in ancient Greece and Italy (Etruria and subsequently Rome). Here it took the form mostly of liver divination (hepatoscopy). While it is possible that it arose in both Greece and Italy independent of Mesopotamian influence, the similarity of some Etruscan liver models to models of Mesopotamian derivation makes this influence a near certainty in the case of the later development of Etruscan hepatoscopy.[31] Thus a third-century BC Etruscan clay model of a liver displays both the *mazzazu* and the *padanu* markings, central to Babylonian hepatoscopy.[32] The most important differences between the two traditions lie in the greater emphasis placed by the Greeks and Etruscans on the caudate lobe or *processus pyramidalis* (the Mesopotamian *ubanu*), followed next by the gallbladder (the Mesopotamian *martu*), and their less subtle differentiation between the left and right sides of the liver. Whereas in Mesopotamia, each zone and each liver part and marking was divided into a left (hostile) and right (friendly) side, in Greece and Etruria the whole liver was divided in this way, but not the separate zones or features. In Greece, furthermore, divination by entrails was not limited to sheep but extended to the animals used in sacrifice to the Olympians— goats, sheep, and calves—a practice also followed in Italy.[33] There is no evidence for extispicy in Greece or Etruria before the sixth century BC (though this is not to rule out its earlier practice). While it is likely that divination by entrails arose independently in Etruria, it is also probable that the Etruscan practice of liver divination was influenced not only by Mesopotamia but also by contact with the Greeks.[34]

For the Greeks, the liver was the most important organ for inspection, perhaps because of its smooth and receptive surfaces, and perhaps also for its felt connection with the deepest impulses of the soul. It was regarded as the inmost spring of the deeper emotions, sending up to the heart and lungs not only blood but also *thumos*—that energy of soul that was regarded in Homer as the center of waking consciousness.[35] One of the clearest explanations of the relationship of the liver to divination is to be found in Plato's *Timaeus,* where Plato identifies the liver as the organ that corresponds to the lower soul-nature of the human being. In Plato, however, the psychosomatic path of influence is not from the liver upward but from the head downward. The liver is smooth and bright in order that it might reflect "as in a mirror" the power of thought that proceeds from the mind (*nous*), and this, he says, is why the gods made the liver the source of divination.[36]

That the mirrorlike quality of the liver was recognized in Etruria is suggested by the fact that several mirrors have come down to us that have scenes of hepatoscopy depicted on their reverse sides. The old-

*Fig. 9.4. The mythical diviner Kalchas.*

est depiction of Etruscan liver divination is the Kalchas mirror from the second part of the fifth century BC (fig. 9.4). Kalchas was a Greek prophet mentioned in Homer's *Iliad* but has here become a mythical diviner, depicted winged, and holding the liver in his left hand with his left foot resting on a rounded stone or *omphalos*. This was the traditional posture of Etruscan diviners (in contrast to the Greeks who stood on both legs and held the liver in either the left or in both hands).[37] Later Etruscan depictions always show the diviner (or *haruspex*) holding the liver in his left hand, standing with his left foot resting on a stone as in fig. 9.5. There is in these depictions a quality of intense introspection, as if the diviner is reaching mentally into an inner world, where he glimpses the thoughts and intentions of the gods and gains access to a realm normally concealed from humankind.

Extispicy was employed in Greece before any major undertaking—especially military. The classic example of the importance that extispicy had in ancient Greek times is Xenophon's account of his military expedition in the territories of the Persian Empire at the end of the fifth century BC, recorded in his *Anabasis* or *The Persian Expedition*.[38] In this extraordinary book, Xenophon describes a range of situations in which extispicy was performed as a matter of course before major decisions were made. Two examples will suffice to give an impression of how this form of divination was used. On one occasion, when the army was near starvation and in the heart of enemy territory, extispicy was being performed every day in order to ascertain what to do; but the results were repeatedly unfavorable and it was decided each time that it was advisable that no action should be taken until favorable results were obtained. Eventually there were no more sheep left to sacrifice, and an ox had to be used instead, but still the omens for action of any kind were unfavorable. At last, desperate for food, a party set out on a foraging expedition despite the unfavorable omens. No sooner had they ventured beyond the safety of the camp, than they were attacked by overwhelming forces of the enemy and five hundred men were cut down, while the rest fled to the mountains.[39] In the eyes of Xenophon, it was clearly madness to go against the omens in this life-and-death situation. Extispicy was without question the most dependable means of determining the best course of action.

A second example shows us that while extispicy could be relied upon for the dependability of its results, it involved no moral frame of reference. Toward the end of the expedition, having suffered great hardships, but now close to home, in Mysia (modern Turkey), Xenophon hears of a rich Persian living near to where he and his army are camped.

*Fig. 9.5. An Etruscan haruspex studies a liver.*

This man has done nothing to provoke the enmity of the Greeks, and their reason for wanting to attack him is solely to get their hands on his cattle, horses, and other property. When they perform their extispicy, the results are favorable, and sure enough, Xenophon's attack—although fiercely resisted—is eventually successful. He captures the man, his wife, and his children and rob him of all his possessions. Untroubled by the slightest twinges of conscience, Xenophon tells us that indeed he had "good reason to be grateful to the god."[40] From its very first usage in ancient Sumeria to its employment by Xenophon in the late fifth century BC, liver divination was capable of giving the diviner access to the disposition of the gods, but I do not know of a single example of a divination that produced anything resembling *moral* guidance. It was not in the least concerned with the morality of a proposed action.

Extispicy was practiced in Etruria (modern Tuscany) prior to its introduction to Rome and was, in the eyes of the Romans, an Etruscan speciality. Although liver divination was introduced to Rome during the sixth century BC, when Rome was ruled by the Etruscan dynasty of the Tarquins, its subsequent role was extremely limited, if not nonexistent, because it was an Etruscan art and because the Romans had almost zero confidence in the loyalty of the Etruscans. It was not until the Second Punic War, toward the end of the third century, that the Etruscans proved beyond doubt their loyalty to Rome, and from this date onward the activity of *haruspices* markedly increased.[41] It is to this period that the famous bronze model of a liver from Piacenza belongs (fig. 9.6). It shows a radical departure from the Mesopotamian tradition and presumably represents an alternative tradition within—or perhaps as a deeper level of—Etruscan hepatoscopy. The liver is now divided into sixteen regions around the periphery, corresponding to the sixteen regions of the sky. Upon the left lobe is inscribed a "wheel" with six "spokes," each defining a triangle within which is inscribed the name of a god or goddess; and upon the right lobe and gallbladder there is a grid with thirteen names within the rectangles of which the grid is formed. These two figures of the wheel and the grid of rectangles have led some commentators to detect the influence of Vedic symbolism, in which the round wheel represents the present

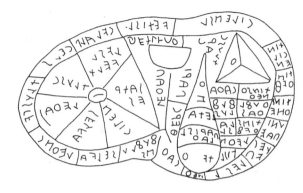

*Fig. 9.6. The bronze liver of Piacenza, late second century BC.*

world and the square represents the celestial world.[42] This interpretation gains support from the fact that the deities inscribed on the regions of the left lobe are the gods of earth and vegetation, the goddess of fate and four boundary gods, while on the right lobe are four gods of heaven and light, along with the gods of water and fate, one (possibly two) goddesses of love, and two protective boundary gods.[43] Between the gallbladder and the wheel on the left lobe, martial gods predominate; but there would appear to be no grounds for interpreting the opposition between the left and right lobes in the traditional way, as respectively *pars hostilis* or unfavorable, and *pars familiaris* or favorable.[44]

The bronze liver of Piacenza makes clear to us the fact that the liver of the sacrificial animal was conceived as a microcosm of the macrocosm. The microcosm of the liver bears upon its surface a picture of the macrocosm: one may therefore gain knowledge of both the heavens and the earth, and of the gods and goddesses of the heavens and the earth, by studying it. As one historian of Roman religion has observed:

Just as the totality of the gods is distributed over the totality of the celestial regions, so this latter totality, with its divine inhabitants, is reflected in the third totality formed by the parts of the liver of the sacrificed sheep: from the organic condition of each of these parts a conclusion may be drawn regarding the mystical condition of the corresponding region and the inclinations of the divinity or divinities who rule it.[45]

The liver and other entrails of the sacrificial animal—be it goat, sheep, or ox—are, while the animal is alive, entirely hidden from view, dwelling within the dark interior of the living beast. There is nothing in the external bearing or countenance of the animal that has the capacity to convey to one who contemplates it an intimation of the secret world of the gods. But if you cut the belly of the beast open, what hitherto has been totally concealed from view is now revealed to your inquiring gaze. At this moment you peer into a world that was previously invisible, hidden from normal sense perception, and a veil is parted between the visible and invisible worlds. In this act, something far more than the observation of physical entrails is involved. One has dramatically gained access to the invisible world—now made visible in these internal organs as in a dark mirror. It was thus that to contemplate the liver was to contemplate cosmic mysteries, to reach into the world of the gods, and to see into their inner life.

In fig. 9.7, a *haruspex* examines the entrails of a bull sacrificed prior to the emperor Trajan setting off on campaign. During Trajan's reign, the Roman Empire reached its greatest extent, and just as in Greece, it was standard practice to perform extispicy before any military venture.

Fig. 9.7. *The examination of the entrails of a bull, sacrificed prior to the emperor Trajan setting out on campaign. From a relief in the Louvre, second century AD.*

Indeed, *haruspices* were attached to the army and went with governors to the provinces as part of the staff, for they were integral to the process of decision making.[46] If we are really to understand what is being depicted here, we have to put aside our modern presumptions. The *haruspex* has cut an opening into the invisible world, and now gazes into a realm of spiritual powers and agencies. His purpose is to determine whether a proposed course of action does or does not harmonize with the spiritual conditions prevailing in the heavens and in the sphere of the gods. On what other basis could human beings make their decisions? To act in concord with the will of the gods one had to consult them, and extispicy in third-century AD Rome had a venerable three-thousand-year history behind it as one of the most effective and reliable ways of doing precisely this.

## THE DECLINE OF THE DIVINATORY CONSCIOUSNESS

One of the main reasons why the practice of divination by entrails came to an end was that there was a growing sense of separation between the world of the gods and the world in which human beings lived and acted. People no longer felt the presence of the gods in their lives as they used to feel it, and thus to make inquiries of the gods before arriving at important decisions came increasingly to be viewed as unnecessary. The sphere of decision making was more and more seen as belonging exclusively to the human being, a matter in which human beings ultimately had to shoulder responsibility. These two factors—the growing sense of separation from the gods, and the desire of human beings to claim the realm of decision making for themselves—began to show in the sixth century BC in ancient Greece with the birth of philosophy.

Although we saw that for Thales, who is generally credited with being the first Greek philosopher, the natural world was "full of gods" and "ensouled and full of spirits (*daimones*)," subsequent Greek philosophers were less sure. Xenophanes, who also lived in the sixth century BC (he was born between forty and fifty years after Thales), was one of the first to express scepticism regarding the existence of the Olympian gods. In the following century this scepticism was taken up by philosophers like Anaxagoras (who flourished in the mid-fifth century BC). While neither Xenophanes nor Anaxagoras were atheists, both were opposed to traditional polytheism and felt drawn toward a new conception of the divine as One rather than Many, and as in some sense transcendent of the natural world. Thus we see in their writings not only an effort to reconceive the divine in a unitary way, but also to explain the natural world in purely physical terms. The sun was not a god, according to Xenophanes—it was made up of "pieces of fire" or "ignited clouds." For Xenophanes, all things in heaven and on earth are made of matter or, as he put it, made of the element earth: "for there are innumerable suns and moons, and all things are made of earth." In other words, all things, both natural and celestial, are material, composed of "earth."[47] Thus the rainbow, which in Homer is seen as a manifestation of the lovely goddess Iris, is, for Xenophanes, simply water vapor or cloud.[48]

In Anaxagoras, who was a contemporary and friend of Pericles, we meet a highly intellectualized conception of the divine as a mind, which is "mixed with nothing but is alone by itself," while matter is conceived as a realm of independently functioning causes.[49] The sun, moon, and stars are divested of divinity: for Anaxagoras they are merely "red-hot stones," and the reason why we do not feel the heat of the stars is because they are so far away.[50] In an equally materialistic vein, the origin of life on Earth is explained not in terms of any divine activity but is attributed to the air, which "contains the seeds of all things."[51] Anaxagoras seems to have delighted in debunking the divinatory consciousness. For him, such phenomena as the eclipse of the moon or sun, or the appearance of a rainbow, which would normally have ominous import, could be explained in purely physical terms.[52] Plutarch famously records one incident in which a ram's head with only one horn growing from the middle of its forehead was brought to Pericles, who was informed by a diviner that this meant that the political contest between Pericles and his rival Thucydides would soon end with victory falling to

Pericles, who would consequently become the single most powerful man in Athens. Anaxagoras cut the skull in two and showed that the growth of the horn in the forehead of the ram was due to natural causes—it was simply that the brain had shifted its place, so the root of the horn came out of the forehead rather than from the side of the head.[53]

What we see here is the clash of two mentalities. For the divinatory consciousness, what manifests physically in the abnormal phenomenon— just as in the deliberately sacralized phenomenon of, for example, a divinatory liver—provides us with a glimpse into the world of spiritual causes, and thereby into forthcoming worldly events. This is because the originating causes of both types of phenomena (omens and historical events) are spiritual, not physical. For the new mentality, so clearly represented in Anaxagoras, the realm of spiritual causes is superfluous. Both so-called omens and the outcome of human affairs can be explained perfectly adequately without recourse to extraneous spiritual causes. No doubt were Anaxagoras presented with a sheep's liver that was missing its caudate lobe, he would explain this abnormality—which throughout the Greek and Roman world was viewed as an extremely unfavorable omen—as being due to disease and nothing more. We recognize Anaxagoras as one of us—a modern man. And yet should we not also feel just a little uneasy at his blithe dismissal of the gods as to all intents and purposes redundant? Is it not possible that *both views* were right? After all, it so happens that the diviner's prophesy was fulfilled: Thucydides was defeated and ostracized in the year 443, shortly after this incident, and Pericles subsequently became the most powerful man in Athens.

The philosophical attack on the divinatory consciousness was not sustained, and for this reason it took a very long time for attitudes to shift. Ten years after the episode with the ram's horn, a law was passed in the Athenian popular assembly that made it a criminal offense not to believe in the gods, and to disseminate rational theories about the heavens. Anaxagoras himself was exiled from Athens for impiety.[54] Despite the hostility of many philosophers, including Platonists and Aristotelians, toward divination, they did not confront it head on. What concerned them most was to carve out a clear field for the human being to exercise an autonomous power of decision making, a subject to which we shall return in the next section.

Meanwhile, within Stoic philosophy, which was probably the most influential philosophy of the period between the third century BC and the second century AD, divination was accommodated into a general understanding of the workings of the divine in the world. With its semimaterialistic, semimetaphysical cosmology, Stoicism was able to hold a kind of middle ground between the old consciousness and the new. For the Stoics, God's substance consists of the whole cosmos, within which the divine is immanent as an active ordering principle or *logos*. Although essentially monotheistic, Stoicism was not antipolytheistic, embracing the old spiritual order of gods and *daimones* as the manifestation in diverse forms of the One. What was different about this new cosmopolitan philosophy was the more materialistic mindset that characterized Stoic thinkers.[55] But within this more materialistic mindset, divination could have its legitimate place. According to Posidonius, one of the most important Stoic philosophers of the late second and early first centuries BC, because the world is conceived as one living whole, all the manifold creatures and things that exist are linked together by a natural affinity or *sympatheia*. Whatever happens in one part of the world will produce a sympathetic reaction in every other part. This notion of *sympatheia* is closely related to the idea of destiny or fate (*heimarmene*), for everything is bound by the power of fate. Because of the mutual interconnection of all things, and the determining influence of fate, divination was seen as a means of coming to know human destiny as it is woven into the spiritual-material fabric that profoundly connects the multitude of diverse phenomena. Thus what reveals itself in a sheep's liver can be understood as bearing on the outcome of a battle.[56] The ideal Stoic sage is one who consciously and willingly follows the path of destiny, and divination can help those striving for wisdom to see where this path leads. For the Stoics, our freedom lies not in our ability to change our fate but in our ability to change our attitude toward our fate, from one of resistance and antagonism to one of acceptance.[57]

Closely associated with the Stoic defense of divination on spiritual-naturalistic lines, both Stoic and Platonically inclined philosophers saw divination in terms of the intervention of *daimones,* understood as spiritual intermediaries between the gods and the human world. This view was as popular among Platonists like Plutarch and Albinus, as it was among Stoics like Posidonius, and goes back to Plato's *Epinomis.*[58] To explain divination on the basis of *daimones* communicating through the sacrificial animal is to come close to the older view, which saw a fusion between the sacrificed animal and the god to whom it was sacrificed, and hence the possibility of reading the soul of the god in the animal's liver. The substitution of the *daimon* for the god does not alter the fundamental direction of thought, which is to attribute divination to supernatural intervention.

Throughout the Greco-Roman period a fragile intellectual consensus was maintained, within which divination was able to continue not only as a respectable but also as an essential practice, holding a central place both in decisions of state and in military decisions. It was only in the fourth century AD that this consensus unraveled with the Christianization of the Empire, but even then divination by entrails was permitted by Constantine, and was not officially banned until AD 391 by the emperor Theodosius.[59] One feels, however, that a certain lack of conviction crept into and slowly ate away at the venerable tradition, leading to accusations of corruption and debasement as early as the second and first centuries BC.[60] In Cicero's *De Divinatione,* written in the middle of the first century BC, the unsuppressed antipathy of the rationalist to what he regards as sheer superstition erupts into the philosophical arena. Cicero's soul is stirred up in opposition to the outmoded divinatory consciousness, which he sees as belonging to the past. For him, nature is simply nature, and all natural events should be explained either in terms of natural laws or, failing that, as the products of chance or accident. It is the height of folly to hold that the gods are the agents of those things that can be explained by natural causes, just as it is to attribute those things that happen by chance to spiritual causes or the principle of *sympatheia.*[61] In Cicero, we hear the voice of the modern consciousness speaking from out of the mouth of an aristocratic Roman. But this aristocratic Roman was, paradoxically, at the same time himself an augur, and in another treatise wrote in defense of both augury and extispicy![62] Why? Because the practices of augury and extispicy were part of the Roman constitution and should therefore be observed by all good Roman citizens. Thus the consensus in favor of the practice of divination was maintained.

Divination in the Roman Empire was like a very old tree, hollow within, yet held up by the strength of its outward form. This was a time when the old oracles went into terminal decline. For Cicero, the decline of the oracles was a sign of human beings becoming less credulous.[63] For Platonists, like Plutarch, who lived roughly a hundred years after Cicero, it was rather a sign that the gods were withdrawing from the world.[64] Plutarch tells the story of a merchant ship that was sailing past the island of Paxi, when suddenly from the island a voice called out loudly for Thamus, which happened to be the name of the Egyptian pilot on board the ship. Thamus at first made no reply, but when the voice called again and then a third time, he answered. The mysterious voice then said: "When you come opposite Palodes, tell them that Great Pan is dead." In consternation, everyone on board ship discussed the matter and it was decided that if there were a breeze, they would sail past Palodes and say nothing, but if the sea were smooth near Palodes, Thamus would make his announcement. It happened that the sea was smooth, and so Thamus shouted out "Great Pan is dead." Then, continues Plutarch, "before he had finished speaking a great wailing arose, not from one voice but from many, and mingled with the wailings were cries of amazement." This story was soon told in Rome, and Thamus was even summoned to appear before Tiberius Caesar, to explain exactly what had occurred.[65]

Plutarch's haunting story of the death of Pan marks a turning point in the decline of the old divinatory consciousness. Whether it was because, as Cicero believed, people were simply less credulous, or whether it was because, as Plutarch thought, the gods themselves were withdrawing or dying, nobody could escape noticing that nature was no longer "full of gods" as it used to be. The inside of the old tree was hollow. This is why the oracles went into decline and this is why it was no longer possible for people to put their faith in divination in quite the same way as in the past.

## THE RISE OF THE
## AUTONOMOUS MORAL AGENT

The emptying of the world of divine presences was, however, just one side of a larger process. We have seen that behind the divinatory consciousness was a religious attitude toward the making of decisions, according to which it was felt necessary to align one's actions with the will of the gods. As the experience of the gods faded from human awareness, a new sense of human autonomy began to assert itself: human decision making was felt to be a matter for human beings to work out from their own inner resources. In the figure of Socrates, especially, we see a kind of reversal of the divinatory consciousness: the philosopher is less concerned to know the will of the gods than to follow the Delphic maxim of knowing oneself, and from this starting point to strive to know how to act rightly, in conformity with virtue. This, for Socrates, is the key to human happiness.[66]

The ancient Greek word for "happiness" was *eudaimonia*. The *eu* has the connotation of "good" so the literal meaning of *eudaimonia* is "to have a good *daimon*" or guardian spirit. In the earliest Greek literature, the *daimon* was seen as a superhuman power that drives a hero forward with an unstoppable energy, if he acts with it; but if he stands against his *daimon,* then everything will turn against him.[67] Thus it became identified with luck or fate, which was not arbitrary but derived from a person's relationship not only to their *daimon* but also to the gods. According to Pindar, "The great mind of Zeus steers the *daimon* of the men whom he loves."[68]

While one could do certain things toward securing one's happiness, it was ultimately not something a person could control because it depended on the favor of the gods. This is why we find Hesiod, at the end of eighth century BC, linking *eudaimonia* to observing omens and not violating taboos, for only thus would one stay on good terms with the gods.[69]

Two hundred years later, at the end of the sixth century BC, something had begun to change, for we find in Heraclitus the groundbreaking statement that "Man's character (*ethos*) is his *daimon*."[70] The *daimon* is no longer located outwardly, as the spirit responsible for what happens to a person in terms of their good or bad fortune: it has become internalized as nothing less than their character. It has, one might say, taken up its abode within the soul, and in so doing it has become far more intimately conjoined with a person's experience of him- or herself. It is Socrates who coins the phrase "care of the soul"—a phrase, which implies a new attitude of responsibility toward one's inner life. And it is Socrates, too, who discovers within the depths of his own soul the voice of his own personal *daimon*. It is, for him, an experience of the divine as a voice that speaks from within himself.

Xenophon, whom we have already met as an avid diviner in his Persian expedition, was a friend and biographer of Socrates. He relates that, rather than placing confidence in divination, auguries, omens, symbols, and sacrifices, Socrates "so asserted concerning these matters as he knew them from an internal consciousness; declaring it was his genius (*daimonion*) from whom he received his information."[71]

In his *Apology,* Xenophon has Socrates say:

> Whereas they say it is from auguries, omens, symbols, and diviners whence they have their notices of the future, I, on the contrary, impute all those premonitions wherewith I am favored to a genius (*daimonion*) and I think that, in so doing, I have spoken not only more truly but more piously than they who attribute to birds the divine privilege of declaring things to come.[72]

In asserting that he regards following the voice of his own inner *daimon* as both more true and more pious than divining by birds (he could as well have included divining by entrails), Socrates both breaks with the past and points the way to the future.

Plato shares with his teacher Socrates the premise that there is a divine element within the human psyche, and that if one is to attain *eudaimonia,* then it is not to the gods without, but to the psyche within, that one must turn one's attention. In his dialogue *Timaeus,* Plato gives us the extraordinary image of the human being as like an upturned plant, with our head corresponding to the root. That is to say, we are a plant with our root in heaven, and the *daimon* is that which in each one of us raises us up toward, and reconnects us with, the heavenly world of the gods:

> As regards the most important part of our soul we must think this: that a god has given it as a *daimon* to each of us, that which we say dwells in the top part of the body, to lift us from the earth to its kindred in heaven, for we are not of earthly but of divine nature . . .[73]

For Plato, the *daimon* remains the key to human happiness, for in the same passage he goes on to say that the wise person is one who cherishes that which is divine in him or herself, and in so doing attains *eudaimonia:* "But he who has been earnest in the love of knowledge and of true wisdom . . . since he is ever cherishing the divine power, and has the *daimon* within him in perfect order, he will be singularly happy."[74]

It is by living in accordance with the inner *daimon* that Aristotle also sees the secret of happiness. In his *Nicomachean Ethics,* Aristotle concerns himself much with the process of decision making, and never refers once to any of the traditional forms of divination. What he is concerned with is how human beings can come to make decisions, not through the examination of the livers of sheep, the observation of birds, or by observing any other omens, but through a moral enquiry, which bypasses all external referents, spiralling inward toward the *daimonic* self: "For a man stops enquiring how he shall act as soon as he has carried back the origin of action to himself, and to the dominant part of himself, for it is this part that chooses."[75]

This "dominant part" of the self is the *nous,* which is the equivalent of the Platonic *daimon.* For Aristotle it has become more closely identified with the sense of self than Socrates' admonitory voice, which spoke from within him but as a mystical "other." In Aristotle we engage the *nous,* the faculty of contemplation and intellectual intuition, as active participants, and its voice is our own most intimate and truest voice.

It follows that for Aristotle *eudaimonia* or happiness is the activity of contemplative thinking, because it is the activity of the divine element within us:

> Such a life as this will be higher than the human level: not in virtue
> of his humanity will a man achieve it, but in virtue of something
> within him that is divine.[76]

Closely related to *nous* is what Aristotle calls *synesis* ("understanding"), which deals with those things about which one may be in doubt and concerning that which it is necessary to deliberate.[77] In other words, *synesis* deals with precisely those issues concerning that which the divinatory consciousness would have felt the need to resort to the study of omens or entrails. This word *synesis* has an interesting history. Its seems to have entered the popular vocabulary during the period before the beginning of the Peloponnesian War (431–405 BC). This, it will be recalled, was at the time when Anaxagoras was debunking the divinatory consciousness, and was then prosecuted for impiety. We find it first used in a literary work by Euripides in circa 431 BC in his play, *Medea.* It occurs in a scene in the play where Medea tells Jason that, no matter what the gods would say to Jason, his *synesis* must tell him that he has not kept faith with her. In this context the meaning of *synesis* is best conveyed by our word "conscience." [78]

The Aristotelian concept of *synesis* is used in a philosophical rather than a literary way. It could be seen as a further development or refinement of the Socratic *daimonion.* Unlike the latter, which is too numinous, too awesome, to be termed a "virtue," Aristotle makes *synesis* one of three intellectual virtues alongside wisdom (*sophia*) and prudence (*phronesis*).[79] While it is usually translated as "understanding," what it refers to is our capacity to make right judgments. During the second and first centuries BC, the form of the word *synesis* changed to *syneidesis,* and then to *syneides,* which is how it appears in Philo and again in St. Paul's epistles. It is in St. Paul that a fuller resonance of the concept is attained, swelling to replace the *daimon* as that element within the human soul through which we are in touch with the divine. For St. Paul, conscience (*syneides*) takes the place of obedience to external law, and is the source of love (agape).[80] Most significantly, for St. Paul, to wound someone else's conscience is to sin against Christ.[81]

When St. Paul's epistles were translated into Latin, *syneides* was translated as *conscientia.*[82] The concept of conscience was subsequently discussed a great deal during the Middle Ages by theologians such as St. Bonaventure and St. Thomas Aquinas. It was understood as an inner light, a *lumen innatum* that has come to live within the human being as a result of Christ's incarnation. It is through this inner light that we know what is right and wrong, and thus it has a direct bearing on the decisions we make.[83] Conscience has an authority of a completely different order from that which the gods of antiquity could exert. For St. Thomas, it constrains us, as does God's law, which is the law of the triune God beyond the gods of old. So, for St. Thomas, to go against conscience is to contravene the law of God. It is thus a higher authority within us than any civil authority, and we are bound to it as we are bound to the image of God within us.[84] Thus for St. Thomas Aquinas, "Every judgment of conscience, be it right or wrong, be it about things evil in themselves or morally indifferent, is obligatory, in such wise that he who acts against his conscience always sins."[85]

For many of us today, the voice of conscience is our highest moral authority. We respect and admire those who follow their consciences, especially when this involves a person sacrificing their career, their freedom, or even their life. And yet, post-Freud, a certain unease has crept into our feelings about this authoritative voice that has installed itself within our psyche. For is it not just the internalized reproving parent whom we have, since childhood, learned to please? Whether or not we accept Freud's reductionist view of conscience, our faith in its authority is less sure than it used to be. To what extent is it truly our own voice? How free are we when we obey the proddings of conscience? Does it not work on us in such a way that it exercises a kind of tyranny over us? Do we not feel bound to obey it, and guilty as sin if we don't?

If what lived in the Middle Ages as a high ideal can now seem to us constraining or even coercive, could this mean that we have in some way outgrown it, and need therefore to conceive of something else, something beyond it? Rudolf Steiner pointed to the inner need today to advance from a morality based on authority to one that is based on the moral insight of each individual, so that our actions derive neither from external rules nor from the internal authority of our consciences, but from our own love of, and commitment to, a moral ideal that we enact for its own sake.[86] When an ideal lives in us in such a way that we truly want to realize it in action, then that action becomes wholly our own. We have found within ourselves the ground for our action, which is the love of the objective that we want to realize. And this is what makes it truly free.[87] Here, then, we attain our full moral autonomy as individuals.

## BEING ANCIENT IN A MODERN WAY

I began by proposing that the contemporary revival of interest in divination could be understood as the expression of a yearning to reconnect with the dimensions of soul and spirit, which have been excluded from the modern scientific worldview. In order to give the diviner access to the realm of archetypes, the act of divination entails a resacralization of time and space to the extent that a divinatory moment and a divinatory place are set aside in order to create a particular kind of imaginative space in which we once more engage in dialogue with the gods and spirits.[88] In antiquity, the divinatory consciousness arose out of a religious attitude toward both nature and the inner life of the soul, an attitude, which underpins its revival today. We find ourselves today, however, in the opposite position of the Greeks and Romans in relation to the spirit world. Whereas for them the gods were withdrawing, for us the gods and spirits are returning, and we need to have the means of meeting them. Divination is precisely one such means. The twentieth century, largely thanks to the influence of Jung, saw enormous advances in understanding and utilizing divinatory techniques. Oracles like the I Ching with its deep wisdom are available and once more meaningful to us, the subtle divinatory science of astrology once again enables us to experience the attunement of psyche to cosmos, while imaginative divinatory systems like the Tarot link us to the archetypal level of a given situation that would otherwise remain unconscious.[89]

It is not my intention, therefore, to argue against the revival of divination. Far from it. Divination enables us to become more aware of the subtle psychic and spiritual forces that are at work in the background of our lives, determining the events that arise. Contemporary divinatory systems are by no means atavistic throwbacks to an age long since surpassed, but are underpinned by a new and living understanding of the subtle energies that are active behind the scenes of our conscious knowing. Marie-Louise von Franz has described divination as a way of opening a window between the personal unconscious and the collective unconscious, a kind of "airhole" where these two realms—which in antiquity would have been called the human world and the world of the gods—are able to meet.[90] It is especially in what she calls "the tense situation," in which an archetype of the collective unconscious is constellated, that the act of divination can create an image of the qualitative field defined by the archetype and give a reading of its "dynamic load."[91]

This is also Stephen Karcher's understanding. For him, what one may consciously experience as a problem or difficulty is transformed by the oracle into a sign or symbolic occurrence that links us to the creative energies of the spirit world. Every encounter with "trouble" is an opening to this world, and in any critical situation divination is the means of giving voice to the hidden complement of that which our ego is unconscious.[92] Divination is based on neither superstition nor belief, but is a way of interacting with the dynamic forces underlying a situation, so that one can understand what is the most appropriate way to act.[93]

Nevertheless, divination does need to be approached in a different way from how it was approached in antiquity, because although it may reveal to us the spiritual and archetypal conditions that lie behind a given situation, our relationship to these factors cannot be the same as that of people in antiquity. It cannot be the same because there is something that has now come to exist in the human psychological make-up that did not previously exist. We have seen how this was initially experienced as the personal *daimon,* in relation to which Socrates felt a greater obligation than to the gods. As the *daimon* became increasingly integrated within the psyche, it became identified with the higher self, or spiritual center, of the individual, contacted most powerfully in the act of contemplation. Already in pre-Christian times, there were the first glimmerings of the experience of conscience, which became central to Christian religious life during the Middle Ages, and has remained so. But in more recent times, the need to act from out of our own freedom, rather than from obedience to any authority, outer or inner, has placed us in a position diametrically opposed to that of a pious ancient Mesopotamian or Greek. For Naram-Sin, the refusal to abide by the results of divination was tantamount to a denial of his own humanity. For us, by contrast, we fail to realize our true human potential to the extent that we do not act freely. Much as we may long to be told what to do, our deeper spiritual desire is in the end to act as autonomous moral agents today, and to own the source of our action as lying nowhere else but within ourselves. If, therefore, we practice divination, we do not do so in order to submit ourselves to the will of the gods, but rather to gain greater insight into our situation in order to come to a freely chosen decision as to how best to act.

In antiquity the psychic life of human beings was wide open to the influence of the gods, and less belonged to, than was participated in, by the human individuality. Now the psychic sphere is claimed by each person as their own. From one point of view this could be regarded as something of a vain illusion. There are tremendously powerful forces that live in this sphere, which, as we know, are archetypal and do not necessarily respect a person's conscious view of himself or herself. But in relation to these archetypal forces, as Jung wrote in *Memories, Dreams, Reflections,* "In the final analysis the decisive factor is always consciousness, which can understand the manifestations of the unconscious and take up a position toward them."[94]

It is this need to "take up a position" toward the manifestations of the unconscious (gods by any other name) that is the crucial thing that differentiates the modern diviner from the ancient.

If we meet the gods again today, through divinatory or other practices, we need to meet them as free individuals who bear ultimate responsibility for our decisions and actions. Whether we attribute the source of our decisions to our *daimon,* to the voice of conscience or to our own freely chosen moral ideal, in each case the responsibility comes back to us and to us alone. Only then is it possible for divination to be healthy, for only then do we consciously "take up a position" in relation to the world of archetypes or spirit world. It was precisely Xenophon's failure to do this in his assault and robbery of the guiltless rich Persian that differentiates the ancient from the modern divinatory consciousness. Had he paused to reflect on the morality of his proposed action, and decided not to act because it was morally unjustified, he would have stepped out of the matrix of the old divinatory consciousness into the new.

When the Greek philosophers began to conceive of a divine core to the human individuality, it was not so much divination itself that was undermined as the ancient relationship to the gods. The focus of divining had to shift from simply divining the will of the gods and attuning ourselves to it, to divining our own deepest will as morally free agents. As we go forward again to meet the gods, divination once more gains credibility, but in order for *us* not to lose *our* credibility, we must take pains to ground our decision making in our own moral insight into what constitutes the right course of action, even if this means going against the oracles. Each of us has to take up our stance, and for the stance that we take each of us alone bears responsibility.

# 10

## THE FUTURE OF THE ANCIENT WORLD

History is a mysterious approach to closeness. Every
spiral of its path leads us into deeper corruption and at
the same time into more fundamental return.

MARTIN BUBER, *I AND THOU*

*More and more people today are interested in the religions of antiquity,
and feel drawn to the spirituality of the ancient world. What does this
tell us about the historical development of consciousness? Why is it that
we find ourselves looking back to the ancient world as if in the manner of
gesturing toward the future rather than the past?*

*The following essay is based on a talk given on May 22, 1993, at a
symposium held in Oxford on "The Future of the Ancient World: The
Relevance of Ancient Religion and Spirituality for us Today."*[1]

### MEANING IN HISTORY

After a long period of collective amnesia, we are becoming aware again
of dimensions of existence with which, in ancient times, people were
already very familiar. It is as if our culture is awakening from a sleep

of some two thousand years or more, during which time a conscious relationship to energies, powers, and forces that the ancients attributed to, or identified with, the gods was almost entirely eclipsed. With the exception of small esoteric groups working, for instance, within the Hermetic, Rosicrucian, and magical traditions, this conscious relationship was banished from mainstream culture.

But now the gods are once more arising on the horizons of our awareness. We find ourselves referring to them as "archetypes," as "energy fields," or as "landscape energies." But whatever language we use to describe what it is we are becoming sensitive to, there is, it seems, a new level of reality, which is coming into focus for us. It is a "new" level of reality that, we sense, is at the same time very old. Has it not always been there? And isn't the truth of the matter that we, as a culture, have simply been looking the other way?

The question therefore arises: why is it that this awareness was lost in the first place? The answer to this question is critical to the way in which we today choose to relate both to the cultures of the ancient world and to the realities of which they were aware. While it may be that we come to know and live consciously again with these more subtle planes of existence, it may not be appropriate to do so in the same way as the ancients did. So the question "why was this awareness lost?" is, I think, a fundamental one for us today as we reorient ourselves toward the rising myths, symbols, energies, and archetypes.

To ask the question "why?" of the historical process is to assume that the forces at work in history are not arbitrary but, on the contrary, harbor an inherent meaning. Of course it is possible to deny meaning in history, but in so doing one risks driving out the possibility not only of attaining insight into the historical development of human consciousness, but also of appreciating the full import of our present situation. How we perceive and grasp hold of meaning in history bears directly on the way in which we poise ourselves for the future. In allowing our gaze to be drawn back to the past, we can equip ourselves all the better to work creatively with what has yet to unfold.

## GODS IN THE PSYCHE

The question "Why has the awareness of the gods been lost?" was already being asked as the sun was setting on the ancient world, by the great essayist of the first century AD, Plutarch. In his essay *On the Decline of the Oracles,* written in all likelihood sometime during the reign of the emperor Trajan, Plutarch poignantly asks: "Why is it that the gods are no longer speaking to us?" Both Cicero, in the first century BC, and Strabo a little later, had commented on the declining prestige of the official oracles.[2] And, if we are to believe Clement of Alexandria, within fifty years of Plutarch's essay all the official oracles were dead.[3] The literature of this period reveals that in the Roman world people were acutely aware that the gods were not as *present* as they used to be. Many leading thinkers in the Roman period were writing essays on the gods, a favorite title being *On the Nature of the Gods.*[4] It was as if, precisely because the gods were no longer so alive to human experience, they became subjects of learned treatises.

It is important to realize that during this period, in the centuries around the birth of Christ, when people looked back into their past they were aware of a history stretching behind them for thousands of years in which divination, myth, ritual, and direct interaction with the gods had been integral to human experience. These formed the context of all dealings with nature, were intrinsic to the healing arts, and informed the process of human psychological integration and spiritual development. The withdrawal of the gods, the undermining of faith in the divinatory arts, the waning of ritual, and the usurpation of mythical thinking by abstract reasoning together constituted a momentous watershed in the history of human consciousness. How were people to understand what was happening?

Plutarch's essay is somewhat rambling and inconclusive, but the point that he seeks to make is this: Direct awareness of the gods entails entering a state of consciousness called *enthusiasmos,* in which the experience of the presence of a god overwhelms one's ordinary sense of self. It is in such a state that prophetic insight becomes possible. However, this state of *enthusiasmos* has become harder and harder to attain, and that is why the oracles are declining, and human beings in general are no longer aware of the gods. While the presence of divinities is necessary for shrines and oracles to be active, the condition of the human soul is also a necessary factor. The decline of the oracles is due, not to the gods absenting themselves, but to changes in human consciousness. By implication—and here Plutarch is less than explicit—the eclipse of human awareness of the gods is necessary in order for a certain development of consciousness to take place.

Plutarch was addressing the specific question of the decline of the ancient oracles. But in so doing he points to two distinct components in any act involving awareness of the gods. On the one hand there is the divine presence; on the other hand there is the condition of the human soul, which is more or less receptive to this divine presence. This is an important distinction, and it bears directly on the line of thought I want to pursue in this essay.

Let us go back some six hundred years before Plutarch lived, to ancient Egypt, a culture in which the experience of the gods was still fully a part of people's lives. Fig. 10.1 shows a procession in honor of the goddess Hathor, recorded on a soapstone bowl toward the end of the sixth century BC in Coptos. Hathor was a goddess associated with love, eroticism, music, dancing, and general intoxication. On the left we see a man playing a double-reed flute, while just in front of him a woman bends over and, hitching up her skirt, slaps her buttock in time to the music. In front of her, another woman dances sensuously and bangs a pair of clappers. Leading them is a man playing a lyre. All the celebrants are wearing lotus flowers on their heads, symbolic of spiritual regeneration. The mood here is one of joyful self-abandonment, which is preeminently the mood of the goddess.

Now although we cannot see her here, we can sense the presence of the goddess in the gestures and movements of the men and women and in the atmosphere exude from their procession. From one point of view, the procession is itself an invocation of the goddess, so that she becomes an almost tangible presence among her devotees. Their consciousness is

*Fig. 10.1. Procession of devotees in honor of the goddess Hathor.*

lifted to another level, and the transpersonal energy of the goddess takes possession of them.

Not every deity was experienced in this way, in a throwing off of normal inhibitions. But in ancient Egyptian times, even in more introverted activities, a god was invariably implicated. In fig.10.2, Thoth, in his manifestation as a baboon, inspires an Egyptian scribe. The ancient Egyptians did not feel it was possible to have wise or powerful thoughts without Thoth being involved. The sacred art of writing, by which the invisible was rendered visible through the skill of the scribe, was regarded as Thoth's calling, and scribes were referred to as "Followers of Thoth."[5] Both the wisdom-content and the magical efficacy of a thought were attributed to a source specifically beyond the merely human sphere.

In this respect the Egyptians were not so different from the ancient Greeks of Homer's time. We are reminded, for example, of Phemius the minstrel's statement in Homer's *Odyssey*.

I am self-taught: it was a god who implanted all sorts of lays in my mind.[6]

In Homer, whose works were committed to writing in the sixth century BC, the activity of the gods in what are now understood to be normal human psychological processes is particularly notable. The *Iliad*, for instance, opens with a famous example of the way in which a deity could

*Fig. 10.2. The god Thoth inspires the scribe Nebmertef.*

intervene in the psyche. It describes how Achilles is only prevented from drawing his sword in anger and killing king Agamemnon by the timely intervention of the goddesses Hera and Athene, the latter seizing Achilles by the hair and admonishing him to take his hand from his sword.

> "Lady," says Achilles to Athene, "when you two goddesses command, a man must obey, however angry he may be in his heart."[7]

It seems that the act of reflection, which in modern times has assumed a position of psychic centrality, was as recently as in Homer's day experienced as involving extraneous agencies.

One might say that in ancient times people lived more deeply than we do today. They lived from archetypal levels. The ancient ego did not block out this archetypal awareness but was constantly being dipped into it—the state of *enthusiasmos* being the basic prototype of a variety of such transpersonal experiences. The essential characteristic of the ancient consciousness was that the ego was continually having its boundaries dissolved in the face of extremely powerful transpersonal forces. In this respect it may further be characterized as a type of *unitary* consciousness in which for us, the "normal" experience of separation from the divine world was continually being breached. There was such an intermingling of the divine and human in the arena of the human soul that, as often as not, the source of what occurred therein was regarded as a god or some power transcendent of the individual.

Perhaps we should say that the ancient ego was not as "strong" as it is today. The sense that an individual has today of being the source of their own thoughts, feelings, desires, and intentions was not nearly so developed in ancient times as it has since become. The *real* agents in all-important matters of the soul were transhuman powers. And the ancient attitude was that one should cooperate with them as best one could in order to achieve one's aims. As Achilles said to Athene at the end of the incident that I referred to:

The man who listens to the gods is listened to by them.[8]

It is an attitude by no means restricted to Homer. In all the cultures of the ancient world one finds a similar attitude toward the gods. This, of course, was the reason why people consulted oracles and performed rites of divination. Not to do so—to proceed entirely according to one's own will—was, as the great Mesopotamian king Naram-Sin once said, to act like an outlaw to the divine-cosmic order, to which human beings aboriginally belong.[9] In the ancient world, therefore, there was not the same sense of autonomy as we have today. People felt it necessary constantly to refer to sources "outside" themselves, if the gods may be so described: that is, to sources extraneous to the self-contained ego. In fig. 10.3, we see the god Seth teaching Thutmose III how to use a bow and arrow. In ancient Egypt, even the ability to make trouble was regarded as being due to a god. Seth is the extraneous source of a king's manic strength and capacity to do violence, qualities that it was necessary for him to tap in time of war. In the account of the battle of Megiddo,

*Fig. 10.3. The god Seth teaches Thutmose III to shoot.*

the strength of Seth was said to pervade Thutmose's limbs; and in the height of the battle of Kadesh, Ramesses II was perceived as the very embodiment of Seth by the enemy, who fled before him.[10] Examples of such interweaving of divine and human energies in the ancient world could be multiplied almost ad infinitum. May these few suffice to make the point.

## GODS IN NATURE

The gods, however, were not simply encountered as agencies acting into the human soul-life. To no lesser extent than they were encountered as "external" forces acting upon the arena of the human soul, they were also encountered as "internal" forces operating, so to speak, on the inner side of nature. The ancient experience of nature, far from being something "out there," perceptible only to the senses, was as much an experience of inner powers as outward forms. Nature had a soul-life, and this soul-life was essentially that of the gods who clothed themselves in natural forms and enacted their eternal myths in natural processes. Hence from the standpoint of exact scientific observation, we find the most outlandish representations of natural objects and events. It is as if the ancients were constantly *seeing through* the outward appearances of things to some noumenal world of which the natural phenomena were but the outermost expression.

*Fig. 10.4. The goddess Nut swallows the evening sun.*

Fig. 10.4 shows an ancient Egyptian representation of a sunset. What in fact is portrayed is a relationship between two mighty cosmic powers: the great cosmic mother Nut, and Ra, the source of universal light, whose principal physical vehicle is the sun. Every evening the sun enters the body of the sky goddess who is here shown about to swallow it. It then passes through her body during the hours of the night and is reborn from her the following morning. The journey of the sun symbolizes the relationship of Ra to the cosmic mother, who encloses within herself an even deeper zone of interiority to which the sun god must eternally return in order to be renewed and reborn.

In fig 10.5, the same cosmic goddess, or a daemonic aspect of her, reveals herself in a sycamore fig. This is because the Egyptians regarded this tree as a likeness of the heavens. Looking up at the starry sky each night, they perceived the heavens as a vast cosmic tree, like the sycamore fig, whose leaves and fruits were the stars in which the gods resided. Most trees and plants in Egypt were sacred, as they were across the ancient world, for they were experienced in terms of the specific divine qualities that they enshrined.

*Fig. 10.5. Nut appears in her sacred tree, the sycamore fig.*

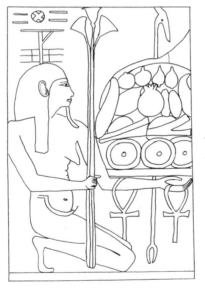

*Fig. 10.6. A Nile deity, in the likeness of Hapi.*

One further example from Egypt is shown in fig. 10.6. In Egypt, one of the most important landscape features in the country is the Nile River. But nowhere in ancient Egyptian art do we see the river portrayed. Instead we see only the spirit of the river, Hapi. He is depicted as an androgynous human being, always bearing fruits or some produce that was his gift to the country. He is, as one hymn describes him,

*Food provider, bounty maker,*
*who creates all that is good.*[11]

Perhaps we have become so inured to this ancient animistic "convention" that we overlook just how remarkable it is. What? Are we to take this pot-bellied, bearded, and bosomed man seriously as a depiction of the River Nile? Yet could it be *our* blindness that causes us *not* to see him?

This type of awareness was still alive in ancient Greek times, when rivers possessed their own priests, and sacrifices and dedications were commonly made to them.[12] Fig. 10.7, which reproduces an image from a sixth-century BC red figure vase, shows the spirit of a river with bull's horns and ears. Quite often, river gods were portrayed as having the form of a horse. In both cases, they must be regarded as daemonic aspects of the great god Poseidon. It was clearly regarded as necessary at this period to show both god and river together, as if to make certain we realize the inseparable connection of the river's outer and inner forms.

*Fig. 10.7. Greek river god.*

Even down to Plutarch's time, at the end of first century AD and through to the end of the second, this fundamental tendency to look beyond or through the outward appearances of things to their inner spirit continued, albeit in an attenuated way. In fig.10.8, we see the spirit of the storm that saved Marcus Aurelius's army from defeat in Germany. The spirit is depicted with beard and wings, and from both

*Fig. 10.8. Storm god, saving Marcus Aurelius's army from catastrophe.*

his beard and his outstretched arms the rain falls torrentially. It is not, as we might wish to put it, that the god *causes* the rain to fall. Rather the rain falling *is* the god: it is the manifestation of the god. There is, in other words, an intrinsic union of the sense-perceptible phenomenon of the rainstorm and the nonsense-perceptible spirit of the rainstorm.

## ANCIENT CONSCIOUSNESS
## OF THE GODS

If we return to Plutarch's question again. "Why is it that the gods are no longer speaking to us?" we can, I think, say two things about the ancient awareness of the divine world, which the people of his time experienced as steadily waning. On the one hand, the ancient consciousness was such that the inner life of human beings was open to influences that were not regarded as originating within the human soul. So a person might quite often have to say: "This thought, this feeling, this desire, and so on, originates not within me, but stems from an agency external to me, namely a god." This, it seems, was a common enough experience.

On the other hand, the ancient consciousness experienced the "external" world of nature as opening onto an inner world, so that everything that appears to us in an outer, sense-perceptible way was experienced in ancient times as also full of divine powers. The boundaries between "inner" and "outer," between "subjective" and "objective," which until recently we felt we could rely upon, were differently drawn in those days. The "outer" world of nature had an inner, spiritual aspect, just as the "inner" world of the human psyche was acted upon from "without" by the gods.

Crucial to this difference of boundaries is the fact that in ancient times it was recognized that the very same beings that were encountered in the depths of the psyche were also working in the depths of nature. One did not, for instance, only meet Hathor in love and a state of intoxication. One also met her in the papyrus thicket and in the wild cow, both of which were sacred to her. One even saw her in the starry sky at night when she revealed herself as but another aspect of the cosmic goddess. In the same way Thoth was encountered in the ibis, the baboon, and, cosmically, as the spirit whose outward manifestation was the moon. Insofar as the gods were experienced as operating, as it were, from two directions—from the interiority of nature outward, and from the periphery of the human psyche inward—there was an essential unity between humanity and nature. What was met on the inner side of nature was known also to be working upon the psyche in the guise of "external" spiritual agencies.

It is, however, necessary to qualify the argument I am putting forward, for if people felt the need to consult oracles, must they not to some extent have felt *cut off* from knowledge of the divine will? If they built temples to house their gods, must they not have felt their gods to be in danger of slipping away from them? And if they composed beautiful hymns to their gods, must not a degree of separation between the human and divine already be presupposed? In contemplating the ancient world we are, after all, turning to an epoch of history *prior to which* we know of no oracles, no temples, no literature. It is a feature, then, of the ancient consciousness that while it constantly refers to the gods, it does so with an underlying awareness that the process of separation from them is already under way.

## THE SOUL COMES OF AGE

If we were to ask: "What, then, has happened to human consciousness since ancient times?" we would have to give a double reply, taking into account both human self-consciousness and our consciousness of nature. Whereas in antiquity the presence of the gods was a factor in both consciousness of self and of nature; this presence has since become a notable absence. So how are we to understand the transformation that took place?

The evolution of human consciousness reached a watershed in the Greek period, the culminating moment of which is reflected in the philosophy of Aristotle. One can trace this evolution from the sixth century on, through Homer to the pre-Socratics, and then on through Socrates and Plato to Aristotle. In fact, what one finds is better described as an *involution* than an evolution, for consciousness developed more and more toward its own center, toward an ever greater self-involvement. This centripetal movement of contraction from the spheres of divine influence resulted in the experience of the centricity of a distinct, individual ego becoming paramount.

At the heart of this experience was the act of reflection, the act of thinking turned upon itself, which was the driving force of the new discipline of philosophy. The acknowledgement of the primacy of the act of thinking is the central theme that connects the pre-Socratic philosophers, causing them to question the validity of any other source of knowledge than that mediated by the thinking function. It led them to claim, as Anaxagoras, writing in the fifth century BC did, that all things are known by the thinking mind (*nous*).[13] Previously one might have maintained that the state of *enthusiasmos,* or some variation of that state, gave access to the deepest knowledge. Now, one philosopher after another claims that thinking goes deeper. It goes deeper into the underlying structure of the cosmos, because this is itself conceived as a kind of intelligence: Anaxagoras declares it to be nothing other than infinite mind (*nous*), while Heraclitus sees it as the cosmic *logos*.[14]

At the same time, thinking takes us more deeply into the source of our own existence. Through the act of thinking, the philosophers argue, we connect with something in ourselves that is truly and essentially us. This line of thought is most fully articulated in Aristotle, who sees the faculty of thinking (*nous*) as "the true self of each person" and adds: "Therefore it would be a strange thing if a person should choose to live not their own life but the life of someone other than themselves."[15]

This passage provides the key to the liberation of the human soul from the gods. For insofar as each person exercises their faculty of thinking, they themselves become the source of their own thoughts, desires, intentions, and actions. Indeed, Aristotle goes so far as to redefine human beings as the originators of their own actions.[16] Thus human autonomy is born. Aristotle follows through the idea of freedom with compelling simplicity.

For where we are free to act we are also free to refrain from acting, and where we are able to say No we are also able to say Yes. If, therefore, we are responsible for doing a thing when to do it is right, we are also responsible for not doing it when not to do it is wrong;

and if we are responsible for rightly not doing a thing, we are also responsible for wrongly doing it . . . [It] consequently depends on us whether we are virtuous or vicious.[17]

The radical nature of this statement is all but lost on us, who have come to take such a viewpoint as little more than a statement of the obvious. But for the ancient Greek, versed in Homer, such thoughts were truly challenging. For throughout the works of Homer, as in the literature of the ancient world as a whole, it is precisely such freedom that is denied human beings by the incessant interventions of the gods. Did Achilles have any choice but to obey the commands of Hera and Athene? And was it not, after all, Zeus who set off the quarrel between Agamemnon and Achilles in the first place? We are referring here to deep-seated assumptions about the forces involved in the processes of the psyche. The vocabulary used throughout the ancient world was one that incorporated extraneous agencies into the very fabric of an individual's psychic functioning. As the individual begins to claim the latter for him or herself alone, so the gods are necessarily ejected from the human soul.

But the gods could not be cast out from the human soul without at the same time being cast out from nature. If all extraneous agencies were to be expunged from (or is it more accurate to say *absorbed into?*) the newly emerged self-referring psyche, so by the same token had the interior life of nature to be denied. The objectification of nature was intrinsic to the process by which *enthusiasmos* (and its variants) was replaced by the act of reflection. In order for human beings to define themselves independently of the gods, so too had nature to be defined in the same way: in time the faculty simply was no longer available with which to apprehend the divine presences within nature. It had been superseded. Human beings therefore came to define themselves as much over against a nature that was increasingly experienced as being "out there" and lacking interiority, as against the divine world. Why? Because the old awareness of the gods, whether they were perceived as forces acting into the psyche or as energies within nature, dissolved the boundaries of the ego. The new primacy of the act of thinking established fresh boundaries, which meant that what occurred within the human soul was all "inner"—internal to the psyche—while what occurred "beyond" the soul was necessarily an "outer" event, lacking an interior. The very notion of interiority became exclusive—applicable only to the human psyche.

This double development—of the interiorization of the soul-life and the exteriorization of nature—must be understood as a process occurring over centuries. Indeed, millennia. In the philosophy of Aristotle, nature is still granted an inner life, albeit one that is no longer understood in terms of the direct engagement of the gods. Rather, we have Aristotle's categories, which may be regarded as the ossified remains of the gods.[18] But the whole tenor of Aristotle's philosophy of nature is nevertheless animistic: nature, on all levels, displays the interior workings of soul. It is really not until the Middle Ages, in the nominalist thinkers of the time—notably William of Ockham—that the inner life of nature is systematically negated.[19] We should understand, therefore, that Decartes' elegant exposition some centuries later of a dualistic universe, divided between "thinking substances" and "extended substances"—a view, which has received so much adverse criticism in recent years—was the product of a long process stretching back not only to Aristotle but to the dawn of history. It is a process bigger than any one human being or group of human beings: rather it is a process of humanity itself.

## FUTURE RETURN

Such is the strength of the polarization between psyche and nature in the universe that we now inhabit, that it still tends to determine the way people think today, although we are perhaps increasingly uncomfortable with it. Even for Jung, the gods are firmly located on the psychic side of the divide: they must be understood not as powers intrinsic to nature but as "symbolic expressions of the inner, unconscious drama of the psyche."[20] To explain their existence, we are obliged to think of the ancients as having *projected* onto nature their own psychic contents, which were then rediscovered in nature in the form of apparently external spiritual beings. For Jung, modern science obliges us to think in this way because its objectivizing methods have so thoroughly "despiritualized" nature. Any latent psychic qualities still to be discovered within the natural world must be understood by us as nothing other than "projections" of the unconscious human psyche.[21] For Jung, the "despiritualization" of the world, through the supposed withdrawal of our projections, was an inevitable outcome of the historical process.

> Since the development of consciousness requires the withdrawal of all the projections we can lay our hands on, it is not possible to maintain any nonpsychological doctrine about the gods. If the historical process of world despiritualization continues as hitherto, then everything of a divine or daemonic character outside us must return to the psyche, to the inside of the unknown man, whence it apparently originated.[22]

From the religious viewpoint of antiquity, however, the historical process would more accurately be interpreted as having involved, not the withdrawal of our psychic projections from the world, but a process of *introjection,* by which the gods dwelling in the interiority of nature have been appropriated by the modern psyche: a subtle but important difference of perspective. What right have we moderns to assume than the world experienced as despiritualized is any more valid or true than an enspirited world? While the historical process of world despiritualization may have had an inevitability about it, this does not mean that we have today arrived at a greater truth than the ancients. It is rather that our vision has drastically narrowed. Thus, far from it being our task to deploy our intellective energies in returning the divine to the psyche, our efforts should be directed toward returning the psyche to the divine. Implicit in this task is the cultivation of a unitive mode of awareness in which what we discover or uncover in the depths of contemplative consciousness is experienced as nothing other than that which lives and works in the depths of nature. It is a mode of awareness in which a deepened sensitivity toward nature leads to a greater understanding of the forces that live and work at archetypal levels in the psyche. In a century during which the so-called withdrawal of projections has accompanied the increasingly catastrophic process of world-despiritualization, it makes more sense to envisage the future as involving *the restoration to nature of our introjections* as a precondition of the respiritualization of the world.

The conceptual and experiential boundaries demarcated by the Greek philosophers and crystallized in the dualism of Descartes are not final. Nature and psyche need not forever confront each other as completely separate spheres of existence, but—as Jung also clearly saw—it is possible to develop a type of consciousness in which these boundaries begin to be transcended.* It is possible, that is to say, to conceive of a kind of consciousness in which the modern nature-psyche, outer-inner divide is once again overcome, but overcome on the basis of a totally free relationship to the realm of the gods. In working toward this objective, we may take our inspiration from those ancient cultures in which a living relationship to the gods was the norm, and in which the polarization of nature and psyche had not yet arisen. This is the future of the ancient world—a future that differs from the past in one fundamental respect: that the renewed relationship to the world of spirit will be based on the autonomy of the individual whose center of consciousness is the free reflective act.

More and more people today are turning their attention toward the cultures of the ancient world, not I suspect purely as an interesting pastime, but for far more profound reasons. The ancient cultures are *reminding* them of something that has lain buried in the depths of the psyche and is at last awakening again. Perhaps we could call it "imagination"; but not the subjective imagination of this or that individual personality, but a contemplative imagination that reaches out to connect us as much with the inner life of nature as with the archetypal energies of the human soul. The consciousness of the ancients was preeminently image based because

---

*The transcendental background to both outer empirical reality and inner psychic reality was referred to by Jung as the *unus mundus*—a concept elaborated in his last major work, *Mysterium Coniunctionis,* paras 759–75. For Jung, the experience of the *unus mundus* is the final stage of the alchemical opus of the transformation of consciousness.

the symbolic image is the medium by which one is able to apprehend the causative powers in which both nature and psyche are rooted. And so we find ourselves looking back to the ancient world as if in the manner of gesturing toward the future rather than the past.

Whether or not it falls within the remit of contemporary archaeology, we may conceive that the task of the archaeology of the future will be less to endlessly uncover sites and "finds," and more to uncover a mode of consciousness long since lost, which, once revealed, strikes a chord of recognition in our hearts. While I have referred to the ancient Greeks of Homer's time, it was the ancient Egyptians in whom the old unitive consciousness was most purely alive, and it fell to the Greeks to steer humanity away from this older consciousness. It was already a dying consciousness in Greece from the sixth century BC onward, whereas in the earlier culture of ancient Egypt we contact a far deeper and altogether richer experience. It is for this reason that Egyptology today has a particularly important role for contemporary Western culture. In an essay written in 1970, the Egyptologist A. A. Baarb reflected on the wider significance of Egyptology for us today, concluding with these inspired words:

> We are today in a similar position as regards the absorption of Egyptian thought as Europe was at the end of the Middle Ages regarding the assimilation of the legacy of Greece, when scholars of the Renaissance started to read Greek again. Perhaps the legacy of Egypt could somehow influence the thinking of the next generations in a similar way to that in which classical studies influenced the centuries of humanism up into our age.[23]

The study of the cultures of antiquity in general, and of ancient Egypt in particular, can serve to guide us out of the secular and dualistic impasse that we now face. This is not to advocate a revival of ancient spirituality today. The reason why such a thing is neither possible nor appropriate is that the ancient consciousness operated on the other side of the Great Divide that came into being in ancient Greek and Roman times. Theirs was a consciousness intent upon maintaining the presence of the gods in their experiential world, whereas ours is a consciousness struggling to reconnect with the divine, having been through the disorientating experience of separation. Theirs was a consciousness in which the fissure between nature and psyche had not yet been opened, whereas ours is a consciousness striving to heal this fissure that, by the time of the Greeks, could no longer be prevented from opening.

We have taken the separation from the divine into ourselves, into our very identity: it has become crucial to our sense of identity as such. And the division between nature and ourselves will always be with us; no matter if we succeed in healing it, it will remain with us like the scar of an old wound. This is the distinctive and fateful path of the West. We have grown apart from the gods, apart from nature, and—socially—apart from the group. And the outcome of this whole process has been to find ourselves within ourselves, at the center of our own soul-life and the source of our own actions. Our self-definition is thus placed in our own hands.

But for that very reason we can return all the more powerfully to a unifying consciousness in which nature and psyche attain a new synthesis, and the world of spirit becomes alive for us once again. We can return all the more powerfully because this can be achieved from the ground of separation and division that has been the precondition of the Western path of individuation. If we learn to relate once more to the gods, we shall do so in freedom and from our own reflective center. And if we rediscover in nature that which at the same time belongs most intimately to ourselves, we shall do so without losing our individual autonomy. The separative consciousness is the ground from which such rediscovery and reunion must spring, but it can only be so through the cultivation of the unitive mode of awareness that, in its first degree at least, depends on the cultivation of the contemplative imagination.[24]

I began this essay with the question posed by Plutarch in Roman times: "Why are the gods no longer speaking to us?" Perhaps, two thousand years later, we are in a position to offer a reply. In fact, the great German philosopher, Hegel, was already offering a reply at the beginning of the nineteenth century. It is with his words that I would like to end these reflections:

> The life of the Spirit is not one that shuns death and keeps clear of destruction; it endures death and in death maintains itself. It only wins to its truth when it finds itself utterly torn asunder. It is this mighty power not by being a positive, which turns away from the negative, as when we say of anything it is nothing or it is false and—being done with it—pass on to something else. On the contrary, spirit is this power only by looking the negative in the face and dwelling with it. This dwelling with it is the magic power that converts the negative into *being*.[25]

# 11

## CHRIST AND THE GODS

And he (Jesus) said:
The human being is like a wise fisherman, who cast
his net into the sea and drew it up from the sea full of
small fish. Among them the wise fisherman found a
large good fish. He threw down all the small fish into
the sea: he chose the large fish without hesitation.

GOSPEL OF THOMAS, 8

*Modern depth psychology has made people aware once again of the gods and their myths as powerful forces active in the psyche. But in recognizing the gods, and the "polytheistic" nature of the unconscious, there is a danger that we overlook the central divine-human archetype. This cannot simply be equated with any single god, but is rather the still point around which the multiplicity of gods revolves. This essay traces the relationship of the One and the Many historically, focusing on the incarnation of the Logos as a pivotal moment in the evolution of human consciousness.*

*This essay arose out of a talk "On the Multiplicity of the Divine Unity: Reflections on Gods and Angels" given at The Burford Old George Meetings on March 6, 1993, and a day workshop on "Angels" given at the Stanton Guildhouse on October 18, 1993.[1]*

## BETWEEN POLYTHEISM
## AND MONOTHEISM

It is usually believed that the cultures of antiquity were polytheistic. Insofar as they recognized a multiplicity of gods, this is of course true. But insofar as the term polytheism is taken to mean that the peoples to whom it refers *only* recognized the divine as a multiplicity, and did not conceive of the divine as a unity, it would not be right to describe the ancients as polytheistic. The many gods were thought of each as originating from one primordial source, which permeated the divine multiplicity and bound it into a single whole (see chapter 6).

In most ancient cultures, therefore, the word "god" was used both in the plural ("the gods") to denote the manifold energies and powers of the divine, and in the singular ("God") to denote the divine in both a general and an absolute sense, as the Godhead of which the many gods were each a specific manifestation. This is the case, for example, both with the ancient Egyptian use of the word *neter* (plural *neteru*—the gods) and with the ancient Greek use of the word *theos* (plural *theoi*—the gods). We should also not overlook the fact that our own word "god," which is of Teutonic origin, likewise has a similar facility for slipping from a singular into a plural mode. The vocabulary of ancient polytheism was as monotheistic as our modern monotheistic vocabulary is potentially polytheistic.

Rather than "polytheism," the religious outlook of the ancient world is better described as *henotheism* (*heno*—"one" in Greek). The henotheistic orientation is one in which the divine is conceived as being fundamentally a unity, but a unity that reveals itself in a multiplicity of forms. The ancients recognized a plurality of spiritual beings, of spiritual agencies and forces, operating in different ways and with varying degrees of power. But these were regarded as emanations of a single divine source. Henotheism could be described as monotheism in a polytheistic mode. It sees both the unity of the divine multiplicity, and the multiplicity of the divine unity. Just how it does this is made clear in the creation myths of ancient Egypt, in which the process by which the One becomes a multiplicity is described.

In the Heliopolitan creation myth, the original divine unity is referred to as Nun, visualized as a vast and infinite ocean within which every possibility of existence is contained, but in a state of potentiality. Nun is formless and indefinable, beyond space, time, and beyond even the category of being. Nun is a great abyss or emptiness, but it is a fecund emptiness, which contains within itself the fullness of all existence, but held in potentiality. Nun is not exactly a god, for Nun is beyond the gods, and yet "father" of them all. Within Nun is a creative principle, a seed of creativity that as it germinates, differentiates itself within Nun. As the life-potential of Nun is activated, something solid appears in the midst of the ocean of potentiality, and this is Atum. Atum is not other than Nun, but is rather a phase in the self-revelation of Nun. Why does Atum not rest content in the ocean of potentiality that is Nun? It is because Atum yearns for something on which to place his feet. Atum—the creative seed—yearns to germinate, to bring potentiality into actuality. And so Atum comes into being out of the nonbeing of Nun and, in the very act of Atum's becoming, a third principle arises: Kheprer, the Becoming One. The completion of this first phase of Nun's self-manifestation is in the unfolding of light within the darkness of the infinite waters, imaged as the appearance of a broad-winged "light-bird" settling upon the solid earth that has emerged in the ocean's midst. The light-bird symbolizes a fourth aspect of Nun's self-unfoldment: Ra. In this manner the One "becomes" Four.

It is now from Ra, or Atum-Ra, that the pantheon of gods issue: Shu and Tefnut, Geb and Nut, Isis, Osiris, Seth, and Horus. Ra, the principle of light is also the creative principle, and the gods who come forth from him are likened to his limbs or members. Through their generation the whole universe of stars, of heaven and earth, of time, of death and the overcoming of death takes on existence. In the Heliopolitan cosmogony, Ra stands at the crossing point between nonbeing and being.

But it is not that Ra, Kheprer, or Atum are other than Nun. Nun is their very substance, and Nun will remain the substance of all the gods that come into being through Ra. The classic statement of this

henotheistic view is found in the Book of the Dead, chapter 17, where
Nun states:

> *I am Atum in rising up.*
> *I am the only One.*
> *I came into existence (Kheprer-na) in Nun.*
> *I am Ra in his rising in the beginning . . .*
> *I am the Great God who came into existence (Kheprer*
> *t'esef ) by himself.*
> *That is, I am Nun who created his name: "Substance of*
> *the Gods."*[2]

The emanation of the multiplicity of the gods from the one divine
source is a theme that every creation myth of the ancient world repeats
in its own way. Often the process involves conflict between the leader
of the gods and the formless divine substratum, or abyss, from which
they emerged. Marduk must battle with Tiamat just as must Zeus with
Kronos, who swallows the gods back into himself as they are born.
Whether involving conflict or not, the succession of gods is described
in terms of a sequence of generations, each one linked to the subsequent
one by virtue of parentage. Each generation of gods is born from—in
other words it *arises out of*—the previous generation. The multiplicity
of gods constitute a single family. And the elaborate genealogies of the
gods described in the ancient creation myths are best understood as a
basic theology concerning the way in which different divine energies
form part of an interrelated whole.

Thus the One is regarded as being present in the Many. And in
the more fluid type of thinking of the ancients, it becomes possible
for a prominent god or goddess to represent the All. The henotheistic
approach to the divine is to regard every deity as a manifestation of
the Godhead, and hence as a conduit, an energy-channel, leading both
to and from the Absolute. As but one manifestation, or aspect of, the
divine totality, each god conveys a portion of the Absolute, and each
god provides a certain pathway, a limited approach to the unlimited.

Hence the necessity of acknowledging a multiplicity of gods—and the more the better—in order to provide as many avenues of approach to the divine as is consistent with the manifold energies emanating from the Godhead. This was understood in pre-Christian times right up to the end of the "polytheistic" era. And so Maximus of Madaura, writing toward the end of the fourth century AD, could state (and this is an attitude typical of the henotheistic mentality):

> There is only one God, sole and supreme, without beginning or parentage, whose energies, diffused through the world, we invoke under various names because we are ignorant of his real name. By successively addressing our supplications to his different members we intend to honor him in his entirety. Through the mediation of the subordinate gods the common father both of themselves and of all men is honored in a thousand different ways by mortals, who are thus in accord in spite of their discord.[3]

In the Roman empire, at the time Maximus was writing, the supreme Godhead was also equally conceived as the Great Mother (*Magna Mater*) under the form of Cybele or Isis—"the One who is in All." From the henotheistic standpoint, the multiplicity of cults were not rivals to each other, they were complementary.

## THE GODS AND THE PSYCHE

While the gods were spiritual beings whose manner of existence was different from that of the natural landscape, plants, or animals, they were nevertheless closely involved in nature. The particular quality of a landscape or landscape feature (such as a mountain or river), plant or animal could often be recognized as characteristic of a certain god or goddess. The gods were experienced in and through nature in this way: not as identified with natural phenomena but rather as underlying energy-patterns that a range of natural phenomena might express through their characteristic forms or modes of behavior.

Likewise the gods were present within the psychic life of human beings: again, not as *identified* with emotions, desires, thoughts, or intentions, but rather as the deeper archetypal patterns underlying these psychological events. Instead of regarding these inner experiences as belonging to oneself, the ancient attitude was that each human soul participated in a "psychic world," common to all. In the depths of this psychic world, the gods were at work, and hence could be located at the source of certain types of soul-experience that people might have.

For this reason, the sense of self-identity was, in ancient times, experienced differently from how most people experience it today. For at the bottom of the soul one discovered the gods, and it was through bringing one's consciousness into a harmonious relationship with the gods that one achieved a sense of self-integration. Our experience today of personal identity being associated with a certain claim over the contents of one's inner life as belonging to oneself, or as expressing oneself, was not the experience of people in antiquity. In ancient times, all psychic experiences brought one into relationship with transpersonal agencies and, rather than denying their reality or ignoring their power, the ancients sought constantly to put themselves into a beneficial relationship to them. Only in this way did they feel they were living rightly.

Under such conditions, the path that led to an experience of oneself as a spiritually autonomous being was open only to the few. This path is vividly described in the ancient Egyptian Pyramid Texts as a journey undertaken in a cosmic setting, in which one god after another is met with and overcome, and their magic appropriated by the spiritual traveler.

> *He is the one who eats men and lives on gods,*
> *He is the one who eats their magic*
> *and devours their glory.*
> *The biggest of them are for his breakfast,*
> *the middle-sized are for his dinner,*
> *and the smallest of them are for his supper.*[4]

The energies of each god are here assimilated, literally ingested, by the person who encounters them. Elsewhere this text makes it clear that this eating of the gods occurs not on earth but in the heavens. The destination of the ancient Egyptian, seeking to attain an experience of existing as a spiritually independent being, was ultimately celestial. It was to board "the boat of Ra" and to sail upon it. For in reaching Ra, one had reached a source transcendent of the multiplicity of gods. Sometimes the aim is described as being to become Ra's servant, his scribe, or his helmsman. At other times it is described as being simply to become one with Ra, the source of the gods.[5] It was only in this experience, achieved among the stars, that the polycentric psyche attained to an experience of its fundamental unity, and it did so through a process involving dominance over the gods.

In the mythology of the ancient Egyptians, the psychic, or psychospiritual, shift from polycentrism to monocentrism involved the experience of psychic fragmentation and reintegration.[6] This was the prelude to becoming one with Ra—the spiritual source—and it was pictured in terms of the death, dismemberment, and reconstitution of Osiris. The Osiris myth describes the experiences that a person had to

*Fig. 11.1. The celestial self, in the image of Ra, looks down upon mummiform Osiris, upon whom Horus radiates light.*

go through in order to come to a realization of their spiritual essence. Fig. 11.1 shows how the person who has won through to this state, and has become a "shining one" (*Akh*) akin to Ra in his celestial boat, could only achieve this by going through a prior death as Osiris, shown mummiform below. But between the two figures is a third—the falcon head of Horus, the son of Osiris who is born upon his death. Horus radiates rays of spiritual light upon Osiris, and it is this radiant quality of Horus that is particularly significant. For the condition of soul that Horus represents is that of Osiris reborn, and equally of Ra grounded—in other words the celestial self that has become incarnate. Horus, to the ancient Egyptians, was the earthly image of Ra: the radiant source of light physically embodied. And the place where Horus came to reside in the initiate's psychophysical organism was the heart.*

The theme of death, dismemberment, and rebirth is of course by no means exclusively Egyptian. It is central to all ancient initiatory myths, many of which dwell particularly on the "Osiris" or underworld aspect of the experience. In Mesopotamia there is the comparable myth of Inanna, whose descent into the underworld, and immolation there, is a prelude to her triumphant resurrection. In Canaan the god Baal must journey into the underworld in order to be reborn again. In Greece we find the mystery cults of Orpheus, Dionysos, Persephone, and Demeter. These myths all conform to an underlying pattern, and they all served to provide the imaginal context in which people were able in a sense to reverse the creation myths, traveling back through a polycentric and polytheistic experience of their inner life to a monocentric experience of the divine source of their human nature.

## THE JUDAIC PATH TO MONOTHEISM

Jesus was born into a society, and into a religious context, that had developed in a quite unique way. This development began, significantly perhaps, in Egypt. It is likely that the Israelites were in Egypt for about

---

*As the Book of the Dead, chapter 29, states, "I am Horus, who dwells in the heart, who dwells in the middle of the body."

four hundred and fifty years, within the period ca. 1700–1250 BC, for the most part during the brilliant eighteenth dynasty. The date of the Exodus is usually placed somewhere between 1280 and 1220 BC.[7] At least in the later years of their stay in Egypt, they were in bondage to the Egyptian state, and were no doubt treated harshly. The Egyptians are certainly portrayed in the Bible as monsters of wickedness, practicing black magic and worshipping idols, their minds entrapped by a grossly materialistic view of the world. Given this picture of the Egyptians, it is clear that none of the Egyptian gods or goddesses was likely to help the Israelites in their plight.

Into this situation came Moses. He has a vision of a burning bush and he hears a voice proclaim that it is the god of the Israelites that speaks to him. The god of the Israelites had been known before Moses's time of course—known to Abraham, Isaac, and Jacob (who originally led the Israelite family into Egypt)—but he was little more than a tribal god. Yet now this god communicates with Moses in an unexpectedly intimate way. The text describes this famous interview as follows:

> *Then Moses said to God: "I am to go, then, to the sons of Israel and say to them: The God of your fathers has sent me to you. But if they ask me what his name is, what am I to tell them?" And God said to Moses: "I am who I am. (Ehyeh asher ehyeh). That is what you must say to the sons of Israel. I am (ehyeh) has sent me to you." And God said to Moses: "You are to say to the sons of Israel, Yahweh (lit. 'He is') . . . has sent me to you." (Exodus 3: 13–15)[8]*

By comparison with other ancient gods, the name of this god of the Israelites is extremely odd. It is extremely odd because it is given in the first person singular. How can one imagine a god with such a name? How can one represent "I am" to oneself? How can one objectify "I am" in a statue or image? The names of gods such as Ra or Horus or Isis all contained within themselves an indication of their cosmic function or status. Ra, "the One Who Creates"; Horus, "He Who is Above"; Isis, "the Throne," and so on. And each could be represented in characteristic ways: Ra, for instance, as a falcon, a ram, sometimes as a calf. Each image symbolically conveyed an aspect of the nature of the deity in question, and indeed could provide the medium through which the deity could become present to human consciousness. And so it was with all the gods, whose energies were aligned to certain animals, natural phenomena, and plants. But "I am" is not a name suggestive of any such alignment of divine and natural energies.

As we might expect, there follows an interesting exchange between Moses and the King of Egypt. Moses says to the Pharaoh:

> *Yahweh, the god of Israel has said "Let my people go."*

Pharaoh replies:

> *Who is Yahweh that I should listen to him and let*
> *Israel go? I know nothing of Yahweh and I will not let*
> *Israel go.* (Exodus 5: 1–2)

It must be remembered that the kings of Egypt were not ignorant of spiritual realities. On the contrary, they ruled as initiate kings, aware as much of the sphere of existence in which the gods moved as they were of the political, social, and economic dimensions of life.

The interview between Moses and Pharaoh suggests that Moses had become conscious of something that the ancient Egyptian religious consciousness was not able to recognize or grasp hold of. And that "something" was an experience in which the divine and the human coalesced in a very particular way. In speaking the name of their god, each Israelite at the same time affirmed their own self-identity, a self-identity purged of every god save the one whose holiest appellation was nothing more nor less than *pure subjectivity;* "I am who I am." Not that they thereby felt themselves to be instantly united with their god each time they said or thought his name, but rather that the whole direction in which the divine was sought, and in which it manifested, was the same direction as that in which they came to experience themselves as individuals.[9]

The accentuation of this experience of the divine as a purely internal experience that positively and vehemently excluded every other manifestation of divinity is what now characterizes the subsequent history of the Israelites.

It is a troubled history because the exclusive concentration of worship on one god alone went against the ancient feeling of reverence toward the divine, which was always regarded as manifesting as a multiplicity of different energies. The first of the Ten Commandments, not to revere other gods, was one that risked catastrophic consequences. By not worshipping, for instance, Baal, one would incur his disfavor, which might be expressed in all manner of destructive ways—pestilence, drought, military defeat, and so on. The worship of such gods had thus to be forcibly suppressed, a task Moses swiftly and mercilessly took in hand.

There was also a profound psychological cost too. The ancient gods were felt to be as much active in the psyche as they were in nature. For this reason we must suppose that the ancient consciousness did not experience nature and psyche as two spheres of existence standing over against each other, or clearly distinguished from each other, as we have today come to experience them.

Rather, the divine forces operating in nature were felt also to be active within the psyche, with the consequence that many experiences that people had—which today we would tend to regard as belonging to our subjectivity—were interpreted as the movements of objectively existing divine powers. The psyche did not belong to a person; each person participated in a psychic world in which the gods were active. Not to revere these gods, and not to make any images of them—in obedience to the second of the Ten Commandments—was to loosen the psyche from all its traditional reference points. How was one to identify what one was experiencing—in love, in anger, in celebration, in thoughtfulness? The ancients attributed to each of these soul-experiences a specific divine agency that stood behind the psychological process. But for the Israelites only one divine agency was allowed to be acknowledged: the "I am" resounding in the depths of the inner life. And only one image of God was acceptable within the Mosaic faith: the *human* archetype, Adam, created in the image of God on the sixth day.

Just as much as a new consciousness of the divine is here indicated, so also is a new psychological order. While the ancient psyche was polycentric, the Israelite psyche became, through the denial of the gods, monocentric. It became concentrated upon the single psychic center of the soul that focused all its most intense spiritual longings, its prayers, its devotion, on the One God—Yahweh.

> *Yahweh, my God, I call for help all day,*
> *I weep to you all night;*
> *May my prayer reach you,*
> *hear my cries for help.* (Psalm 89)

Yahweh became the single reference point for all that passed through the soul.

> *In you, Yahweh, I take shelter;*
> *Never let me be disgraced.*
> *In your righteousness rescue me, deliver me,*
> *turn your ear to me and save me.* (Psalm 71)

Inasmuch as Yahweh was the single reference point of the righteous soul, so too were Yahweh's laws, commandments, and prohibitions. The Israelite soul was subjected to a regimen of dictates that were to be obeyed in preference to the archetypal impulses welling up within the psyche.

And Yahweh increasingly was not discoverable in any natural phenomena: the exclusive relationship to the one God required not only the centralization of consciousness, fortified by a bulwark of moral and legal codes, but also the deanimation of nature. For if the gods are denied in the psyche, they must as surely be denied in nature. Thus were nature and psyche forced apart, for the very factor that had guaranteed their union was an awareness that underlying both were the very same gods.

Yahweh's final repudiation of the gods in the eighth century BC ("I am the first and the last: there is no other god besides me." Isaiah 44: 6) also marked the final severance of nature from psyche. For this god Yahweh was too far removed from both nature and psyche for the experience of the divine presence to have the ability to mediate between them. He cannot be likened to "anything that is in heaven above, or that is in the earth beneath, or that is in the water under the earth" (Exodus 20: 4). From the psychological side, he is so powerful and unfamiliar to the soul that "a human being may not see him and live" (Exodus 33:30). The exclusive monotheism of the Jews thus, in a sense, left both nature and psyche bereft of the divine presence. Faith came to replace experience as the principal relationship to the divine; but not only faith. For God's increased distance also meant that the spiritual life was made reliant upon an intensification of inner activity, each individual having to draw from deep within their own resources in order to turn toward their God. It might be that the parameters of the psyche—insofar as the gods were excluded from it—were now diminished. But in place of the gods there arose a heightened sense of individual autonomy, intrinsic to which was the dawning awareness that within the human subjectivity— in the deepest depths of the soul—it was possible to contact a greater "I am."

If, therefore, we were to attempt to contrast the emerging consciousness of the Israelites with that of the ancient Egyptians, with whom they had made such a radical physical and spiritual rupture, we might say: in ancient Egyptian spiritual life there existed two levels of self-consciousness. On the more "mundane" level, people experienced their psychological processes as originating from, and as tied up with, the activity of the gods. They would thus identify their psychological processes less as their own and more as arising from the gods, with whom they felt the necessity to relate themselves. Beyond this, at a higher level, there existed the possibility of mastering the gods and achieving an experience of union with the divine creative source from whom all the gods derived their power. But in order to achieve such a union with Ra, or Atum-Ra—"to look upon his face" as the Book of the Dead[10] expresses it—a person had to come to experience the polycentric consciousness as involving an inner fragmentation or dismemberment of the soul. This "Osiris" experience was the necessary prelude to the reconstitution of the soul about a single divine center.

For the Israelite, by contrast, at the level of ordinary awareness, the activity of the gods was constantly negated in the psyche. The soul was no longer an arena in which the gods were seen as actively giving rise to psychic events. Whatever occurred therein was ultimately to be claimed by a person as belonging to him or herself alone. At the same time, the "liberated" personality referred more and more to moral and legal exhortations and prohibitions as a way of maintaining a relationship to the divine, now conceived as the One God Yahweh.

But unlike Ra, Yahweh was not a god that any human being could become identified with, in the sense that the ancient Egyptian initiate might identify with Ra. Yahweh was a god unlike any other god in that it was not possible to become united with him. Except for the prophets through whom Yahweh spoke, no Israelite would dare to say "I am Yahweh" as an ancient Egyptian—in an exalted state of consciousness—might say, "I am Ra." And yet Yahweh's absence was curiously and uniquely present in the still depths of the human soul, demanding an allegiance, which was to be forged in a specifically moral way. That is, through the burgeoning moral sense, nurtured and guided by the divine commandments, which now took precedence over supplication of the gods:

> If you come on your enemy's ox or donkey going astray, you must lead it back to him. If you see the donkey of a man who hates you fallen under its load, instead of keeping out of his way, go to help him. (Exodus 23:5–5)

It is a new voice that can be heard coming out of Israel. It is as if the god of the Israelites had in some uncertain way made common ground with what was noblest in the human spirit. And this god, despite his forbidding persona, was at the same time felt to be a "personal God."

He was both far away yet also strangely close to hand. And it is this closeness, this intimacy of Yahweh and the human spirit, that distinguishes the Israelite from the ancient Egyptian (or Mesopotamian or Canaanite) relationship to the divine.

## THE GREEK RETREAT FROM THE GODS

In Greek culture, a comparable evolution in human consciousness was also beginning to occur, though it took place in the more leisured atmosphere of the Greek settlements and cities on the present Turkish coast. Here it was the contemplation of philosophers, rather than the thunder and travail of prophets, that brought into focus a new relationship to the divine. And here it was less the yearnings of the soul than a more objective concern to lay bare the underlying causative principles operating in nature that most preoccupied the philosophers. Throughout the sixth century BC we find in these Greek cities one philosopher after another seeking abstract or semiabstract principles rather than the old gods as the key to their understanding of the natural world. According to Anaximenes, writing at some time during the middle of the sixth century BC (his exact dates are unknown), all natural phenomena can be understood in terms of the element air. Now this element would previously have been referred to as Zeus. But Anaximenes bypasses the god in favor of the semi-abstract principle, explaining the generation of the world solely through the condensation and rarefaction of this element air.[11]

At about the same time as Anaximenes, Anaximander postulated the wholly abstract principle of the "Boundless" (*Apeiron*) as his First Cause, from which all else derives. It is an indefinite, unlimited power that cannot be equated with anything in nature, nor any god, though it is nevertheless divine.[12] Here, then, in this notion of the Boundless, imagery and personification become redundant in the face of the all-encompassing abstract idea. One could no more make an image of the Boundless, nor conceive of it as one or other god or goddess, than could the Israelite of Yahweh.

This movement of thought came to a head toward the end of the

sixth century in the writings of Heraclitus. For Heraclitus, the first principle of all things is the Logos—an ordering principle that channels the
creative powers of the universe into harmonious and ordered forms. The
word *Logos* has the connotation of "proportion" and "ordered pattern."
The cosmic Logos (like the Boundless of Anaximander) is superior to
the gods; it governs all things. But Heraclitus does not simply talk of
the Logos in cosmic terms. He also refers to it as living on the inner
boundaries of the human soul.[13] It is from this inner Logos, this Logos
in the soul, that Heraclitus claims to speak. His thoughts stem from a
level of experience in which the duality between self and world—that
necessarily arises with the demise of the gods—is freshly transcended.

> *Listening not to me, but to the Logos, it is wise to agree*
> *that all things are one.*[14]

The Greek word *Logos* is closely associated with the notion of thinking
(it is, after all, the word from which "logic" is derived). Heraclitus really
sets the agenda for all subsequent Greek thinking, which is characterized
by this fundamental assumption: that the human faculty of thinking is,
at its deepest level, of the same essential nature as the creative power
that gives rise to the universe. Later philosophers, like Anaxagoras and
Aristotle, referred to both as Mind (*Nous*). For these philosophers, there
is the universal cosmic mind, and there is in each individual a "microcosmic" mind, and ultimately they are one and the same.[15] For Aristotle,
the *Nous* is the "highest" and "best" thing in us, the source not only of
contemplative activity but also of moral intuition, and we should do
all that we can to live in conformity with it, "for though it is small in
bulk, in power and value it far surpasses everything else."[16] The presupposition here is that the human faculty of thinking has the potential to
reach deeper into the divine than the previous polytheistic consciousness based on image, personification, and myth.

While this whole trend of thought is being carried forward—toward
the cosmic Logos appearing on the far horizon of the natural world, and
toward the microcosmic Logos beginning to stir within the depths of

the human soul—the traditional gods of the Greeks came increasingly under attack. Outflanked by these profound intellective experiences, the gods were dismissed by some as mere projections of the human psyche, the latter on the one hand being clearly demarcated from nature, and on the other hand discovering within itself a new experience of interiority, which apparently bypasses the gods through an activity at once personal and universal. This is the view of Xenophanes, writing in the sixth century BC.[17] Other philosophers, such as Prodicus and Critias were to follow suit, denying the existence of the gods altogether.[18]

What was happening in Greece, therefore, was a parallel process to what had already occurred with the Jews. Whereas the history of the Israelites is one in which the gods were forcibly driven from people's awareness both of nature and of the psyche, in Greece the gods simply faded from awareness as part of the process of the unfolding of the new philosophical consciousness, If, among the Jews, the gods were replaced by the One God Yahweh, then among the Greeks they were increasingly overshadowed by the cosmic Logos or Mind (*Nous*). And while with the Jews we can point to a developing moral consciousness and a certain intimacy as characterizing each person's relationship to their god Yahweh, with the Greeks we see the emergence of a new intellective center within the psyche, which, at the most profound level of experience, was felt to be of the same essence as the cosmic Mind. It was this apprehension that gave rise to the possibility of wresting from the gods the decision concerning the rightness of human actions. Moral choice and judgment could be carried into the human sphere just because there was this new coalescence of the human and the divine. Both the Israelites and the Greeks were beginning to experience a type of self-consciousness in which, instead of finding one's self-identity through harmonization or conjunction with gods or a god, one discovered this self-identity to be *intrinsically* divine.

The historical consequence of the Judaeo-Hellenic liberation of the "personal space" of the entirely humanized psyche from the domination of the gods may have been that the ego was thereby born;[19] but this fact alone does not itself constitute the meaning of the historical process. The meaning resides in the capacity of this ego to find a universal identity in its own individual core. So there is a moral dimension here. The ego that has dogged European history, and which has more recently become a major world player, was and is the means by which the human soul turns toward itself, toward its own interior, in the manner of claiming its own world, freed from the interventions of the gods. Having expunged the gods from the psyche, it became possible for individuals to "find themselves" within the attitude that they adopted toward this or that psychic force, experienced as an impulse, feeling, intuition, or desire. That is, it became possible for each person to claim that attitude as their own, as the expression of *their* individuality. But at the same time, each person could find within themselves a deeper reference point by which their individual consciousness could become grounded in something essentially transcendent of their ego. This deeper reference point, as much as it was reached through contemplation, was also the source of ethical awareness. Hence the birth of the ego was at once the birth of the moral self, and involved becoming aware of the distinctively human capacity of moral insight and selfless action, not attributable to the intervention of any god, but arising—as Aristotle put it—from "the ruling part" of ourselves—namely the "divine" *nous*.[20] The divine and the human were indeed beginning to form a new kind of alliance.

## THE LOGOS INCARNATE

Now it is into this whole spiritual environment—not only Judaic but also Hellenic—that Jesus was born. Historically speaking, he was born into an age when truly momentous changes in consciousness had already occurred. And if one looks beyond the Jews and the Greeks toward other civilizations of the ancient world, in particular the Mesopotamian and Egyptian, it is possible to trace the earlier stages of this developmental path toward, on the one hand, a growing emphasis on the One God (the cult of Amon, for instance, in Egypt) and on the other hand an increased sense of personal autonomy and also individual responsibility (as evidenced, for example, in the legal codes of the Mesopotamians).

Because of the greater antiquity of these cultures, this twin development is less pronounced in Mesopotamia and Egypt, but it is nevertheless possible to discern significant changes in religious practice and of
spiritual attitude in both cultures. These point toward the same basic
fact: that the gods as a multiplicity were beginning to lose their vitality, and in their place a more self-possessed, more individualized self-
consciousness was emerging, the spiritual focus of which was on the
cosmic creative source transcendent of the multiplicity of gods.

One approach to understanding the significance of Jesus, then, is
that he—as an individual—carried this process to fruition. He attained
a level of consciousness in which he experienced the cosmic Logos as his
own self. His individuality, his individual self-consciousness, he experienced as completely merged with the divine cosmic creative principle.
The cosmic Logos thus came to fill the consciousness of this individual
human being who lived his individuality to its divine depth. This was
an experience of the fusion of the lesser "I am" of the monocentric ego
with the greater "I am" of the Godhead.

Such an experience could only take place in a psychic environment
from which the gods had withdrawn, for only in such an environment
was it possible for a person to come into a relationship of full responsibility for their psychic life. No longer under the sway of the gods, something specifically human in the soul-life had become the central reference
point of all psychic events. This was the sense of individual selfhood,
of ego or "I," that had emerged as the gods faded from consciousness.
But with the emergence of this specifically human element of individual
self-consciousness, there also arose, as something wholly intrinsic to it,
the possibility of self-transcendence. And in that very movement of self-
transcendence there arose the potentiality of the human to realize itself
as divine, and as identical with the cosmic Logos.

This realization of the human *as* divine could not, however, have
the character of the ecstatic ascent of the ancient Egyptian toward
union with the god Ra in the heavens. For its intrinsic meaning lay in
the discovery within the distinctively human sphere—and hence within
not only the humanized psyche but also within the psychophysical

organism—of a divine, indeed cosmic, identity. The experience was thus expressed in terms of the "descent" of the divine into the human, the descent of the cosmic Logos (whom the ancient Egyptians had known as Ra) into the human soul, which all the time retained its purely human sense of self-identity.

From this perspective, various statements made by Jesus concerning self-knowledge shed light on what he himself must have experienced. They also point the way forward to those following in his path. In "The Book of Thomas the Contender" (from the Nag Hammadi library) a dialogue between the resurrected Jesus and his brother Judas Thomas is recorded. Thomas represents all human beings who understand themselves to be companions of Jesus. Jesus says to him:

> Now since it has been said that you are my twin and true companion, examine yourself that you may understand who you are, in what way you exist, and how you will come to be. Since you are called my brother, it is not fitting that you be ignorant of yourself. And I know that you have understood, because you had already understood that I am the knowledge of the truth. So while you accompany me, although you are uncomprehending, you have in fact already come to know, and you will be called "the one who knows himself." For he who has not known himself has known nothing, but he who has known himself has at the same time already achieved knowledge about the depth of the All.[21]

## POLYTHEISTIC PERSPECTIVES ON CHRIST

In the ancient Egyptian religious literature, it is possible to discern a shift of emphasis in the cult of Ra, as this evolves over the centuries. In the Old Kingdom (the age of The Pyramid Texts), Ra is supremely and unequivocally a celestial deity. His home is among the stars. But by the time of the New Kingdom, there are a plethora of esoteric writings (such as The Book of Gates, The Book of What Is in the Underworld, and so forth) that concern themselves exclusively with Ra's sojourn in a subcelestial region between heaven and earth—namely the Dwat (usually translated as the Underworld). These writings describe how Ra enters this twilight region, which is really the realm of psychic energies, and travels through it, in order to bring his glorious light to those who dwell therein. It is as if, in the course of ancient Egyptian history, Ra was perceived to be drawing nearer to the earth, and to the human world. In the Book of the Dead, from the same period of Egyptian history, it is revealed that Ra and Osiris, the god with a human face who undergoes death, are in fact one.[22] The two gods are said to meet in the Dwat, the intermediate region between heaven and earth. It remained only for Ra to fully incarnate in human form for the long journey of his descent to be fulfilled.

From the polytheistic perspective of antiquity, Christ (who described himself as the Light of the World) was readily understood, by some at least, as an incarnation of the sun god. It is well known that Constantine, in his first vision of Christ while on campaign in Gaul, mistook him for Apollo. And in the cemetery under St. Peter's in Rome, there is a famous portrayal of Christ as Helios in his sun chariot (fig. 11.2).

In the second century AD, when many of the people drawn to Christianity were still thinking in polytheistic terms, such an identification seemed virtually self-evident. Thus Melito of Sardis, in a passage in which he describes the sun god's daily circuit of the earth and descent into the Ocean, refers to Christ in the following terms: "King of Heaven, prince of creation, sun of the eastern sky who appeared both to the dead in Hades and to mortals upon earth, he, the only true Helios, arose for us out of the highest summits of heaven."[23]

According to the ancient Egyptian understanding, the great solar god Ra preexisted the sun that we see in the sky. Ra was never simply the *sun* personified. His existence did not derive from the sun's existence, but rather the sun's existence derived from his existence. The extent to which he was thought of as identified with the sun was only so far as the sun—as source of light for the cosmos—had an inherent kinship with Ra's own nature as the light-principle in the universe. The relationship between Ra and the sun was often expressed as being like

*Fig. 11.2. Christ portrayed as Helios, third century AD.*

that of a person to their eye. The sun was the "Eye of Ra" by means of which his purely spiritual light was conveyed to the world, in such a manner that the world became visible to him. Ra, therefore, while solar in quality, was conceived as a being far greater than the sun. He was conceived as the living agency who brought the cosmos into existence by radiating his spiritual substance outward into a multiplicity of gods, likened to his limbs, each of which became manifest in some feature of the universe—in the stars, the earth, the atmosphere, and so on.

What is stated in the opening verses of St. John's Gospel concerning the Logos, could as well have been stated concerning Ra who—as we have seen—was originally one with the Father of the gods, Nun.

> *In the beginning was the Logos,*
> *and the Logos was with God,*
> *and the Logos was God.*

*He was in the beginning with God;*
*all things were made through him,*
*and without him was not anything made*
*that was made.*
*In him was life,*
*and the life was the light of men.*
*The light shines in the darkness,*
*and the darkness has not overcome it.*

(Gospel of John 1:1–5)

I have argued that the Logos idea and the associated idea of the universal *Nous* or Mind, was intimate to the development of Greek philosophical thinking, and had the effect of gravitating the life of reflection toward a central point. This central point focused attention away from the multiplicity of gods and on to the single divine source, of which the multiplicity of gods were deemed a manifestation.

In the mainstream Stoic philosophy, which held a dominant position in the Roman period during the centuries immediately preceding Jesus's birth, the Logos was conceived as containing within itself certain "seed principles" (*logoi spermatikoi*) from which all forms derived. These archetypal principles are similar in conception to the Ideas of Plato and the later Reason-Principles (or "seminal reasons") of Plotinus. There was of course, a reluctance among the philosophers to identify these abstractly conceived principles with the gods, but Plotinus comes very close to it in his discussion of the Reason-Principles in *Enneads* IV.[24] In the world of Hellenic and Hellenistic philosophical speculation, with its exaltation of the divine Mind (as *Nous* or Logos) over the gods, it is not entirely surprising that—insofar as they are accounted for in abstract, philosophical terms—the gods tend to be regarded as creative ideas within the divine Mind. That is, ideas, which are not simply objects of thought but are the archetypal forms of thinking, through which the divine Mind expresses itself. In Plato, who was able to move with such facility between strictly philosophical and imaginative or mythological modes of expression, we find the gods or *daimones* assembled in the

*Timaeus* around the central Logos-figure (the *Demiourgos*) in order to assist in the work of creation, performing thereby a similar function to the Ideas elsewhere in his philosophy.[25] Plato is a good example of a philosopher who knows that while the language of philosophy may be abstract, what philosophy refers to in abstract terms are in fact concrete spiritual realities, and hence can equally well be treated mythically.

The conception of seminal reasons continues into Christian philosophy, playing a prominent (though somewhat differently conceived) role in St. Augustine's creation theology as the *rationes seminales,* and from thence into the mainstream of orthodox theology. According to Maximos the Confessor (writing in the seventh century AD) there are a multiplicity of logoi or inner principles, which are contained within, or "embraced by" the Logos. For St. Maximos,

> The whole Logos of God is neither diffuse nor prolix but is a unity embracing a diversity of principles, each of which is an aspect of the Logos.[26]

It is interesting to compare such a statement with the view of the last great pagan Neoplatonist, Proclus, who—writing contemporaneously with Augustine in the fifth century—saw that

> the entire series of gods has the form of unity and the form of goodness as a single character . . . As derivative terms proceeding from the First Principle they have the form of goodness and unity, inasmuch as that Principle is One and Good. . . .
>
> For the non-Christian henotheist, there is no metaphysical difficulty in accommodating the gods within a theology centered on the One. But neither, really, need be a problem for the Christian to allow that another way of understanding the "diversity of principles" is as the very same gods, "each of which is an aspect of the Logos."[27]

There is a plaque in the Louvre, dating from Roman times, which has the busts of the twelve Olympians gathered in a circle, the center of which is left empty (fig. 11.3). This powerful image clearly illustrates the fundamental unity of the gods, much as Proclus describes it. It is significant that the unifying principle is not portrayed, for it is, in Neoplatonic philosophy, essentially beyond depiction. As Proclus says, "not all the gods together may be matched with the One, so far does it overpass the divine multitude."[28]

The plaque may be taken as a henotheistic mandala. There are all the mighty gods of Olympus, but each one is peripheral to the central Godhead that cannot be framed in an image. In the Neoplatonic metaphysics in which Proclus was steeped, the One is comparable to the Nun in the ancient Egyptian theology, while the divine Mind (*Nous*) is comparable to Atum-Ra. The goal of Neoplatonic spiritual striving is the experience of union with the One through an ecstatic ascent from the physical realm.

Such an image had to be transformed in order to become compatible with the new Christian understanding. But the transformation was needed less because of the presence of the twelve Olympians than because of the absence of Christ in the center. In the pre-Christian age,

*Fig. 11.3. The twelve Olympians gather around a common center.*

the Logos-function, insofar as it was conceived mythically, was ascribed primarily to the sun god. The fourth-century AD mosaic illustrated in fig. 11.4 is particularly interesting because it occupies an intermediate position between the ancient polytheistic or henotheistic conception of the divine, and the later Christian conception in which the emphasis is thrown onto the central figure of the divine-human archetype.

In the outer circle of the mandala, the twelve Olympians are replaced by the twelve signs of the zodiac. Already in the Roman Empire, the siderealization of the gods was common place. And in fact in the previous illustration (fig. 11.3), each of the Olympians is depicted with their zodiacal insignia. Now the gods have vanished altogether and are superseded by the zodiacal principles. But in the center of the circle, there is the extraordinary image of Helios in his sun chariot, drawn by four spirit-beasts through a star-filled sky. The presence of Helios is all the more extraordinary because the mandala is from a fourth-century pavement mosaic in a synagogue in Israel. Hence the four archangels in each corner of the outer square were presiding over the different seasons of the year.

*Fig. 11.4. Helios in his sun chariot, in the center
of a zodiac, with archangels in the four corners.*

A further stage in the evolution of this type of mandala can be seen in fig. 11.5—a Christian mosaic from Ravenna, created but a century later. The mosaic shows the twelve Olympians transformed into the twelve apostles, who stride purposefully around the outer circle. In the center of the circle, Jesus is baptized by St. John.

*Fig. 11.5. The baptism of Christ, with the twelve apostles.*

The baptism is the moment when, from the Christian point of view, the whole world order changes. At this moment the cosmic Logos unites with the human being Jesus, who now becomes the *Christos*—the anointed one. In this event, the spiritual emphasis shifts from the rapturous ascent of the soul to God, to God's *descent* into the human soul. What is essentially cosmic becomes human, and thus there are no longer any gods to be seen. It is as if the dazzling reality of what is taking place here is so overpowering that the gods become invisible. They are dispersed to the very margins of human awareness. At the same time, the twelve apostles may be understood as each representing a particular divine or zodiacal energy, but this energy is as fully embodied, and as unequivocally humanized, as the Logos is in Jesus.

Beyond the imagery of the twelve apostles surrounding Christ, is a further variation in which the figure of the Logos-incarnate, the God-man, is returned to the cosmic setting from whence he originated, and to which he belongs as cosmic Logos. Here Christ is the representative of all humanity, and indeed the whole creation, which originally issued from his creative word. All is now brought back through him to the source, in an ultimate *Apokatastasis* or Restoration of all Things to God. The Christ that Giotto has given us in the fresco illustrated in fig. 11.6 may be viewed in this light. It forms part of a much larger scene of the *Last Judgment*. This detail shows Christ surrounded by twelve angels, and thereby epitomizes a changed relationship between human consciousness and the divine multiplicity. How are we to understand this metamorphosis of the Olympians into angels? Are the angels simply the gods in Christian disguise? Or is it that, with the total

*Fig. 11.6. Christ surrounded by twelve angels.*

coalescence of the human and the divine in Christ, a transformation is thereby wrought in the world of the gods, the effect of which is that they actually *become* angelic beings? What is it, exactly, that constitutes the difference between the gods and the angels?

## GODS AND ANGELS

For the pagan thinkers of the Roman Empire, the Christian belief in angels was extremely perplexing. The third-century AD Neoplatonist, Porphyry, could not see the difference between angels and gods, and hence could neither understand the Christians' refusal to honor the traditional gods, nor their reluctance to make sacrifices to the angels.[29] What Porphyry failed to grasp was that the angels differ from the gods less in their relation to the Godhead, than in their relation to the human being. The critical experience upon which Christianity is based is that of an inner conjunction of the human essence with the Logos. This alters the relationship between the Godhead and humanity, and it thereby affects the relationship between the gods and human beings.

It was therefore still possible for Christian writers to use virtually the same language in describing the relationship of the angelic hierarchies to the Godhead as pagans (such as Proclus) did in describing the relationship of the "series of gods" to the One. So, for example, Dionysius the Areopagite, referring to the Godhead in the Helios imagery of light, could say:

> This light can never be deprived of its own intrinsic unity; and although in goodness, as is fitting, it becomes a manyness and proceeds into manifestation [i.e. in the hierarchies of angels] . . . yet it abides eternally within Itself in changeless sameness, firmly established in its own unity.[30]

It is a thought echoed by Dante in the Middle Ages who, in his journey through Paradise, learns to recognize the nine angelic choirs in

> *that Living Light which from its radiant Source*
> *streams forth its light but never parts from it . . .*
> *(and) of its own grace sends down its rays, as if*
> *reflected through the nine subsistencies,*
> *but in itself eternally One remains.*[31]

If Christians could thus acknowledge the divine multiplicity one thousand years into their monotheistic faith, it makes it all the more important to understand how and why this multiplicity differs from that of the old polytheism.

I have suggested that in the historical process leading up to, and then brought to a fulfillment in, the Logos experience of Jesus, something was in fact changing between human beings and the divine world. One sign of a crucial shift occurring can be seen in the spiritual history of the Jews, when the old gods are replaced by angels. But what did this really signify?

The nature of the altered relationship between the human and the divine world, as experienced in the Jewish context, can, I think, be gleaned from a story recorded in one of the apocryphal "Books of Adam and Eve."[32] This tells of how, when God created Adam—the human archetype—he commanded all the angels to bow down before this human "image of God" and to worship him. All the angels obeyed, save one—namely Samael or Satan. Now the attitude of Satan in this story is not much different from what we might expect from one of the ancient gods. This is what he says:

> I will not worship an inferior and younger being than myself. I am
> his senior in the Creation. Before he was made I was already made.
> It is his duty to worship me.

Thus spoke Satan. And all the angels under him likewise refused to bow down before this new creature made of clay. As we know, God was very angry and banished Satan and his followers from heaven as a consequence of their refusal to worship Adam.

The story pinpoints where the pre-Christian conception of gods and the Judaeo-Christian conception of angels part company. In ancient times people worshipped the gods, and they did so because their aspirations were heavenward, toward aligning conditions here on earth with conditions in heaven. Heaven was regarded as the source of all that came into being on earth, including humanity. The gods were indeed both older than, and superior to, humans, because they were closer to the Godhead.

The early Christians not only objected to worshipping the gods, they also desisted from worship of the angels. Their reason was that the location of the divine source of the gods had shifted from heaven to earth, and specifically to within the human being as "image of God." This was already presaged in Judaism, and our story indicates just where we are to look for what it is that distinguishes the angels from the gods. The gods demand from human beings an attitude of worship. But the angels, insofar as they acknowledge the cosmic Logos-nature of the human archetype, feel compelled to worship the divine *within* the human. For the divine presence within the human being is greater than all the divine multitude (whether conceived of as gods or angels) precisely because it is, even if but potentially realized, a presence closer to the Godhead than they. For it is the creative Logos from which they—both gods and angels—have sprung. This was the insight that had seized hold of the early Greek philosophers, who ranked the cosmic Logos or *Nous* above the gods, just as it had caused the Jewish prophets to denounce worship of any other divinities than the One God Yahweh. We could say, therefore, that the angels differ from the gods by virtue of this fundamental reorientation, which was, as it were, clinched by the fully realized "incarnation" of the Logos in Jesus, the second Adam.

In the ancient world, the gods stood between the human soul and its self-integration, and ultimately its union with the cosmic creative principle in a higher experience of self-identity. The angels—from the point of view of human individuation at least—must surely have a comparable role. But where their role differs from that of the gods is insofar as the cosmic creative principle is now acknowledged as conjoined with the human essence. Now this is something that obviously implicates us, in our own attitude toward, and experience of, our own deeper self-identity.

The angels stand between the individual self-consciousness and the universal Logos in a manner that must be distinguished from the way in which the gods of ancient times mediated between human soul experiences and the Godhead. For the place of the angels is between the monocentric consciousness of the ego and its self-transcendent union with the Logos, whereas the place of the gods was between a far less individualized, polycentric psychic life and the experience of individual spiritual autonomy achieved in an ecstatic out-of-the-body state of consciousness. Union with Ra occurred in a celestial context. At the heart of the Christian experience is the *descent* of the Logos, the Logos made flesh. The context is earthly. And the quality of the experience one in which the monocentric ego comes through to a deeper realization of the divine within the human.

The gods were, and still are, forces that are active within the psychic world, which in ancient times was recognized as permeating all of nature as the *Anima Mundi* or Soul of the World. Each individual shared or participated in this psychic world. And it is most interesting to observe how the activity of the gods was still widely acknowledged throughout the Medieval and Renaissance periods of European history, both in astrology and in the doctrine of correspondences. Each planet bore the name of a god and was pictured as a god. These planetary energies are psychic—literally astral; they belong to the psyche, in the sense of the "psychic world" in which we, as ensouled beings, participate.

But the angels were never really conceived in psychic terms, and while there exist traditions regarding the planetary associations of the different archangels, the attempt to conflate the angels with the gods never really succeeds. This is because they represent less psychic energies than the means by which the psychic level is transcended. They represent those powers that are really supra-astral. For this reason, they are more usually shown in Medieval and Renaissance illustrations as residing beyond the planetary spheres, beyond even the zodiac, occupying a place the other side of the world.

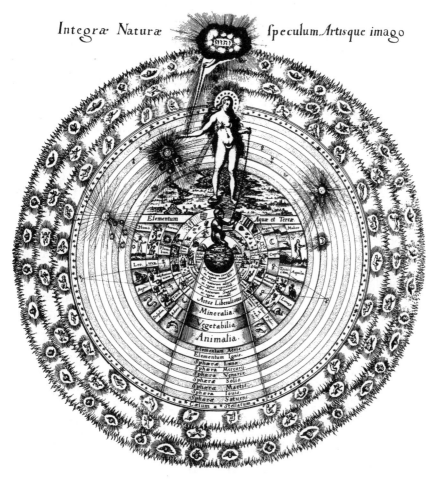

*Fig. 11.7. The Earth, the World Soul, the planets, and the angels.*
*From a diagram by Robert Fludd, 1617.*

Fig. 11.7 is from Robert Fludd's *De Macrocosmi Historia* of 1617. Although relatively late in date, it continues a tradition going back hundreds of years. It shows a geocentric cosmos, in which the Earth is surrounded by the spheres of the planets, each one radiating their influence down upon the various kingdoms of nature, and human activities, below. Beyond the sphere of the fixed stars, the world of the angels is depicted, grouped in three ranks. In the center of the picture, in a dominant position, is the feminine figure of the Soul of the World, the *Anima Mundi*. Her right foot stands on earth, her left on water; her body extends upward into the spheres of the planets, and her head is crowned with stars. It is she who mediates the astral energies of the stars and planets to all her creatures. But she herself is but a link in the great chain of being, which stretches upward from her right hand to the Godhead, passing through the realms occupied by the angels.

It is because of their spiritual location between the astral, or psychic, level and the Godhead that angels have the quality of leaving people free, precisely where the ancient gods would intervene in the psychic life. Their sphere of activity in relation to humanity is in our moral life—i.e., in that area of our lives in which we struggle to take up an independent stance toward the forces operative in the psyche. Could it be for this reason that angelic beings all bear the same sublime countenance, whereas the gods each have their specific archetypal character? In contrast to the gods, the angels present to us a universal face, full of serenity, strength, and compassion, but without distinctive personality, or even gender. They show us the countenance of the human being deified. Perhaps for this reason the angelic world is so often pictured as revolving around the central figure of Christ, the divine-human archetype, as in fig. 11.8.

In contrast to the angels, the gods may be understood primarily, but not exclusively, as psychic energies, active in the psychic fundaments of both the human and the natural worlds. The angels then assume the role of guides and sustainers of the ego-bound soul striving toward the divine center of love and wisdom within its core. Formulating it in this way, however, it is necessary to resist clinging too tightly to our formulation. The gods may also act as angels, just as angels may take on the appearance of gods. Too stark a distinction between the gods and the angels would, I think, be counterproductive. What is important is less the different ways in which they are conceived, and less also our own orientation to either the gods or the angels, and more our own conception and experience of ourselves, and our willingness to travel more deeply into our own center, about which ultimately both gods and angels revolve.

*Fig. 11.8. Angels surround Christ.*

## RETURN TO SOURCE

Today, across the spectrum of contemporary depth psychology, there is a strong tendency to rediscover the ancient gods in the archetypal energies that move in the unconscious. From the standpoint that I have taken, it seems unavoidable that the recovery of awareness of the gods in a newly polycentric depth psychology requires that the angels be acknowledged as well. For it is they that enable the gods to become centered on that which is divine in the human being. The question therefore arises: what exactly is this human capacity that is both our point of contact with the divine yet is not in itself identifiable with any one deity? How are we to describe this capacity that touches the hidden spiritual essence of our humanity? For it is from this point in ourselves that our relationship to the gods finds anchorage.

Many Christian mystics, especially those writing within the Orthodox tradition, have continued to use the same term as was used by the early Greek philosophers to refer to this capacity in us. It is said to dwell in the depths of the soul, and it is identified as the *Nous*.[33] What is this *Nous*? In the language of Christian mysticism it is spoken of as "the eye of the heart." Insofar as it is an eye, it is an organ of perception, of insight, and of understanding. But insofar as it is of the heart, it functions not through the analytical or discursive mind, but through an intuitive knowing filled with love for that toward which its attention is turned.

The "eye of the heart" is not any object of thought, for it is no more objectifiable than the seeing eye is seeable. But neither is it a subject as opposed to an object, but rather it is the transcendent ground on which a meeting between one's individual self and the universal Logos can take place. To experience this transcendent ground is to become aware of a universal creative source from which our individual self-consciousness derives. One experiences a higher sense of self-identity, a higher "I am."

But this higher "I am" is not simply internal to the soul. It has the character of internality insofar as we can approach it through an interior movement, a movement inward. But it also enables us to direct our consciousness toward beings other than ourselves, and to adopt as our own standpoint the inner life of these beings. Because it links us to the creative source from which both psychic and physical realities arise, this interior movement turns into a movement outward. It leads us to an experience of self-identity that goes beyond conventional distinctions between "I" and "world," for it is beyond both, yet immanent within both.

Speaking from this transcendent standpoint, in which one experiences one's deepest self in union with the Logos, Jesus said:

*I am the light that is over them all.*
*I am the All.*

*The All has come forth from me,*
*and the All has attained unto me.*
*Cleave the wood: I am there.*
*Raise up the stone,*
*and you will find me there.*[34]

The statement implies that it is possible, through an outgoing movement of attentiveness toward the natural world, to discover at its core precisely the same creative principle as one can discover within oneself. On the way, we meet the gods, just as we meet the gods in the psyche.

It may be that the recovery of the awareness of the gods gives us the living, experiential foundation for the respiritualization of nature and the transcendence of the ego. But at the bottom of this reawakening to the divine as multiplicity, there lies the further dimension of a new awareness of the divine as unity. Just as the old polytheism was in fact monocentric, so does the emerging polytheism need to recognize a new principle of unity at its center. A principle of unity that cannot be reduced to any god, for it is the specifically human energy of transcendence, which links us with the One that embraces all multiplicity.

# 12

## PATHWAYS INTO
## THE FUTURE FROM
## THE DEEP PAST

*The cultures of the ancient world did everything possible to harmonize conditions on earth with conditions in heaven, and the spiritual journey of each individual ultimately led one to union with the divine in the realm of the stars. But can the ancient religious consciousness still be valid for us today? Rather than seeking to revive the past, should we not be finding the pathways that lead from the past into our own future?*

*This essay is based on a talk given at the launch of the Jupiter Trust in Oxford, on May 20, 1995.[1]*

### THE COSMOLOGICAL CONTEXT:
### REFLECTIONS ON AN OLD HINDU MYTH

I want to try to view our present situation from the standpoint of a wide cosmological and historical perspective. I believe we need to relate to the times we live in from a perspective that is bigger than these times, for then the initiatives that we take can be carried through with an awareness that extends beyond the narrow limits of our own lives, to the much larger spiritual and historical process with which we are engaged. Those of us who are working today for the spiritual renewal of our culture need, I think, to achieve an insight into how the development of consciousness in the West relates to the wider spiritual picture of the whole human evolutionary journey, because it then becomes more possible to work with genuine optimism for the future.

According to one ancient Hindu text, this evolutionary journey of humanity is inextricably linked to the unfolding of universal Spirit. The text is from the *Brihadāranyaka Upanishad,* and it recounts an early myth concerning Spirit (*ātman*).[2] It tells of how in the beginning there is only Spirit. But Spirit, being alone, is not happy. Spirit longs for the companionship of something that is other than itself. The consciousness that Spirit has of itself is in some sense inadequate. It lacks the full realization of knowing itself in and through another.

So it divides itself into two, one part male and the other female. And the male unites with the female, and as a result of this union human beings are born. The female tries to hide herself from the male, and takes the form of a cow. But he turns himself into a bull, they unite again, and this time cattle are born. She becomes a mare and he a stallion, she a she-ass and he an ass, they unite and so horses and donkeys are born. She becomes a she-goat, he a goat; she a ewe and he a ram, and so goats and sheep are born. In this way Spirit, dividing against itself but constantly overcoming this division within itself, brings forth the whole universe.

The universe, however, is not aware of Spirit, because Spirit is so closely identified with creation. The unity of Spirit has become a multiplicity, but as such, Spirit has lost the "completeness" that it originally had. The text states,

> [Spirit] entered into everything, even to the tips of fingers, just as a razor fits into a razor case, or fire into a brazier. Yet he [Spirit] cannot be seen, for he is incomplete.[3]

Despite having poured itself into the world, Spirit is "incomplete" in the world, for its outpouring entails a fragmentation of itself. It can only achieve completion or fulfillment when it is known or "seen" in its true essence of Oneness, rather than in all its fragmented parts.

We could say that Spirit is unconscious of itself in the world to the extent that the world is unconscious of it. The fulfillment of Spirit is thus dependent on its coming to self-knowledge in the midst of what it has created. The text explains:

> What introduces differentiation is name and form. . . . One who reveres any of these individually has no right knowledge: for he [Spirit] is incomplete in any of these individually. Let a person revere him rather as the Self, for therein do all these works become one.[4]

Only when we who are caught up in external life turn inward, realizing our unity with Spirit, will Spirit become fully consonant with itself and therefore have the possibility of attaining perfect self-consciousness. For it is one thing for Spirit to dream itself in the multiplicity of creatures, but it is another thing for Spirit to wake up to knowledge of itself within the consciousness of these creatures.

A third phase in the journey of Spirit toward fulfillment or self-realization is thus required: the return of its externalized self back to itself, and the overcoming of the division of Spirit against itself that this implies. This third phase will result in a state distinct both from that in which Spirit existed in the beginning as an undifferentiated unity, and from the state that Spirit is in when it has created a world that remains ignorant of its true identity. The third state will be a richer condition altogether, because it will involve the incorporation of the finite, the limited, and the temporal back into the infinite, the unlimited, and the eternal. It will involve the self-knowledge of Spirit within and through the temporal and finite world.

A basic cosmological scheme is given here, which I believe can still serve us today. Although the text to which I have referred is Indian and dates from around 700 BC, the truths that it expresses have been expressed and reexpressed in different religious and philosophical forms over the millennia in many different cultures and times. More recently, it was the guiding inspiration of one of the greatest of modern philosophers, Georg Wilhelm Friedrich Hegel. In the following passage, Hegel succinctly defines Spirit in a manner wholly compatible with the way in which Spirit is discussed in the *Brihadāranyaka Upanishad* to which I have just referred.

[Spirit] attains actuality not by fleeing from the Other but by overcoming it. Spirit can step out of its abstract, self-existent universality, out of its simple self-relation, can posit within itself a determinate, actual difference, something other than the simple "I" and hence a negative. And this relation to the Other is, for Spirit, not merely possible but necessary, because it is through the Other and by the triumph over it, that Spirit comes to authenticate itself and to be in fact what it ought to be according to its concept, namely the ideality of the external, the idea, which returns to itself out of its otherness. Or, expressed more abstractly, the self-differentiating universal, which in its difference is at home with itself and for itself.[5]

Hegel and the *Brihadāranyaka Upanishad* share an understanding of Spirit's involvement in the world of time and matter: it is that there is a certain mutual dependency between Spirit and the Other that is its reflection, a dependency that places a quite definite burden of responsibility upon human beings in the unfolding of Spirit. As Meister Eckhart once said, "God can no more do without us than we can do without him."[6] Human attitudes are therefore important for God. The human historical process, and the changes in consciousness that define it, have a significance that reaches beyond the merely human into the sphere of Spirit.

Today, it may seem that we have come to a stage in the unfolding of history at which the process of Spirit's "self-negation"—of Spirit positing an Other, which is apparently separate and different from itself—has achieved a kind of limit. It is as if we cannot get more materialistic or egotistical than we already are. But in the midst of a historical epoch in which secular values and reductionist perspectives dominate culture, there are signs of a growing impulse to reverse the process, to reconnect with the spiritual dimension, to expand our consciousness, and to work toward a future in which human beings freely cooperate with the spiritual world.

The contemporary resurgence of interest in spirituality, be it New Age or traditional, suggests that we are being moved at a deep level by the desire of Spirit to "return to itself out of its otherness." But what is the appropriate pathway for this return? Can it be the same as that which was deemed appropriate four or five thousand years ago? The question must be asked because—according to the cosmological perspective I have outlined—we ourselves are inescapably involved, and yet humanity's consciousness has not stayed static. On the one hand, Spirit's return to itself depends upon our return to Spirit, so how we set about doing this has a significance that extends beyond ourselves. On the other hand, how we set about "the return" today may need to be very different from how people set about it in the second or third millenniums BC.

In order to answer this question of what is the appropriate pathway of return, therefore, I want first to examine some of the features of the spirituality, which prevailed in the ancient world, some four or five thousand years ago. I want to focus particularly on the ancient cultures of Egypt and Mesopotamia. These civilizations belong to a cultural epoch that preceded our own, which is essentially the product of the later Greek and Roman ages. By extending our historical perspective into these earlier periods, we can become aware of developments in the unfolding of human consciousness over time that may help us to see more clearly what is the appropriate pathway of return for today.

## ANCIENT STAR WISDOM: THE PATH TO COSMIC UNION

One of the characteristics of ancient cultures is their tremendous respect for the past. In both Egypt and Mesopotamia one meets the same attitude to time, which is that there used to be a Golden Age when the world was wholly attuned to the gods. The earth was still not completely separated from heaven. This was an age before war, strife, violence, old age, and death; an age before there was noise, confusion, and disturbance. Everything proceeded in harmony with heaven. In the ancient Egyptian Pyramid Texts, §1463, for example, we read of conditions in the cosmos:

> *When no anger had yet arisen,*
> *when no noise had yet arisen,*
> *when no conflict had yet arisen,*
> *when no confusion had yet arisen*

Both Mesopotamian and Egyptian chronologies look back far into the past. The early Sumerian King Lists cover an immense period of time—several hundred thousand years, with the earliest kings reigning for extraordinarily long periods. In one King List, two early kings reign each for seventy-two thousand years, while three kings are each given reigns of twenty-eight thousand years. These figures relate to significant cosmic cycles, and are clearly intended to show that in early times conditions on earth were assimilated to conditions in heaven.[7] Ancient Egyptian chronologies record that in the distant past a succession of gods ruled over Egypt: there were no human rulers until comparatively recently. The first human god-kings were the immediate descendants of divine beings who had ensured that Egypt remained absorbed within the heavenly world.

The actual succession of the gods who ruled over Egypt can be seen in fig. 12.1, which shows the divine crew of the sun boat. At the prow of the boat stands the hawk-headed sun god Ra who, according to one King List, reigned over Egypt for thirty thousand years. Behind him is Atum, the eternal fount of all creation, from whom Ra emerged at the beginning of time. Behind Atum is Shu, the god who succeeded Ra as ruler over Egypt, with his wife Tefnut. Behind Tefnut is Geb, the earth god, who became king of Egypt after Shu, and his wife Nut. Then come Osiris and Isis. Osiris was the last king of Egypt before the human rulers, each of whom was considered to be an embodiment of his son Horus. One of these human rulers is shown at the back of the sun boat; his name is Tutankhamun.

*Fig. 12.1. The divine sun boat, whose crew includes the succession of gods who ruled over Egypt before human kings.*

A common feature of ancient Egyptian chronologies is that the length of the reigns of the gods diminishes as they succeed each other, until their reigns finally attain human length with human rulers of the earliest dynasties.[8] Because the age of the god-kings was a golden age, the ancient Egyptians viewed the passage of time, as did the Mesopotamians, as a degenerative process. The further back they looked, the less did it seem to them that earth and heaven were separated from each other. The passage of time involved a gradual falling away from, or a falling out of, the lap of the gods, as earth tended increasingly to go a separate way from heaven.

One of the major orientations of ancient spirituality could therefore be described as a longing for the past. The Egyptians referred to it as "The First Time." It was the "time" before time as we know it existed. The First Time is essentially the world of myth, of archetypal patterns of myth in which the gods live and move. It was to this world that religious rituals constantly referred. The aim was to align the mundane temporal world with this world of spiritual archetypes that shone out from the First Time. But the First Time also had a cosmic location. It was regarded as indissolubly linked to the rhythms of the stars, where the gods have their home. And so the ancient spiritual longing was not only for a past in which time was merged with the trans-temporal world of the gods, it was also a longing to return to our cosmic home among the stars.

In fig. 12.2, a procession of Egyptian deities can be seen marching against a background of stars. This is the context in which they belong. Comparable pictures can be found from ancient Mesopotamian sources. The ancient understanding of the gods was that they belonged to the world of the stars. Great pains were therefore taken in these ancient cultures to observe the stars. Calendars were ruled by the movements of stars; and sacred buildings were sited especially to reflect star groupings and alignments.[9] In Egypt specialist priests devoted themselves to observing the movements of constellations, and every temple in Mesopotamia had its observatory called The House of Observation.[10]

Everything possible was done in these ancient cultures to try to conform conditions on earth to conditions in heaven. But also, and this is more relevant to our theme, human spiritual realization was understood to

*Fig. 12.2. A procession of Egyptian deities makes its way across the heavens. Tomb of Seti I.*

require an initiatory journey that took one beyond the earth to the realm of the stars. The Egyptians conceived the highest spiritual attainment as being to become inwardly radiant like the sun. The source of this inner radiance was located beyond normal everyday consciousness. One reached this source by following the sun out of this world—the world of one's normal consciousness—into the star world. The spiritual journey was felt to involve a movement out of, and away from, the sphere of the earth and normal sensory awareness. In the Egyptian Book of the Dead we read of how a person changes into a falcon in order to ascend to the sky.

> *I am risen,*
> *I am risen from the secret chamber*
> *as a golden falcon, broken out of its egg.*
> *I fly, I hover,*
> *I am a huge falcon with emerald wings*
> *...Thus am I merged with my father Ra.*[11]

In Mesopotamia, a number of images have survived, which portray a man flying on the back of an eagle to the heavens (fig. 12.3). This image may well correspond to the mythical prototype of a king named Etana who traveled in this fashion when he ascended through the heavens. But other vehicles of ascent are also described or portrayed in the ancient cultures: in Mesopotamia the snake god Nirah provided a further prototype of flight that is paralleled in Egyptian images of initiates riding to the stars on the back of snakes (fig. 12.4).[12]

*Fig. 12.3. Flying to heaven on the back of an eagle. Akkadian cylinder seal.*

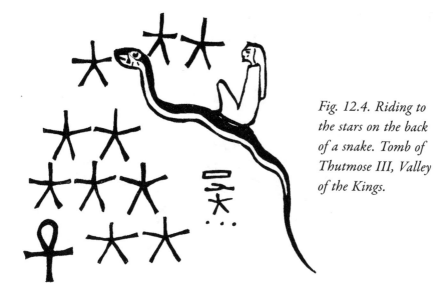

*Fig. 12.4. Riding to the stars on the back of a snake. Tomb of Thutmose III, Valley of the Kings.*

In Egypt the king is also described as ascending by means of a range of other methods: using ladders made by the gods, rising up on the smoke of incense, or traveling up a sunbeam to the heavens.[13] In Crete, a griffin is the animal vehicle on which the ecstatic spiritual traveler rides.*

Such imagery is best interpreted as picturing states of consciousness in which the soul is lifted above itself and transported to a completely different level, a distinctively *higher* level, in order to commune with the gods among the stars. We should probably understand the experiences described by this imagery as arising in a state of consciousness that is freed entirely from the body. These star travelers are moving in a disembodied state.

In fig. 12.5, we see an Egyptian initiate standing on the back of the universe. He has transcended the world of time altogether, for this is shown on the inside of the circle formed by the cosmic serpent and the twelve female figures who personify the hours marking the sun's journey. Remote from the earth, he stands on the back of the great

---

*For example there is an engraved gold ring with just such an image in the Hearakleion Museum, (Case 88, no. 1017). This image is reproduced in chapter 2, fig. 18.

serpent that enfolds the Egyptian universe, and gazes into an utterly transcendent world in which he perceives the spiritual form of the sun in its cosmic home among the stars.

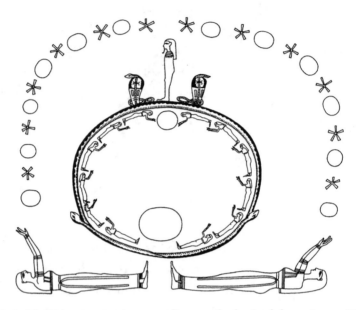

*Fig. 12.5. The Egyptian initiate standing on the back of the universe. Tomb of Ramesses III.*

This mystical experience was described by Plato more than a thousand years later. It should be remembered that Plato spent some time in Egypt—according to one early biographer, studying at Heliopolis, the cult center of the god Ra—and many essential features of his philosophy can be linked to the earlier Egyptian wisdom.[14] This is how Plato describes the experience of the immortalized soul in his dialogue *Phaedrus*:

Now the souls that are termed immortal, when they reach the summit of the arch [which supports the outer heaven] go outside the vault [of heaven] and stand upon the back of the universe; standing there they are carried round by its revolution while they contemplate what lies outside the heavens.[15]

He goes on to describe the region contemplated as

> the abode of the reality with which true knowledge is concerned . . .
> intangible but utterly real, apprehensible only by intellect (*nous*).[16]

The title of the priest who is shown in fig. 12.6 is "Master of the Secrets of Heaven." This priest is named Amenanen, and during the New Kingdom he held the office of High Priest at Heliopolis, cult center of the sun god Ra. He wears the traditional garment of the priesthood, a leopard skin draped around his body. But the spots of the

*Fig. 12.6. The High Priest Amenanen wears the mantle of priesthood, a leopard skin whose spots have been changed into stars. New Kingdom, reign of Amenhotep III.*

leopard have all been transformed into stars. Such a person would have been able to guide souls into the realm of the gods, and to act as mediator between the gods and the lower world. The priestly function was both to open ways between the mundane world and the sphere of the gods, and to channel divine, cosmic energy into the mundane world, thereby helping to keep the latter attuned to the cosmic order.

I have quoted Plato, who may be regarded as one of the last representatives of the type of spirituality that characterized the earlier, pre-Greek cultures of Mesopotamia and Egypt. Plato himself lived from the later part of the fifth century to the middle of the fourth century BC. But the main lines of his thinking would have been entirely familiar to the earlier Middle Eastern cultures. There are two tenets of Platonic philosophy in particular, which express attitudes central to the older spiritual traditions. First, for Plato, the spiritual source both of the natural world and of ourselves is to be found by ascending away from the body and from all sensory experience, and "traveling" in a state of consciousness free of the body into a dimension of existence beyond that of which we are normally aware.[17] This dimension is the purely spiritual World of Forms, or Ideas from which both the forms in the natural world and the thoughts in our minds derive.[18] Second, in Plato's view, the truly spiritual does not participate in matter. It is not tainted by immersion or involvement in matter. Hence the relationship between the purely spiritual Forms or Ideas and the natural forms we perceive in the world around us, as well as the sense-based ideas we normally think, is described by Plato in terms of the latter being reflections or pale images of the former.[19] In order to participate in the true Reality, from which what appears real to us derives, we must sever our connection with the material world and sense-based consciousness. We cannot experience our true self on earth: it is necessary to go upward and backward in a movement of self-recovery, which transports the soul into a pristine, pre-earthly state of self-remembrance.[20] Plato's message is an initiatory one: we must learn to die to our incarnate selves, for death is the secret of life.[21]

Fig. 12.7 shows a detail of a famous portrait of Plato, painted

*Fig. 12.7. Plato and Aristotle portrayed by Raphael.*
*Plato, to the left, gestures heavenward, Aristotle, to the right,*
*gestures forward. Detail from* The School of Athens.

by Raphael early in the sixteenth century, in which he stands beside
Aristotle, the leading thinker of the next generation of philosophers
at Athens. Since it was painted nearly two thousand years after Plato's
death, a physical likeness of Plato was not the artist's purpose. It was
rather the portrayal of the spirit of Plato's philosophy, expressed in the
manner and bearing of the bearded old man, the way in which he holds
himself, his gestures, and attitude. In his left hand he carries his great

mystical-cosmological work, the *Timaeus,* while with his right hand he points upward toward the heavens. The artist has subtly portrayed the relationship of Plato's philosophy to the earth in the way in which his feet are placed only tentatively upon the ground. So tentatively that we cannot be sure whether he is walking forward or backward. He almost hovers above the ground, his feet lacking commitment to the earth.

The figure of Aristotle next to Plato is an equally eloquent statement of the spirit of Aristotle's philosophical outlook. In his left hand, he carries his masterly treatise on how to act rightly in the world, the *Ethics.* His right arm, in contrast to Plato's, which gestures toward the heavens, is stretched out ahead of him and points forward rather than upward. Aristotle's stance is full of the vigor of a man in his prime. He stands with complete commitment to this world, his feet firmly placed on the ground.

## COMMITMENT TO THE EARTH: ARISTOTLE, CHRIST, AND MODERN SPIRITUALITY

Aristotle's philosophy marked a radical departure from the spiritual traditions of which Plato was one of the last representatives. In his philosophy is enshrined a spirituality that does not require an ascent to the heavens in order to discover the spiritual source either of the world or of ourselves, for Spirit is engaged in the world and can be discovered everywhere in nature. For Aristotle nature is the outpouring of Spirit, which is the active or creative principle in all things. For him, the concept form does not belong to a World of Ideas separate from the world that we perceive with our senses. The sense-perceptible world is not a copy or pale imitation of a transcendent world of spiritual archetypes. Rather, these archetypes are embodied in the sense-perceptible world. Spirit is utterly committed to nature.[22] Furthermore, in human consciousness Spirit has the possibility of knowing and recognizing itself. Aristotle refers to this in the twelfth book of the *Metaphysics,* where he describes the meditative act in which a transcendent self-consciousness is attained without traveling to the stars, a "self"-consciousness in which universal Spirit comes to know *itself* in and through human consciousness. Or, put in another but equally valid way, the individual human being comes to a deeper experience of "self" as none other than the universal source of life and consciousness.[23]

In terms of the Hindu myth with which we began, Aristotle's view of the spiritual path (like Hegel's) no longer looks back toward the original Unity (or the Egyptian First Time), but looks forward to a new reunion with Spirit on the basis of an independent self-consciousness that knows the infinite without departing from the finite. An acceptance of our embodiment, of our belonging to the earth, runs through Aristotle's philosophy just as an unwillingness to accept the reality of incarnate life runs through the writings of Plato. For Aristotle, Spirit has made its habitation here on earth; it is part of the destiny of Spirit to become implicated in matter. Spirit and matter together make the world.[24]

Here, then, is a very different attitude toward our spiritual destiny from that which prevailed in the star-oriented cultures of Mesopotamia and Egypt, whose wisdom Plato transmitted to the Greek world. Aristotle's attitude is definitively modern: he no longer harks back to an earlier epoch, to a "First Time" in which the human spirit still existed within the embrace of the cosmos, and had not yet separated out from the original divine unity. Aristotle is too much in love with the world to see withdrawal from it as a valid spiritual path. The two emphases of his philosophy are on pursuing knowledge of nature, and on developing a thoroughly grounded ethics. As regards the former, he seeks everywhere the working of the divine within the natural world.[25] As regards the latter, the basis of right action is brought back to the spiritual intuition of the free and fully responsible human agent.[26]

These two key aspects of Aristotle's philosophy can resonate with us today, even though Aristotle himself lived right at the beginning of the modern era. To approach the natural world as the harborer of spirit, rather than as an obstacle, which we must overcome if we are to reach the truly spiritual, is fundamental to contemporary ecological awareness. It implies an attitude of devotion to nature that constitutes an essentially different orientation to that of the pre-Greek world. It is as if the ancient consciousness was impelled to "see through" nature to the gods who lived and moved in a dimension that was strictly supernatural—a mythological world of archetypal energies—whereas for Aristotle the perception of the supernatural occurs at the same time as a deepened apprehension of the natural. The two go together.

The ethical aspect of Aristotle's philosophy is equally important. Aristotle was utterly opposed to making any moral rules or "imperatives." For him, the key to right action is that the source of an action stems from the element in our nature that transcends the ego, "for though this may be small in bulk, in power and value it far surpasses all the rest."[27] Right action presupposes connectedness with the indwelling spiritual power that we experience in the act of contemplative thinking, which takes us beyond thought to an intensified consciousness of the universal source of thought. Herein lies the "true self" of a person, the spiritual ground of their being, that is both universal, and at one and the same time the source of their individuality. Once again the point is that the divine is encountered within ourselves, not in another world—it is encountered through the intensification of normal consciousness rather than through its negation.

Aristotle grasps the fact that humanity has entered a new stage in the unfolding cosmological drama, and that this stage is to do with the infinite rediscovering itself within the sphere of the finite. In human understanding, particularly in our capacity for intellectual or spiritual intuition, Aristotle sees a cosmic and eternal activity at work within human consciousness. The source of human thinking is infinite, but it is locked within the confines of finitude. Human beings thus have a vital mediating role of releasing the infinite from its entanglement within the finite, thereby allowing the divine to know itself within the human.[28]

Now this cosmic and eternal creative activity was identified by the ancient Egyptians as emanating from the sun god Ra. In terms of the ancient Egyptian understanding, Aristotle might have said that we should look no more for the universal creativity of the sun god in the outer cosmos, for we can discover his activity as interwoven with the deepest processes in human consciousness. In this crucial respect Aristotle's experience is a precursor of the baptismal experience of Jesus, realizing his inward identity with the cosmic Logos.

Fig. 12.8 is an early portrayal of the Baptism of Christ. The bird that previously might have transported the initiate away from the earth to the heavens has here turned around and brings cosmic consciousness down from heaven to earth. The significance of the Baptism is that instead of experiencing cosmic consciousness in a discarnate state, Christ experiences it in an embodied state. The experience is of the union of the soul with the universal creative spirit, but now the union takes place on earth instead of in the heavens.

In the illustration, Jesus is shown elementally balanced. He stands on earth, the lower part of his body is in water, the upper in air, while the fire of spiritual inspiration descends from above. On his right (to the left of the picture) is the god of the Jordan River with horns on his head. This god represents the old polytheistic order. He stands for all the gods of the old spirituality who must now defer to this event of the fusion of the divine with the human. His gesture conveys to us the sense that human spiritual development is no longer held in trust by the gods, but rather the development of Spirit is entrusted to human beings. The human soul will no longer ascend to heaven on a ladder made by the gods with their own hands. For a new coalescence has occurred between human nature and the divine, in which the divine and the human are fused in mutual dependency. Something cosmic has broken through, into the midst of the world, and the stage is set here on earth for the next phase of the cosmological drama—the *apokatastasis* or restoration of all of creation to the divine.

We have seen that the ancient Egyptians regarded the sun as the locus of human spiritual striving, and understood the process of initiation to involve following the sun into the realm of the stars. Now this locus has shifted to the earth. In esoteric Christianity the central mystery is this union of the sun with the earth.[29] It becomes possible to unite with the spiritual source of the universe without journeying beyond the earth.[30] The *apokatastasis* or reciprocal union of the finite

*Fig. 12.8. The baptism of Christ (detail). Baptistry of
the Arians, Ravenna, fifth century AD.*

and the infinite, the temporal and the eternal, should be understood as
occurring through Spirit's unconditional embrace of the realm of finitude and temporality.

If modern consciousness is more earthbound than the consciousness
of the ancients, this is because the cosmic process has involved division
and separation at its very heart, which has in modern times, been carried through to its extreme point. In the face of this extremity, a tremendous longing for ancient forms of spirituality may arise, a longing
to trace back the process of separation, in order to regain the experience
of unity with the divine that was the original state of spiritual bliss.

This is essentially the Platonic path, and Platonism (not necessarily explicit or conscious, but Platonism nevertheless) is a strong current in much New Age spirituality.

It is important that we place beside it the Aristotelian path, of which Hegel's philosophy is the outstanding modern representative.[31] This Aristotelian path again may not necessarily be explicitly or consciously held as Aristotelian, but nevertheless constitutes a powerful spiritual current in the West, all the more powerful for its close allegiance to the root Christian experience. It can be summarized in this contrasting thought: Spirit has unraveled itself so completely into materiality, into that which is divided from itself, that this division must itself form the basis of reunion. The fullest experience of Spirit's division from itself is carried by human consciousness, aware of itself as cut off from the divine, yet pivotally placed as the medium through which the divine can affect a return to itself. We bear within ourselves both the rupture of the original divine unity and the potentiality to heal that rupture. It is a wound that we carry within our own nature, the healing of which is at the same time the realization—in the midst of our separateness and limitation—of our inner identity with Spirit, and of Spirit's self-knowledge within us.

# NOTES

In the following notes, on occasion the sources of some translations have not been cited. In these cases, the responsibility for the translations is mine alone. —J.N.

## CHAPTER ONE. THE RESTITUTION OF THE EAR

1. Jeremy Naydler, published as *The Restitution of the Ear* (Oxford: Abzu Press, 1993).

2. D. Wolkstein and S. N. Kramer, *Inanna* (London: Rider, 1984), 12.

3. Ibid., 52.

4. Ibid., xvi–xvii.

5. Miriam Lichtheim, "The Instruction of Ptahhotep," §575, *Ancient Egyptian Literature,* vol. 1 (Berkeley: University of California Press, 1975), 74.

6. Ibid., 74.

7. H. G. Liddell and R. Scott, *Greek-English Lexicon (Abridged)* (Oxford: Oxford University Press, 1974), for *theoria* and *theorein,* 317; for *idein* and *oida,* see ibid., 195. See also David Ross, *Plato's Theory of Ideas* (London: Oxford University Press, 1951), 12–15. For an illuminating discussion of the use of the words *eidos* and *idea* in Plato (who was writing in the first half of the fourth century BC), we read (on page 13): "Both *eidos* and *idea* are derived from *idein,* 'to see' and the original meaning of both words is no doubt 'visible form.'"

8. Plato, *The Republic,* §511, trans. H. D. P. Lee (Harmondsworth: Penguin, 1955), 278.

9. Aristotle, "Physics," §184a, in *Physics,* vol. 1, trans. Philip Wicksteed and Francis Cornford (London: William Heinemann, 1970), 11.

10. Thomas Aquinas, *Summa Theologiae,* 2.2 : q. 8, a1., vol. 32 (London: Blackfriars, Eyre and Spottiswode, 1974).

11. Z. Barbu, *Problems of Historical Psychology* (New York: Grove Press, 1960), 22, for a discussion of Febvre's work.

12. Jean Gebser, *The Ever-Present Origin,* trans. Noel Barstad with Algis Mickunas (Athens, Ohio: Ohio University Press, 1985). This is a point thoroughly understood by Gebser. See, for example, page 19 for his comments on the "antithetical nature of perspective."

13. Galileo, *Il Saggiatore,* quoted in E. Burtt, *The Metaphysical Foundations of Modern Physical Science* (London: Routledge and Kegan Paul, 1932), 78.

14. John Locke, *An Essay Concerning Human Understanding* (Oxford: Oxford University Press, 1975), book 2, ch. 8.

15. See Ernst Lehrs, *Man or Matter* (London: Faber and Faber, 1951), ch. 2.

## CHAPTER TWO. THE HEART OF THE LILY

1. Jeremy Naydler, published as *Perceptions of the Divine in Nature. Part One: The Heart of the Lily* (Oxford: Abzu Press, 1993).

2. The symbolism of the plants in this picture is discussed in Julia Berrall, *The Garden: An Illustrated History* (Harmondsworth: Penguin Books, 1978), 96.

3. Allen G. Debus, *Man and Nature in the Renaissance* (Cambridge: Cambridge University Press, 1978), 43–45.

4. Martyn Rix, *The Art of Botanical Illustration* (London: Bracken Books, 1981), 30f.

5. Francis Bacon, *Novum Organum* (London: Joannem Billium Typographum Regium, 1620), 1.124.

6. Josef Pieper, *Leisure the Basis of Culture* (London: Fontana, 1965), 27f. "The Middle Ages drew a distinction between the understanding as *ratio* and the understanding as *intellectus. Ratio* is the power of discursive, logical thought, of searching and of examination, of abstraction, of definition, and drawing conclusions. *Intellectus,* on the other hand, is the name for the understanding insofar as it is the capacity of *simplex intuitus,* of that simple vision to which truth offers itself like a landscape to the eye."

7. R. G. Collingwood, *The Idea of Nature* (Oxford: Oxford University Press, 1965), 103.

8. A. N. Whitehead, *Science and the Modern World* (New York: Free Press, 1967), 51.

9. J. C. Cooper, *An Illustrated Encyclopaedia of Traditional Symbols* (London: Thames and Hudson, 1978), 98.

10. Anne Baring and Jules Cashford, *The Myth of the Goddess* (London: Penguin Books, 1991), 323.

11. Rodney Castleden, *The Knossos Labyrinth: A New View of the "Palace of Minos" at Knossos* (London: Routledge, 1990), 117–18.

## CHAPTER THREE. THE SOUL OF THE WEATHER

1. Jeremy Naydler, published as *Perceptions of the Divine in Nature. Part Two: Baal Hadad at Bracknell* (Oxford: Abzu Press, 1993).

2. Aristotle, *De Anima*, §425b, 26–426a, 1; §430a, 10–20. For Aristotle's epistemology, see David Ross, *Aristotle* (London: Methuen, 1964), 136–39, 148–51.

3. *The Ancient Egyptian Book of the Dead,* trans. R. O. Faulkner (London: British Museum Publications, 1985), 66.

4. M. D. Müller, *Egyptian Mythology* (London: G. G. Harrap, 1918), 65.

5. Jeremy Black and Anthony Green, *Gods, Demons and Symbols of Ancient Mesopotamia* (London: British Museum Press, 1992), 147.

6. Z. A. Ragozin, *Chaldea: From the Earliest Times to the Rise of Assyria* (London: T. Fisher and Unwin, 1886), 170.

7. Jane Harrison, *Prolegomena to the Study of Greek Religion* (London: Merlin Press, 1962), 181f.

8. Ibid., 67.

9. Pausanias, *Hellados Perlegesis,* II.34.3, quoted in Harrison, *Prolegomena to the Study of Greek Religion,* 67.

10. Jean Seznec, *The Survival of the Pagan Gods* (Princeton: Princeton University Press, 1972), 47.

11. Joscelyn Godwin, *Robert Fludd: Hermetic Philosopher and Surveyor of Two Worlds* (London: Thames and Hudson, 1979), 57.

12. J. D. Bernal, *Science in History,* vol. 2 (Harmondsworth: Penguin Books, 1969), 470.

13. *Enuma Elish,* Tablet IV, in Stephanie Dalley, *Myths from Mesopotamia* (Oxford: Oxford University Press, 1989), 253.

## CHAPTER FOUR.
## THE REALITY THAT IS NOT THERE

1. Jeremy Naydler, published as *The Reality That Is Not There: Reflections on Non-Locational Space* (Oxford: Abzu Press, 2004).

2. The Gospel of Thomas, §113.

3. Rudolf Steiner, *Theosophy* (Hudson, N.Y.: Anthroposophic Press, 1994), 111.

4. C. G. Jung, *Memories, Dreams and Reflections* (London: HarperCollins/ Fontana Press, 1995), 351.

5. Plotinus, *Enneads* IV.3.9, trans. A. H. Armstrong, *Plotinus* (New York: Collier Books, 1962), 91.

6. Henry Corbin, "*Mundus Imaginalis,* or The Imaginary and the Imaginal," in *Swedenborg and Esoteric Islam* (Chester, Penn.: Swedenborg Foundation, 1995), 6.

7. "Liber XXIV philosophorum" quoted in F. Yates, *Giordano Bruno and the Hermetic Tradition* (London: Routledge and Kegan Paul, 1971), 247.

8. Henry Corbin, *Spiritual Body and Celestial Earth* (Princeton: Princeton University Press, 1990), 74.

9. Corbin, *"Mundus Imaginalis,* or The Imaginary and the Imaginal," 5f.

10. Plato, "Phaedrus," §247, in Plato, *Phaedrus and Letters VII and VIII,* trans. Walter Hamilton (Harmondsworth: Penguin, 1973), 52.

11. Mircea Eliade, *Shamanism: Archaic Techniques of Ecstasy* (London: Arkana, 1989), 262f.

12. See Rudolf Steiner, "The Position of Anthroposophy Among the Sciences" (lecture April 8, 1922) referred to in Olive Whicher, *Sun Space: Science at the Threshold of Spiritual Understanding* (London: Rudolf Steiner Press, 1989), 39. See also C. G. Jung, *Aion,* CW 9, part 2 (Princeton: Princeton University Press, 1979), 310.

13. Ibn 'Arabi, "The Earth Which Was Created from What Remained of the Clay of Adam," in Corbin, *Spiritual Body and Celestial Earth,* 136–140.

14. Steiner, "Uniting with the Universal Spirit" (lecture of March 5, 1918) in *Staying Connected,* ed. Christopher Bamford (New York: Anthroposophic Press, 1999), 166–69.

15. C. G. Jung, "The Symbolic Life," *The Symbolic Life,* CW 18 (London: Routledge and Kegan Paul, 1954), 273–74.

16. William Blake, "The Everlasting Gospel," §97–100, in *Blake's Poems and Prophecies,* ed. Max Plowman (London: Everyman, 1970), 350.

17. Whicher, *Sun Space,* 8.

## CHAPTER FIVE. ANCIENT EGYPT AND THE SOUL OF THE WEST

1. Jeremy Naydler, published as *Ancient Egypt and the Soul of the West* (Oxford: Abzu Press, 1996).

2. Plotinus, *Enneads,* 5.8.5.

3. C. G. Jung, *Modern Man in Search of a Soul* (London: Routledge and Kegan Paul, 1961), 130.

4. Robin Lane Fox, *Pagans and Christians* (London: Penguin, 1988), 166–67.

5. For the solidificaion of the world, see René Guénon, *The Reign of Quantity and the Signs of the Times,* trans. Lord Northbourne (London: Luzac and Co., 1953), ch. 17.

6. Plato, *Timaeus,* §21c–22c.

## CHAPTER SIX. ON THE DIVINITY OF THE GODS

1. Jeremy Naydler, published as *On the Divinity of the Gods* (Oxford: Abzu Press, 1994).

2. For Chrysippus's now lost treatise, one of the main sources is Cicero, *De natura deorum,* 1.41. Posidonius's treatise (also lost) is said to have extended to at least five books, for which see John Dillon, *The Middle Platonists* (London: Duckworth, 1996), 107. For Cicero, see *The Nature of the Gods,* trans. Horace C. P. McGregor (Harmondsworth: Penguin, 1972).

3. Alexandre Piankoff, *The Litany of Re* (Bollingen Foundation; Princeton: Princeton University Press, 1964), 19. For the sake of consistency I have amended the spelling of "Re" to "Ra" in all quoted passages.

4. Ibid., 23 (translation adapted).

5. Ibid., 46.

6. From the Berlin "Hymn to Ptah," Twenty-Second Dynasty. Translation adapted from J. P. Allen, *Genesis in Egypt* (New Haven: Yale University, 1988), 38–40.

7. "The Kadesh Battle Inscriptions of Ramesses II," in Miriam Lichtheim, *Ancient Egyptian Literature,* vol. 2 (Los Angeles: University of California Press, 1976), 71.

8. C. G. Jung, "The Archetypes of the Collective Unconscious," *The Archetypes and the Collective Unconscious,* CW 9, part 1 (London: Routledge and Kegan Paul, 1968), paragraph 50.

9. C. G. Jung, *Mysterium Coniunctionis,* CW 14 (Princeton: Princeton University Press, 1970), paragraph 668.

10. James Hillman, *Re-Visioning Psychology* (New York: Harper and Row, 1977), 170.

11. Piankoff, *The Litany of Re,* 29.

12. Ibid., 30 (translation adapted).

13. Ibid.

14. Ibid., 35.

15. Ibid., 39.

## CHAPTER SEVEN. THE ARTIST AS PRIEST

1. Jeremy Naydler, published as *The Artist as Priest: Reflections on the Sacred Art and Culture of Ancient Egypt* (Oxford: Abzu Press, 2007).

2. Erik Hornung, *Idea into Image* (New York: Timken Publishers, 1992), 131f. See also Dimitri Meeks and Christine Favard-Meeks, *Daily Life of the Egyptian Gods* (London: Pimlico, 1999), 66.

3. Siegfried Morenz, *Egyptian Religion* (London: Methuen, 1973), 114.

4. Hornung, *Idea into Image*, 131f. See also Meeks and Favard-Meeks, *Daily Life of the Egyptian Gods,* 140–143.

5. S. H. Nasr, *Religion and the Order of Nature* (Oxford: Oxford University Press, 1996), ch. 2.

6. Siegfried Morenz, *Egyptian Religion,* 113. See also A. Gardiner, *Egyptian Grammar* (Oxford: Oxford University Press, 1973), 541.

7. The story is translated in Adolf Erman, *The Ancient Egyptians: A Sourcebook of Their Writings* (New York: Harper and Row, 1966), 47–49 and in Lichtheim, *Ancient Egyptian Literature,* vol. 2: *The New Kingdom,* 197–99.

8. Richard H. Wilkinson, *Symbol and Magic in Egyptian Art* (London: Thames and Hudson, 1994), 114.

9. Ibid., 108–9.

10. Ibid., 180–181.

11. G. E. Moore, epigraph to *Principia Ethica* (Cambridge: Cambridge University Press, 1903). The quotation is in fact from Bishop Butler, who was writing in the eighteenth century, but it sums up an attitude still prevalent in most areas of academic learning today.

12. For Babi, see Jeremy Naydler, *Shamanic Wisdom in the Pyramid Texts: The Mystical Tradition of Ancient Egypt* (Rochester, Vt.: Inner Traditions, 2005), 301, 307f.

13. Robert K. Ritner, *The Mechanics of Ancient Egyptian Magical Practice* (Chicago: The Oriental Institue of the University of Chicago, 1993), 17.

14. Ibid., 25.

15. Lanny Bell, "The New Kingdom 'Divine Temple' the Example of Luxor," in *Temples of Ancient Egypt,* ed. Byron E. Shafer (London: I. B. Tauris Publishers, 1998), 151.

16. For a fuller interpretation of these pylon reliefs, see Jeremy Naydler, *Temple of the Cosmos: The Ancient Egyptian Experience of the Sacred* (Rochester, Vt.: Inner Traditions International, 1996), 112–20.

17. Corbin, *"Mundus Imaginalis,* or the Imaginary and the Imaginal," 18f.

18. C. Desroches-Noblecourt, *Tutankhamen* (London: The Connoisseur and Michael Joseph Ltd., 1963), 80–81, 205.

19. P. Derchain, "Symbols and Metaphors in Literature and Representations of Private Life," *Royal Anthropological Institute News* 15 (1976): 7–10.

20. T. G. H. James, *Egyptian Painting* (London: British Museum, 1985), 26–28.

21. Lise Manniche, *Sexual Life in Ancient Egypt* (London: Kegan Paul, 1997), 42.

22. Richard H. Wilkinson, *Symbol and Magic in Egyptian Art,* 182.

23. Ibid. See also Wolfgang Westendorf, "Bemerkungen zur 'Kammer der Wiedergeburt'

im Tutanchamungrab," in *Zeitschrift fur Ägyptische Sprache und Alterumskunde* 94 (1967): 139–50.

24. Betsy M. Bryan, "Painting Techniques and Artisan Organization in the Tomb of Suemniwet, Theban Tomb 92," in *Colour and Painting in Ancient Egypt,* ed. W. V. Davies (London: British Museum Press, 2001), 70. Bryan suggests a total of eighty people, including lesser skilled workers and assistants, were employed on the decoration of the Eighteenth Dynasty Tomb of Suemniwet. Teams of up to one hundred and twenty persons are known to have worked on the decoration of the tombs of the Valley of the Kings. Much smaller teams would have worked on smaller, nonroyal tombs.

25. James, *Egyptian Painting,* 17.

26. Quoted in John A. Wilson, "The Artist of the Egyptian Old Kingdom." *Journal of Near Eastern Studies,* 6 (1947): 245.

27. J. Baines and C. J. Eyre, "Four Notes on Literacy," *Göttinger Miszellen* 61 (1983): 89. Adolf Erman, *Life in Ancient Egypt* (New York: Dover Publications, 1971), 415, points to the significance of one of the titles of the high priest of Memphis (the cult center of the god Ptah), which was "chief leader of the artists." According to Erman, he "really exercised this office." Just as artists could exercise priestly functions, so could the priest be seriously engaged in artistic activities.

28. Richard Temple, *Icons and the Mystical Origins of Christianity* (Shaftesbury: Element Books, 1990), 156. For further comparison between Byzantine and ancient Egyptian artists, see Bryan, "Painting techniques and artisan organization in the Tomb of Suemniwet, Theban Tomb 92," 64.

29. Alan H. Gardiner, "The House of Life," *Journal of Egyptian Archaeology* 24 (1938): 177.

30. Ibid., 157–79. Gardiner has collected much of the source material.

31. Baines and Eyre, "Four Notes on Literacy," 88.

32. E. S. Bogoslovsky, "Hundred Egyptian Draughtsmen," *Zeitschrift fur Ägyptische Sprache und Altertumskunde* 107 (1980): 91–93.

33. Evidence for this can be gleaned from Gardiner, "The House of Life," 161, 173.

34. R. A. Schwaller de Lubicz, *The Temple of Man,* vol. 1 (Rochester, Vt.: Inner Traditions, 1998), ch. 11.

35. Wilson, "The Artist of the Egyptian Old Kingdom," 235.

## CHAPTER EIGHT.
## ANCIENT EGYPT AND MODERN ESOTERICISM

1. Jeremy Naydler, published as *Ancient Egypt and Modern Esotericism* (Oxford: Abzu Press, 2006).

2. Comparison between Thutmose III and Napoleon was first made by J. H. Breasted, *A History of Egypt from the Earliest Times to the Persian Conquest* (London: Hodder and Stoughton, 1912), ch. 16. Since then, it has been reiterated many times. See, for example, Leonard Cottrell, *The Warrior Pharaohs* (London: Evans Brothers Ltd, 1968), ch. 6, entitled "The Napoleon of Ancient Egypt," and Peter A. Clayton, *Chronicle of the Pharaohs* (London: Thames and Hudson, 1994), 109f.

3. Quoted in Jan Assmann, "Death and Initiation in the Funerary Religion of Ancient Egypt," *Religion and Philosophy in Ancient Egypt,* ed. W. K. Simpson (New Haven: Yale University Press, 1989), 142, n41.

4. Eliade, *Shamanism: Archaic Techniques of Ecstasy,* ch. 4.

5. For Egyptology's denial of shamanism in ancient Egypt, see, for example, Jan Assmann, *The Search for God in Ancient Egypt,* trans. David Lorton (Ithaca: Cornell University Press, 2001), 153.

6. Erik Horning, *The Secret Lore of Egypt: Its Impact on the West,* trans. David Lorton (Ithaca: Cornell University Press, 2001), 3.

7. Ibid.

8. Corbin, "*Mundus Imaginalis,* or The Imaginary and the Imaginal," 1–33. See ch. 7, n17.

9. George Hart, *A Dictionary of Egyptian Gods and Goddesses* (London and New York: Routledge and Kegan Paul, 1986), x.

10. Naydler, *Temple of the Cosmos,* 107–20.

11. Christian Jacq, *Egyptian Magic,* trans. Janet M. Davis (Warminster: Aris and Phillips, 1985), 99. The author explains: "On the field of battle, the pharaoh's enemies are not merely human. They are possessed by a hostile force against which the pharaoh must use magical weapons. Before any battle, one must proceed to put a spell on one's enemies, part of the official techniques of war practiced by the State. The sacred model for this is supplied by the rituals, which the priests celebrate in the temples for the purpose of fighting the enemies of the Light."

12. Ibid., 95–99. For the double defeat of Apophis, see "The Book of the Day and The Book of the Night" in A. Piankoff, *The Tomb of Ramesses VI,* Bollingen Series 40/1 (New York: Pantheon Books, 1954), 389–407.

13. For a discussion of the solarization of Amenhotep III at his Sed festival, see W. Raymond Johnson, "Amenhotep III and Amarna: Some New Considerations," *Journal of Egyptian Archaeology* 82 (1996), 67ff. See also Naydler, *Shamanic Wisdom in the Pyramid Texts,* 87f.

14. Naydler, *Temple of the Cosmos,* 26, 215–17.

15. W. Brede Kristensen, *Life Out of Death: Studies in the Religions of Egypt and of*

*Ancient Greece,* trans. H. J. Franken and G. R. H. Wright (Louvain: Peeters Press, 1992), 28. The author comments: "The world of death secreted greater powers and contained richer possibilities than the world of finite experience. It was the basis for the whole existence, which we are apt to call worldly life."

16. The "Annals" at Karnak, recording Thutmose III's campaigns, are couched in mythical and theistic language. The king is described as acting in consort with Amon-Ra against the "wretched enemy"—implicitly identified with the forces of cosmic chaos. The mystical fusion of king and sun god is even more explicit in the so-called poetical stela of Thutmose III found at Karnak. Both texts are translated in Lichtheim, *Ancient Egyptian Literature,* vol. 2, 30–39.

17. *The Ancient Egyptian Book of the Dead,* trans. R. O. Faulkner (London: British Museum Publications, 1972), ch. 130.

18. Alison Roberts, *My Heart, My Mother* (Rottingdean: Northgate, 2000), 174–78. It is explicitly stated in The Book of What Is in the Underworld (*Amduat*), div. 1 that the text is "useful for those who are on earth" and similar indications can be found in The Book of the Dead, which has been compared by Terence DuQuesne in *A Coptic Initiatory Invocation* (Thame: Darengo, 1991), 52, n112, with the Tibetan *Bardo Thödol*—a text clearly intended for spiritual practice.

19. Garth Fowden, *The Egyptian Hermes* (Princeton: Princeton University Press, 1986), ch. 7; David Frankfurter, *Religion in Roman Egypt* (Princeton: Princeton University Press, 1998), ch. 5 and 6.

20. See, for example, Plutarch's essay "The Decline of the Oracles," in *Moral Essays,* trans. Rex Warner (Harmondsworth: Penguin Books, 1971), 31–96. See also ch. 10.

21. Homer, *The Odyssey,* trans. Ennis Rees (Indianapolis: Bobbs-Merrill Publishing, 1977), 188.

22. See Rudolf Steiner, *Universe, Earth and Man,* trans. Harry Collison (London: Rudolf Steiner Publishing Co., 1941), 250f. As Rudolf Steiner stated: "What we call the 'future' must always be rooted in the past; knowledge has no value if not changed into motive power for the future. The purpose for the future must be in accordance with the knowledge of the past, but this knowledge is of little value unless changed into propelling force for the future."

## CHAPTER NINE.
## BEING ANCIENT IN A MODERN WAY

1. Jeremy Naydler, published as *Being Ancient in a Modern Way: Divination in the Light of the History of Consciousness* (Oxford: Abzu Press, 2007).

2. G. S. Kirk and J. E. Raven, *The Presocratic Philosophers* (Cambridge: Cambridge University Press, 1957), 94–95 with §§93–95.

3. Stephen Karcher, *The Illustrated Encyclopedia of Divination* (Shaftesbury: Element, 1997), 10f: "Divination . . . was and is first of all a way to see what is there, what spiritual forces are active in your present situation and how you can successfully interact with them . . . The divinatory way creates a *temenos,* a protected and creative place that allows this symbolic interaction to take place."

4. C. B. F. Walker, "A Sketch of the Development of Mesopotamian Astrology and Horoscopes," *History and Astrology,* ed. Annabel Kitson (London: Unwin Hyman, 1989), 11.

5. H. W. F. Saggs, *The Greatness That Was Babylon* (New York: The New American Library, 1962), 429f.

6. Ivan Starr, *The Rituals of the Diviner* (Malibu: Undena Publications, 1983), 4. Commenting on the unusual importance, which extispicy early acquired in Mesopotamia, Starr writes: "It would seem, in fact, that the variety of divine messages received by various other means, such as dreams, visions, prophecies, or even by means of the observation of celestial phenomena, were often considered inconclusive until confirmed by more reliable means, such as extispicy."

7. O. R. Gurney, "The Babylonians and Hittites," *Divination and Oracles,* ed. Michael Loewe and Carmen Blacker (London: George Allen and Unwin, 1981), 161.

8. Ulla Jeyes, *Old Babylonian Extispicy: Omen Texts in the British Museum* (Istanbul: Nederlands Historisch-Archaeologisch Institut, 1989), 15–19. For the historical development of liver divination (hepatoscopy) into a more general examination of entrails (extispicy), see A. Leo Oppenheim, *Ancient Mesopotamia: Portrait of a Dead Civilization* (Chicago and London: Chicago University Press, 1977), 213.

9. A. Leo Oppenheim, *Ancient Mesopotamia: Portrait of a Dead Civilization* (Chicago: Chicago University Press, 1977), 213. See also Gurney, "The Babylonians and Hittites," 147.

10. For the *barû* as a scholar, see Jeyes, *Old Babylonian Extispicy,* 14. For the preference for the young ram, see Ulla Jeyes, "The Act of Extispicy in Ancient Mesopotamia: An Outline," *Assyriological Miscellanies,* vol. 1, ed. Bendt Alster (Copenhagen: University of Copenhagen Institute of Assyriology, 1980), 16.

11. Morris Jastrow, *Religious Belief in Babylonia and Assyria* (New York: Benjamin Blom, 1911), 165f. A collection of three hundred and twenty-two questions from the State Archives of Assyria can be found in Ivan Starr, *Queries to the Sungod: Divination and Politics in Sargonid Assyria,* State Archives of Assyria, vol. 4 (Helsinki: Helsinki University Press, 1990), 4–299. The words spoken by the *barû* begin with the standard formula: "Shamash, great lord, answer me with a firm 'yes' to what I ask you" and close with "Be present in this ram, place in it an affirmative

answer, favorable designs, favorable, propitious omens of the oracular query by the command of your great divinity so that I may see them."

12. Jeyes, "The Act of Extispicy," 15.

13. Ibid., 17.

14. Starr, *The Rituals of the Diviner,* 26f., and Jeyes, "The Act of Extispicy," 17.

15. Jastrow, *Religious Belief in Babylonia and Assyria,* 148.

16. Ibid., 151f. Jastrow refers to the relatively late (third century BC) buccolic poet Theocritus who describes the lover fatally wounded by the arrows of love as being "hit in the liver." See, however, note 35 below.

17. For the technical terms of the various parts of the liver and their meanings, see Jeyes, *Old Babylonian Extispicy,* 93–95; Starr, *Queries to the Sungod,* pp.xl–lv; and Geoffrey P. Neate, *Akkadian Oracles* (Oxford: University of Oxford thesis, 1973), 8f.

18. For the paradigmatic nature of the opposition between the right and the left and its importance in prognostication, see Starr, *The Rituals of the Diviner,* 16–24. See also Jastrow, *Religious Belief in Babylonia and Assyria,* 170; and Jeyes, "The Act of Extispicy," 22f.

19. Jeyes, "The Act of Extispicy," 14.

20. Jastrow, *Religious Belief in Babylonia and Assyria,* 185.

21. Ibid., 175, 182.

22. Ibid., 183.

23. I follow Jeyes here. According to Starr, *Queries to the Sungod,* xlii, this is located on the left lobe.

24. Neate, *Akkadian Oracles,* 5. See also Oppenheim, *Ancient Mesopotamia,* 212, 214.

25. For the stages of this development, see Starr, *The Rituals of the Diviner,* 6 and 15f. The tabulation and systemization of omens into series was already fully operative in the Old Babylonian period (early second millennium BC).

26. For a discussion of the rules of association, see Jeyes, "The Act of Extispicy," 23f. See also Starr, *The Rituals of the Diviner,* 8–12.

27. Jeyes, "The Act of Extispicy," 21f. Other markings would be seen by the modern anatomist as meaningless wrinkles, possibly caused by pressure of surrounding organs, for which see Georges Dumézil, *Archaic Roman Religion,* vol. 2, trans. Philip Krapp (Chicago and London: University of Chicago Press, 1970), 658.

28. Henri Frankfort, *Kingship and the Gods* (Chicago: University of Chicago Press, 1978), ch. 17.

29. Ibid., 253.

30. Quoted in Oppenheim, *Ancient Mesopotamia,* 227.

31. Dumézil, *Archaic Roman Religion*, vol. 2, 657–59. See also W. R. Halliday, *Greek Divination* (London: MacMillan, 1913), 189–92. Note, however, that the existence of Etruscan liver models that have no Mesopotamian counterparts, such as the bronze liver of Piacenza, testify to an entirely different divinatory tradition existing in Etruria alongside the one subject to Mesopotamian influence.

32. Dumézil, *Archaic Roman Religion*, 658.

33. See L. B. van der Meer, *The Bronze Liver of Piacenza: Analysis of a Polytheistic Structure* (Amsterdam: J. C. Gieben, 1987), 157–64 for an excellent summary of the similarities and differences in liver consultations in Etruria, Greece, and Mesopotamia.

34. Ibid., 163. Most of the Attic vases with hepatoscopy scenes have been found in Etruria, and it is known that the Etruscans had religious contacts with the sanctuaries at Olympia and Delphi from the seventh century BC onward.

35. R. B. Onians, *The Origins of European Thought* (Cambridge: Cambridge University Press, 1988), 85. In Homer, the liver was no longer regarded as the "seat of the soul," but rather its vital energy penetrated the *thumos* whose home had become the chest or lungs.

36. Plato, *Timaeus*, §71b–e; trans. Benjamin Jowett, *The Dialogues of Plato*, vol. 3 (London: Sphere Books, 1970), 276f.

37. Van der Meer, *The Bronze Liver of Piacenza*, 159.

38. Xenophon, *The Persian Expedition*, trans. Rex Warner (Harmondsworth: Penguin Books, 1949). The frequency of the use of extispicy in Xenophon's account is discussed in Robert Temple, *Netherworld* (London: Random House, 2002), 198–209.

39. Xenophon, *Anabasis* (Cambridge: Harvard University Press, 1992), 6.4.9–25 and *The Persian Expedition*, 231–33.

40. Xenophon, *Anabasis*, 7.8.23 and *The Persian Expedition*, 299–301.

41. Dumézil, *Archaic Roman Religion*, vol. 2, 606f. It was only toward the end of the Republic that the *haruspices* became organized into a haruspical college, for which see Mary Beard, John North, and Simon Price, *Religions of Rome*, vol. 1 (Cambridge: Cambridge University Press, 1998), 20.

42. Dumézil, *Archaic Roman Religion*, vol. 2, 652.

43. van der Meer, *The Bronze Liver of Piacenza*, 165f.

44. Ibid., 165.

45. Dumézil, *Archaic Roman Religion*, vol. 650.

46. Beard et al., *Religions of Rome*, vol. 1, 326 and 320.

47. Kirk and Raven, *The Presocratic Philosophers*, 173, §178. For the sun as "pieces of fire," see 172, §178; as "ignited cloud," 73, §180.

48. Ibid., 173, §181. For a general discussion, see Kirk and Raven, *The Presocratic Philosophers*, 168–73.

49. Ibid., 372, §503. For the dualism of Anaxagoras, see ibid., 375.

50. Ibid., 391, §529.

51. Ibid., 393, §533.

52. Ibid., 392, §529; 391, §528.

53. The incident is related in Plutarch, "Life of Pericles," §6, in Plutarch, *The Rise and Fall of Athens*, trans. Ian Scott-Kilvert (Harmondsworth: Penguin, 1960), 170. For a discussion, see Robert Flacelière, *Greek Oracles*, trans. Douglas Garman (London: Elek Books, 1965), 74f.

54. Kirk and Raven, *The Presocratic Philosophers*, 362, §487.

55. For a summary of the "physical theology" of the Stoics, see A. H. Armstrong, *An Introduction to Ancient Philosophy* (Boston: Beacon Press, 1963), 122–25. See also Frederick Copleston, *A History of Philosophy*, vol. 1, part 2 (New York: Image Books, 1962), 132–38.

56. This notion of *sympatheia* seems to have formed the basis of Posidonius's defense of divination in his now lost treatise *On Divination*, of which only fragments are preserved. See Dillon, *The Middle Platonists*, 110. It is interesting to note that Plotinus upheld the Stoic doctrine of *sympatheia* and saw it "as a reasonable basis for divination" thus "the wise man is the man who in any one thing can read another." Plotinus, *Enneads*, trans. Stephen MacKenna (London: Faber and Faber, 1969), II.7. See also *Enneads*, IV.4.32. For a discussion of Plotinus's views, see Wallis, *Neoplatonism*, 70f.

57. Armstrong, *An Introduction to Ancient Philosophy*, 125f.

58. Dillon, *The Middle Platonists*, 288.

59. Beard, North, and Price, *Religions of Rome*, vol. 1, 374. For Constantine's use of *haruspices* to investigate the meaning of lightning striking certain public buildings in Rome in the early fourth century AD, see Beard, et al., 372.

60. See Cicero, *De Divinatione*, trans. W. A. Falconer, (Cambridge: Harvard University Press, 2001), II.51f., who reports that Cato expressed surprise that two *haruspices* could look at each other without laughing, and then lists several examples of the manifest failure of divination by entrails from the time of Hannibal to Pompey.

61. Ibid., II.55.

62. Ibid., see Falconer's introduction, 216. Cicero's other treatise is *On the Republic*.

63. Ibid., II.117.

64. Plutarch, "The Decline of the Oracles" in *Moral Essays*, 52, §15.

65. Ibid., 53f, §17.

66. John Ferguson, *Socrates: A Source Book* (London: Macmillan, 1970), 15f and Armstrong, *An Introduction to Ancient Philosophy*, 29ff.

67. As Menelaus declares in Homer's *Iliad*, 17.98. See also Burkert, *Greek Religion*, 180.

68. Pindar, *Pythian Odes*, 5.122, quoted in Burkert, *Greek Religion*, 181.

69. "Happy (*eudaimon*) and prosperous is he who, knowing all these things does his work, guiltless before the gods, observing omens and not overstepping taboos." Hesiod, *Works and Days*, edited with prolegomena and commentary by M. L. West (Oxford: Clarendon Press, 1978), v. 825. See also the discussion in Jane Harrison, *Themis* (London: Merlin Press, 1963), 95f.

70. Kirk and Raven, *The Presocratic Philosophers*, 213, §250.

71. Xenophon, *Memorabilia*, I.1.4, trans. Ferguson, *Socrates: A Source Book*, 145.

72. Xenophon, *Apology*, 13, trans. Ferguson, *Socrates: A Source Book*, 140f.

73. Plato, *Timaeus*, §90a, trans. G. M. A. Grube, *Plato's Thought* (London: Athlone Press, 1980), 144f.

74. *Timaeus*, §90bc, trans. Jowett, *The Dialogues of Plato*, vol. 3, 296.

75. Aristotle, *Nichomachean Ethics*, trans. H. Rackham (London: Heinemann Loeb, 1975), III.iii.17 (1113a17).

76. Ibid., X.vii.8 (1177b26f).

77. Ibid., VI.x.2 (1142b34f).

78. Euripides, *Medea*, v. 495f, which Frederick Hiebel in *The Gospel of Hellas* (New York: Anthroposophic Press, 1949), 28, translates as follows: "I cannot even understand whether you think that the old gods no longer rule, or that fresh rules are now in vogue among human beings, for your conscience must tell you that you have not kept faith with me." For a discussion of the history of the word *synesis,* see Frederick Hiebel, *The Epistles of Paul and Rudolf Steiner's Philosophy of Freedom* (New York: St. George Publications, 1980), 4–8.

79. Aristotle, *Nichomachean Ethics*, I.xiii.21 (1103a.5).

80. Romans 2:14–15; 1 Timothy 1:5.

81. 1 Corinthians 8:12.

82. Hiebel, *The Gospel of Hellas*, 30, 255. See also Hiebel, *The Epistles of Paul,* 8.

83. In the Middle Ages, discussion centered both on the word *conscientia* and the Greek word *synderesis,* which was used by St. Jerome to denote a power higher than reason that dwells in the human soul, and which is closely related to, if not identical with, conscience. Basing himself on Plato's threefold division of the powers of the soul into the appetitive, the emotional, and the rational, St. Jerome added synderesis as a fourth suprarational power. In his *Commentary on Ezechial*, I.1.1, he relates the four powers to the four animals of Ezechial's vision: the bull to the appetitive, the

lion to the emotional, the man to the rational, and the eagle to synderesis. For a brief survey of medieval theories of synderesis and conscientia, from St. Jerome to St. Bonaventure and St. Thomas Aquinas, see John Rickaby, article on "Conscience" in *The Catholic Encyclopedia,* vol. 4 (New York: Robert Appleton Co., 1908). For Plato's threefold division of the soul, see *Republic,* §439 and *Timaeus,* §§69–71.

84. Thomas Aquinas, *Disputations,* XVII "de Veritate," 4, ad 1 and 5, ad 3, in St. Thomas Aquinas, *Philosophical Texts,* selected and translated with notes and an introduction by Thomas Gilby (London: Oxford University Press, 1951), 291, §810, and §811.

85. Thomas Aquinas, *Quodlibetum,* in *St. Thomas Aquinas, Philosophical Texts,* 291, §808.

86. Rudolf Steiner, *The Philosophy of Freedom* (London: Rudolf Steiner Press, 1970), 130–35.

87. Ibid., 135–38.

88. Stephen Karcher, *I Ching: The Classic Chinese Oracle of Change* (London: Vega, 2002), 8.

89. Juliet Sharman-Burke and Liz Greene, *The Mythic Tarot* (London: Century Hutchinson, 1986), 196f.

90. Marie-Louise von Franz, *On Divination and Synchronicity* (Toronto: Inner City Books, 1980), 108–10.

91. Ibid., 54–57.

92. Karcher, *I Ching: The Classic Chinese Oracle of Change,* 10.

93. Karcher, *The Illustrated Encyclopedia of Divination,* 11.

94. C. G. Jung, *Memories, Dreams, Reflections,* 212.

## CHAPTER TEN.
## THE FUTURE OF THE ANCIENT WORLD

1. Jeremy Naydler, published as *The Future of the Ancient World* (Oxford: Abzu Press, 1994).

2. Cicero, *De Divinatione,* 1.38; 2.117; Strabo: *Geography,* trans. Horace Leonard Jones (London: William Heinemann, 1917), ix.iii.8.

3. Clement, *Protrepticus,* trans. G. W. Butterworth (London William Heinemann, 1919), II.ii.i f.

4. For example Chrysippus of Tarsus (Stoic philosopher of the third century BC), Posidonius of Apamea (Platonic-Stoic philosopher of the first century BC), and most notably Cicero in 45 BC. See also chapter 6, n2.

5. Lichtheim, *Ancient Egyptian Literature,* vol. 2, 168 and 113.

6. Homer, *Odyssey*, 22.347. Translated and discussed in E. R. Dodds, *The Greeks and the Irrational* (Berkeley, Los Angeles and London: University of California Press, 1973), 100.

7. Homer, *Iliad*, 1.187–222. The passage is discussed in Bruno Snell, *The Discovery of the Mind* (New York: Dover, 1982), 155–57.

8. Homer, *Iliad*, 29.

9. Oppenheim, *Ancient Mesopotamia*, 227. See also ch. 9, 161, of this book for a discussion of Naram-Sin.

10. For Thutmose, see "The Annals of Thutmosis III," §85, in Lichtheim, *Ancient Egyptian Literature*, vol. 2, 32. See also ch. 8, 5f. For Ramesses, see "The Kadesh Battle Insctiptions of Ramesses II," §159, in Lichtheim: *Ancient Egyptian Literature*, vol. 2, 67.

11. "Hymn to Hapi" in Lichtheim, *Ancient Egyptian Literature*, vol. 1, 206.

12. Nilsson, *Greek Folk Religion*, 10. See also Halliday, *Greek Divination*, 117.

13. Fragment 12, in Kirk and Raven, *The Presocratic Philosophers*, 372f.

14. For Anaxagoras on mind, see ibid., 372–75. For Heraclitus, see ibid., 187–89, and Fragments 1, 2, and 50.

15. Aristotle, *Nichomachean Ethics*, X.vii.9, (1178a:3).

16. Ibid., III.iii.15, (1112b:30).

17. Ibid., III.v. 2–3, (1113b:2–14), 143–45.

18. See Rudolf Steiner, "Das Bilden von Begriffen und die Kategorienlehre Hegels" (November 13, 1908) in Rudolf Steiner, *Die Beantwortung von Weltfragen und Lebensfragen durch Anthroposophie* (Dornach: Rudolf Steiner Verlag, 1986).

19. See Jeremy Naydler, "The Regeneration of Realism and the Recovery of a Science of Qualities" in *The International Philosophical Quarterly* XXIII, 2 (1983): 163f.

20. Jung's theory of the origin of the gods is outlined in several essays and longer works notably "Archaic Man" reproduced in *Modern Man in Search of a Soul;* "The Psychological Foundations of Belief in Spirits" reproduced in *The Structure and Dynamics of the Psyche,* CW 8 (London: Routledge and Kegan Paul, 1969); and "Psychology and Religion," reproduced in *Psychology and Religion: West and East,* CW 11 (London: Routledge and Kegan Paul, 1958). For the gods as "symbolic expressions of the inner, unconscious drama of the psyche" see "Archetypes of the Collective Unconscious" in *The Archetypes and the Collective Unconscious,* CW9, Part 1, 7.

21. In "Transformation Symbolism in the Mass" in *Psychology and Religion: West and East,* CW 11, 375, Jung writes: "At that time [i.e., in antiquity] and until very much later no one had any idea of the unconscious: consequently all unconscious contents were projected into the object, or rather were found in nature as apparent

objects or properties of matter and were not recognized as purely internal psychic events . . . It remained for science to despiritualize nature through its so-called objective knowledge of matter."

22. Ibid., CW 11, § 141.

23. A. A. Baarb, "Mystery, Myth and Magic" in *The Legacy of Egypt,* ed. J. R. Harris (Oxford: Clarendon Press, 1971), 168.

24. See Owen Barfield, *Saving the Appearances* (London: Faber and Faber, 1957), 146–47. This book cannot be commended too highly to anyone wishing to pursue further the subject of the present essay.

25. Hegel, *Phenomenology of Mind,* trans. J. B. Baillie (London: George Allen and Unwin, 1949), Preface, 93.

## CHAPTER ELEVEN. CHRIST AND THE GODS

1. Jeremy Naydler, published as *Christ and the Gods* (Oxford: Abzu Press, 1994).

2. E. A. Wallis Budge, *The Egyptian Book of the Dead (The Papyrus of Ani): Egyptian Text, Transliteration and Translation* (New York: Dover, 1967), 281.

3. Quoted in Franz Cumont, *Oriental Religions in Roman Paganism* (New York: Dover, 1956), 207. Maximus was a pagan friend of St. Augustine.

4. Pyramid Texts, Utterance 273–74, §403f.

5. James H. Breasted, *Development of Religion and Thought in Ancient Egypt* (Philadelphia: University of Pennsylvania Press, 1972), 120–26.

6. The terminology of "polycentrism" and "monocentrism" with regard to the psychic life is borrowed from Hillman, *Re-Visioning Psychology,* 33–35.

7. Bernhard W. Anderson, *The Living World of the Old Testament* (Harlow: Longman, 1978), 33–45. While it is generally assumed that the Israelites entered Egypt at the time of the Hyksos domination, and that the Exodus occurred during the reign of Ramesses II, it is not possible to ascribe exact dates, and the sojourn in Egypt could have been up to a hundred years shorter.

8. See Anderson, *The Living World of the Old Testament,* 53ff for commentary.

9. As Barfield, *Saving the Appearances,* 113, beautifully put it: "when any true child of Israel perused the unspoken Name, *Yahweh* must have seemed to come whispering up, as it were, from the depths of his own being!"

10. Book of the Dead, ch. 175: 10–13.

11. Kirk and Raven, *The Pre-Socratic Philosophers,* 144f.

12. Ibid., 104ff.

13. Heraclitus: Fr. 45, in ibid., 205, §235: "You would not find out the boundaries of soul, even by traveling along every path: so deep a *logos* does it have."

14. Heraclitus, Fr. 50, in ibid., 188, §199.

15. Anaxagoras, Fr. 12, in ibid., 373, §503, "Mind (*Nous*) is all alike, both the smaller and the greater quantities of it." For Aristotle, *Metaphysics,* 1072b. "The actuality of thought (*nous*) is life, and God is that actuality."

16. Aristotle, *Nicomachean Ethics,* X.7.8; (1173a).

17. Kirk and Raven, *The Presocratic Philosophers,* 168–75 and 179–81.

18. Nilsson, *Greek Folk Religion,* 135. For a general discussion on the rise of atheism in ancient Greece, see Burkert, *Greek Religion,* 313–17.

19. Gebser, *The Ever-Present Origin,* 147: "The centripetal direction toward one God prefigures the centering of the human ego that takes place in the mental structure as ego-consciousness."

20. Aristotle, *Nicomachean Ethics,* 3.3.17 (1113a). For the divinity of *nous,* see *Nicomachean Ethics,* X.7.8f (1172b26–1173a8).

21. "The Book of Thomas the Contender," in *The Other Bible,* ed. Willis Barnstone (New York: Harper and Row, 1984), 583.

22. Book of the Dead, ch. 17, 24: "Who then is this? It is Osiris, or as others say, Ra is his name, even Ra the self-created," trans. Budge, *The Egyptian Book of the Dead (The Papyrus of Ani): Egyptian Text, Transliteration and Translation,* 282.

23. Quoted in Hugo Rahner, *Greek Myths and Christian Mystery* (New York: Harper and Row, 1963), 115.

24. Plotinus, *Enneads,* IV.3.xi, trans. Stephen MacKenna, 270: "Every particular thing is the image within matter of a Reason-Principle, which itself images a prematerial Reason-Principle: thus every particular entity is linked to that Divine Being in whose likeness it is made . . ."

25. Plato, *Timaeus,* 41b, c.

26. "On Theology," 2.20. In *The Philokalia,* vol. 2, ed. G. E. H. Palmer et al. (London: Faber and Faber, 1979), 142.

27. Proclus, *Elements of Theology* (Oxford: Clarendon Press, 1963), L.119.

28. Ibid., L.133.

29. Porphyry, *Against the Christians,* Fr. 76, discussed in E. R. Dodds, *Pagans and Christians in an Age of Anxiety* (Cambridge: Cambridge University Press, 1990), 118.

30. "The Celestial Hierarchies," in Dionysius the Areopagite, *Mystical Theology and Celestial Hierarchies,* trans. The Editors of the Shrine of Wisdom (Godalming: The Shrine of Wisdom, 1965), 21.

31. Dante, *Paradiso,* canto 13: 55–60, translation adapted from Dante Alighieri, *The Divine Comedy Volume III: Paradise,* trans. Mark Musa (London: Penguin Books, 1984). See also canto 29: 133ff.

32. "The Books of Adam and Eve" in *The Apocrypha and the Pseudepigraphia of the*

*Old Testament in English,* vol. 2, ed. R. H. Charles (Oxford: Oxford University Press, 1913), 137.

33. St. Diodochus of Photoki, in *Philokalia,* vol. 1, 280: "We share in the image of God by virtue of the intellectual activity (i.e., the activity of the *nous*) of our soul" and "The grace of God . . . dwells in the very depths of the soul—that is to say, in the intellect (*nous*)"; St, Maximos the Confessor in *Philokalia,* vol. 2, 276, states: "Our intellect (*nous*) possesses the power of apprehension through which it perceives intelligible realities; it also possesses the capacity for a union that transcends its nature and that unites it with what is beyond its natural scope. It is through this union that divine realities are apprehended . . ."

34. "The Book of Thomas the Contender," in Barnstone, *The Other Bible,* 305.

## CHAPTER TWELVE. PATHWAYS INTO THE FUTURE FROM THE DEEP PAST

1. Jeremy Naydler, published as *Pathways into the Future From the Deep Past* (Oxford: Abzu Press, 1995).

2. *Brihadāranyaka Upanishad,* I.iv. In my interpretation of this text, I have drawn on two translations: R. C. Zaehner, *Hindu Scriptures* (London: J. M. Dent and Sons, 1966) and Shree Purohit Swami and W. B. Yeats, *The Ten Principal Upanishads* (London: Faber and Faber, 1938).

3. *Brihadāranyaka Upanishad,* 1.iv, trans. R. C. Zaehner, *Hindu Scriptures* (London: J. M. Dent and Sons, 1966), 36.

4. Ibid.

5. Hegel, *Philosophy of Mind,* §382 Zusätze, 15.

6. Meister Eckhart, quoted in R. Steiner, *Eleven European Mystics* (New York: Rudolf Steiner Publications, 1960), 136. Commenting on this remark of Eckhart's, Steiner writes: "Eckhart realizes that part of the accomplishment of the primordial nature of the world is that it should find itself in the human soul. This primordial nature would be imperfect, even unfinished, if it lacked that component of its frame, which appears in the human soul. What takes place in man belongs to the primordial nature; and if it did not take place the primordial nature would be only a part of itself."

7. For a discussion of the cosmic relevance of the chronologies given in the Sumerian King Lists, see Joseph Campbell, *The Mask of God: Oriental Mythology* (Harmondsworth: Penguin, 1976), 116ff.

8. For a brief survey of ancient Egyptian King Lists, and a fuller treatment of the ancient Egyptian attitude toward time, see Naydler, *Temple of the Cosmos,* ch. 5.

9. For the extensive use of astrological calendars in Mesopotamia in determining the conduct of the king, see M. Jastrow, *Religion of Babylonia and Assyria* (Boston:

Ginn and Company, Athanaeum Press, 1898), 374–81. For the siting of temples in accordance with constellations, see Eric Burrows, "Some Cosmological Patterns in Babylonian Religion" in *The Labyrinth,* ed. S. H. Hooke (New York: MacMillan, 1935), 60ff. For the importance of the stars in the siting and alignment of Egyptian temples, see, E. A. E. Reymond, *The Mythical Origin of the Egyptian Temple* (Manchester: Manchester University Press, 1969), 309 and R. B. Finnestad, *Image of the World and Symbol of the Creator* (Wiesbaden: Otto Harrassowitz, 1985), 56ff. See also Robert Bauval and Adrian Gilbert, *The Orion Mystery* (London: BCA, 1994) for the possible correspondence of the Giza pyramids with the constellation Orion.

10. S. Sauneron, *The Priests of Ancient Egypt* (New York: Grove Press, 1960), 66. For temple observatories in Mesopotamia, see Jastrow, *Religion of Babylonia and Assyria,* 362.

11. Book of the Dead, ch. 77.

12. Images of winged snake-gods (Nirah being the most prominent) are best interpreted in a shamanic context. See Black and Green, *Gods, Demons and Symbols of Ancient Mesopotamia,* 166. For ascent on snakes in Egypt, see The Book of What Is in the Underworld, Div. 11, in Piankoff, *The Tomb of Ramesses VI.*

13. For ascent by ladder, Pyramid Texts, §365; on a sunbeam, Pyramid Texts, §1108.

14. See Jeremy Naydler, "Plato, Shamanism and Ancient Egypt," in *The Temenos Academy Review* 9 (2006): 67–92. See also Karl Luckert, *Egyptian Light and Hebrew Fire* (New York: State University of New York Press, 1991), 227–35.

15. Plato, *Phaedrus,* 247b, in Plato, *Phaedrus and Letters VII and VIII,* trans. Walter Hamilton, (Harmondsworth: Penguin, 1973), 52.

16. Ibid., 247c, 52.

17. This is clearly articulated in Plato, *Phaedo,* 65, trans. Hugh Tredennick, *The Last Days of Socrates,* 111: "So long as we keep to the body and our soul is contaminated with this imperfection, there is no chance of our ever attaining satisfactorily to our object, which we assert to be Truth. . . .We are in fact convinced that if we are ever to have pure knowledge of anything, we must get rid of the body and contemplate things by themselves with the soul by itself." (Plato, *Phaedo,* §65). The "things" referred to are the Forms.

18. For Plato's doctrine of Forms, see especially his dialogues the *Parmenides* and the *Sophist.* Plato's belief that all knowledge is an anamnesis or "remembering" of truths of which the soul was directly aware before it incarnated in a physical body, implies that self-knowledge is also attained through reconnecting with the state of consciousness one had before one incarneted for the doctrine of anamnesis see the *Phaedo* and *Meno,* §§72–75.

19. Plato, *Parmenides*, §§132d–134b.

20. Plato's belief that all knowledge is an *anamnesis* or "remembering" of truths of which the soul was directly aware before it incarnated in a physical body, implies that self-knowledge is also attained through reconnecting with the state of consciousness one had before one incarnated. For the doctrine of *anamnesis* see the *Phaedo* and *Meno*, §§72–75.

21. Thus in *Phaedo*, §64a trans. Tredennick, *The Last Days of Socrates*, 107: "Ordinary people seem not to realize that those who really apply themselves in the right way to philosophy are directly and of their own accord preparing themselves for dying and death."

22. Aristotle's arguments against the Platonic theory of Forms or Ideas are given in the *Metaphysics*, Book One. The following statement is typical of Aristole's approach: "It would seem impossible that the substance and the thing of which it is the substance exist in separation; hence how can the Ideas, if they are the substances of things, exist in separation from them?" *Metaphysics*, 991b, trans. Hugh Tredennick (London: Loeb-Heinemann, 1933), 69.

23. Ibid., 1072b 13–1074b 35.

24. Ibid., Books Seven and Eight, for Aristotle's discussion of substance. Substance, for Aristotle, is form combined with matter. See G. R. G. Mure, *Aristotle* (New York: Oxford University Press, 1964), 101. See also *Physics*, Book Two.

25. Aristotle, *Physics*, §184a 17ff, trans. P. H. Wicksteed and F. M. Cornford (London: Loeb-Heinemann, 1970), 11. "The path of investigation must lie from what is more immediately knowable and clear to us, to what is clearer and more intimately knowable in its own nature; for it is not the same thing to be directly accessible to our cognition and to be intrinsically intelligible. Hence, in advancing to that which is intrinsically more luminous and by its nature accessible to deeper knowledge, we must start from what is more immediately within our cognition, though in its own nature less fully accessible to understanding."

26. Aristotle, *Ethics*, III.iii.17ff. and IX.viii.6, in which he writes of "carrying back the action to oneself, and to the dominant part (*to hegoumenon*) of oneself, for it is this part that choses." (III.iii.17) The "dominant part" here is *nous*, the capacity for intellectual intuition.

27. Ibid., X.vii.8. The quotation in full is as follows: "We should not follow those who tell us that because we are human we should think human thoughts, and because we are mortal we should think the thoughts of mortals, but we ought as far as possible to achieve immortality, and do all that a human being can do to live in accordance with the highest thing in us; for though this may be small in bulk, in power and value it far surpasses all the rest."

28. "Such a life as this however will be higher than the human level; not in virtue of their humanity will a person achieve it, but in virtue of something within them that is divine . . ." Aristotle, *Ethics,* X.vii.8

29. Georg Blattmann, *The Sun, The Ancient Mysteries and a New Physics* (Edinburgh: Floris Books, 1985), 96–97: "the knowledge . . . was self-evident in early Christian times, and only later fell into oblivion: that what was born and went forth from the Baptism, namely Christ, is the *Sol novus,* the newborn Sun-spirit itself. Common invocations of Christ were *O sol salutus* (sun of salvation), *Helios anatoles* (sun of the rising) . . ."

30. David Fideler, *Jesus Christ, Sun of God* (London: Quest Books, 1993), 51–52 comments; "Origen, in his work *Against Celsus,* states that those who follow the example of 'the Sun of Righteousness,' who sent forth His rays from Judaea, become not only followers of Christ, but Christs in their own right. . . . Not only is the Logos the image and manifestation of the otherwise transcendent Source, but it is the connecting principle through which we are joined back to the One, and that is why Jesus is represented as the mediator between heaven and earth in Christian symbolism."

31. G. R. G. Mure, *Introduction to Hegel* (Oxford: Oxford University Press, 1940) for Hegel's philosophy as an extension and development of Aristotle's.

# BIBLIOGRAPHY

Allen, J. P. *Genesis in Egypt*. New Haven: Yale University, 1988.

Alster, Bendt, ed. *Assyriological Miscellanies,* vol. 1. Copenhagen: University of Copenhagen Institute of Assyriology, 1980.

Anderson, Bernhard W. *The Living World of the Old Testament*. Harlow: Longman, 1978.

*The Ancient Egyptian Book of the Dead*. Translated by R. O. Faulkner. London: British Museum Publications, 1985.

*Ancient Egyptian Pyramid Texts*. Translated by R. O. Faulkner. Oxford: Oxford University Press, 1969.

Aquinas, Thomas. *An Aquinas Reader*. Edited by Mary T. Clark. London: Hodder and Stoughton, 1974.

——. *St. Thomas Aquinas: Philosophical Texts*. Edited by Thomas Gilby. London: Oxford University Press, 1951.

——. *Summa Theologiae*. London: Blackfriars, Eyre and Spottiswode, 1974.

Aristotle. *De Anima*. Translated by W. S. Hett. London: William Heinemann, 1975.

——. *Metaphysics*. Translated by H. Tredennick. London: William Heinemann, 1975.

——. *Nichomachean Ethics*. Translated by H. Rackham. London: William Heinemann, 1975.

——. *Physics*. Translated by Philip Wicksteed and Francis Cornford. London: William Heinemann, 1970.

Armstrong, A. H. *An Introduction to Ancient Philosophy*. Boston: Beacon Press, 1963.

——. *Plotinus*. New York: Collier Books, 1962.

Assmann, Jan. "Death and Initiation in the Funerary Religion of Ancient Egypt." In W. K. Simpson, ed., *Religion and Philosophy in Ancient Egypt*. New Haven, Conn.: Yale University Press, 1989.

———. *The Search for God in Ancient Egypt*. Translated by David Lorton. Ithaca: Cornell University Press, 2001.

Baarb, A. A. "Mystery, Myth and Magic." *The Legacy of Egypt*. Oxford: Clarendon Press, 1971.

Bacon, Francis. *Novum Organum*. London: Joannem Billium Typographum Regium, 1620.

Baines, J., and C. J. Eyre. "Four Notes on Literacy." *Göttinger Miszellen,* 61 (1983).

Bamford, Christopher, ed. *Staying Connected*. New York: Anthroposophic Press, 1999.

Barbu, Z. *Problems of Historical Psychology*. New York: Grove Press, 1960.

Barfield, Owen. *Saving the Appearances*. London: Faber and Faber, 1957.

Baring, Anne, and Jules Cashford. *The Myth of the Goddess*. London: Penguin Books, 1991.

Barnstone, Willis, ed. *The Other Bible*. New York: Harper and Row, 1984.

Bauval, Robert, and Adrian Gilbert. *The Orion Mystery*. London: BCA, 1994.

Beard, Mary, John North, and Simon Price. *Religions of Rome*. Cambridge: Cambridge University Press, 1998.

Bell, Lanny. "The New Kingdom 'Divine Temple' the Example of Luxor." In Byron E. Shafer, ed., *Temples of Ancient Egypt*. London: I. B. Tauris Publishers, 1998.

Bernal, J. D. *Science in History,* vol. 2. Harmondsworth: Penguin Books, 1969.

Berrall, Julia. *The Garden: An Illustrated History*. Harmondsworth: Penguin Books, 1978.

Black, Jeremy, and Anthony Green. *Gods, Demons and Symbols of Ancient Mesopotamia*. London: British Museum Press, 1992.

Blake, William, *Poetry and Prose of William Blake*. Edited by Geoffrey Keynes. London: The Nonesuch Library, 1967.

———. *Blake's Poems and Prophecies*. Edited by Max Plowman. London: Everyman, 1970.

Blattmann, Georg. *The Sun, The Ancient Mysteries and a New Physics*. Edinburgh: Floris Books, 1985.

Bogoslovsky, E. S. "Hundred Egyptian Draughtsmen." *Zeitschrift fur Ägyptische Sprache und Altertumskunde* 107, 1980.

Breasted, J. H. *Development of Religion and Thought in Ancient Egypt*. Philadelphia: University of Pennsylvania Press, 1972.

———. *A History of Egypt: from the Earliest Times to the Persian Conquest*. London: Hodder and Stoughton, 1912.

Bryan, Betsy M. "Painting Techniques and Artisan Organization in the Tomb of Suemniwet, Theban Tomb 92." In W. V. Davies, ed., *Colour and Painting in Ancient Egypt*. London: British Museum Press, 2001.

Buber, Martin. *I and Thou.* Translated by Walter Kaufmann. Edinburgh: T. and T. Clark, 1970.

Budge, E. A. Wallis. *The Egyptian Book of the Dead (The Papyrus of Ani): Egyptian Text, Transliteration and Translation.* New York: Dover, 1967.

Burkert, Walter. *Greek Religion.* Oxford: Basil Blackwell, 1985.

Burrows, Eric. "Some Cosmological Patterns in Babylonian Religion." In S. H. Hooke, ed., *The Labyrinth.* New York: MacMillan, 1935.

Burtt, E. *The Metaphysical Foundations of Modern Physical Science.* London: Routledge and Kegan Paul, 1932.

Campbell, Joseph. *The Masks of God: Oriental Mythology.* Harmondsworth: Penguin, 1976.

Castleden, Rodney. *The Knossos Labyrinth: A New View of the "Palace of Minos" at Knossos.* London: Routledge, 1990.

Charles, R. H., ed. *The Apocrypha and the Pseudepigraphia of the Old Testament in English,* vol. 2. Oxford: Oxford University Press, 1913.

Cicero. *De Divinatione.* Translated by W. A. Falconer. London: Harvard University Press, 2001.

———. *The Nature of the Gods (De natura deorum).* Translated by Horace C. P. McGregor. Harmondsworth: Penguin, 1972.

Clark, Mary T., ed. *An Aquinas Reader.* London: Hodder and Stoughton, 1974.

Clayton, Peter A. *Chronicle of the Pharaohs.* London: Thames and Hudson, 1994.

Clement of Alexandria. *Protrepticus.* Translated by G. W. Butterworth. London: Heinemann, 1919.

Collingwood, R. G. *The Idea of Nature.* Oxford: Oxford University Press, 1965.

Cooper, J. C. *An Illustrated Encyclopaedia of Traditional Symbols.* London: Thames and Hudson, 1978.

Copleston, Frederick. *A History of Philosophy.* 9 vols. New York: Image Books, 1962–1977.

Corbin, H. *"Mundus Imaginalis,* or The Imaginary and the Imaginal." *Swedenborg and Esoteric Islam.* Chester, Penn.: Swedenborg Foundation, 1995.

———. *Spiritual Body and Celestial Earth.* Princeton: Princeton University Press, 1990.

Cottrell, Leonard. *The Warrior Pharaohs.* London: Evans Brothers Ltd., 1968.

Cumont, Franz. *Oriental Religions in Roman Paganism.* New York: Dover, 1956.

Dalley, Stephanie. *Myths from Mesopotamia.* Oxford: Oxford University Press, 1989.

Dante Alighieri. *The Divine Comedy.* London: Penguin Books, 1984.

Debus, Allen G. *Man and Nature in the Renaissance.* Cambridge: Cambridge University Press, 1978.

Derchain, P. "Symbols and Metaphors in Literature and Representations of Private Life." *Royal Anthropological Institute News* 15 (1976).

Desroches-Noblecourt, C. *Tutankhamen.* London: The Connoisseur and Michael Joseph Ltd., 1963.

Dillon, John. *The Middle Platonists.* London: Duckworth, 1996.

Dionysius the Areopagite. *Mystical Theology and Celestial Hierarchies.* Godalming: The Shrine of Wisdom, 1965.

Dodds, E. R. *The Greeks and the Irrational.* Los Angeles: University of California Press, 1973.

———. *Pagans and Christians in an Age of Anxiety.* Cambridge: Cambridge University Press, 1990.

Dumézil, Georges. *Archaic Roman Religion,* vol. 2. Translated by Philip Krapp. Chicago: University of Chicago Press, 1970.

DuQuesne, Terence. *A Coptic Initiatory Invocation.* Thame: Darengo, 1991.

Egyptian Book of the Dead in Budge, E. A. Wallis. The Egyptian Book of the Dead (The Papyrus of Ani): Egyptian Text, Transliteration and Translation. New York: Dover, 1967.

Eliade, Mircea. *Shamanism: Archaic Techniques of Ecstasy.* London: Arkana, 1989.

Erman, Adolf. *The Ancient Egyptians: A Sourcebook of their Writings.* New York: Harper and Row, 1966.

———. *Life in Ancient Egypt.* New York: Dover Publications, 1971.

Faulkner, R. O. *The Ancient Egyptian Book of the Dead.* London: British Museum Publications, 1985.

———. *The Ancient Egyptian Pyramid Texts.* Oxford: Oxford University Press, 1969.

Ferguson, John. *Socrates: A Source Book.* London: Macmillan, 1970.

Fideler, David. *Jesus Christ, Sun of God.* London: Quest Books, 1993.

Finnestad, R. B. *Image of the World and Symbol of the Creator.* Wiesbaden: Otto Harrassowitz, 1985.

Fix, William R. *Star Maps.* London: Octopus Books, 1979.

Flacelière, Robert. *Greek Oracles.* Translated by Douglas Garman. London: Elek Books, 1965.

Fowden, Garth. *The Egyptian Hermes.* Princeton: Princeton University Press, 1986.

Fox, Robin Lane. *Pagans and Christians.* London: Penguin, 1988.

Frankfort, Henri. *Kingship and the Gods.* Chicago: University of Chicago Press, 1978.

Frankfurter, David. *Religion in Roman Egypt.* Princeton: Princeton University Press, 1998.

Franz, Marie-Louise von. *On Divination and Synchronicity.* Toronto: Inner City Books, 1980.

Gardiner, A. *Egyptian Grammar.* Oxford: Oxford University Press, 1973.

———. "The House of Life." *Journal of Egyptian Archaeology* 24 (1938).

Gebser, Jean. *The Ever-Present Origin.* Translated by Noel Barstad with Algis Mickunas. Athens, Ohio: Ohio University Press, 1985.

Gilby, Thomas, ed. *St. Thomas Aquinas: Philosophical Texts.* London: Oxford University Press, 1951.

Godwin, Joscelyn. *Robert Fludd: Hermetic Philosopher and Surveyor of Two Worlds.* London: Thames and Hudson, 1979.

*Gospel According to Thomas.* Translated by A. Guillaumont et al. Leiden: E. J. Brill, 1976.

Grube, G. M. A. *Plato's Thought.* London: Athlone Press, 1980.

Guénon, René. *The Reign of Quantity and the Signs of the Times.* Translated by Lord Northbourne. London: Luzac and Co., 1953.

Guillaumont, A. et al. *The Gospel According to Thomas.* Leiden: E. J. Brill, 1976.

Gurney, O. R. "The Babylonians and Hittites." *Divination and Oracles.* London: George Allen and Unwin, 1981.

Halliday, W. R. *Greek Divination.* London: MacMillan, 1913.

Harris, J. R. *The Legacy of Egypt.* Oxford: Clarendon Press, 1971.

Harrison, Jane. *Prolegomena to the Study of Greek Religion.* London: Merlin Press, 1962.

———. *Themis.* London: Merlin Press, 1963.

Hart, George. *A Dictionary of Egyptian Gods and Goddesses.* London and New York: Routledge and Kegan Paul, 1986.

Hegel. *Phenomenology of Mind.* Translated by J. B. Baillie. London: George Allen and Unwin, 1949.

———. *Philosophy of Mind.* Translated by William Wallace and A. V. Miller. Oxford: Oxford University Press, 1971.

Hesiod. *Works and Days.* Edited with prolegomena and commentary by M. L. West. Oxford: Clarendon Press, 1978.

Hiebel, Frederick. *The Epistles of Paul and Rudolf Steiner's Philosophy of Freedom.* New York: St. George Publications, 1980.

———. *The Gospel of Hellas.* New York: Anthroposophic Press, 1949.

Hillman, James. *Re-Visioning Psychology.* New York: Harper and Row, 1977.

Holford, Ingrid. *The Guinness Book of Weather Facts and Feats.* London: Guinness Superlatives Ltd., 1982.

Homer. *Iliad.* Translated by E. V. Rieu. Harmondsworth: Penguin Books, 1950.

———. *Odyssey.* Translated by Ennis Rees. Indianapolis: Bobbs-Merrill Publishing, 1977.

Hooke, S. H., ed. *The Labyrinth.* New York: MacMillan, 1935.

Hornung, Erik. *Idea into Image.* New York: Timken Publishers, 1992.

———. *The Secret Lore of Egypt: Its Impact on the West.* Translated by David Lorton. Ithaca: Cornell University Press, 2001.

Jacq, Christian. *Egyptian Magic.* Translated by Janet M. Davis. Warminster: Aris and Phillips, 1985.

James, T. G. H. *Egyptian Painting.* London: British Museum Publications, 1985.

Jastrow, Morris. *Religion of Babylonia and Assyria.* Boston: Ginn and Company, Athanaeum Press, 1898.

———. *Religious Belief in Babylonia and Assyria.* New York: Benjamin Blom, 1911.

Jeyes, Ullah. "The Act of Extispicy in Ancient Mesopotamia: An Outline." In Bendt Alster, ed., *Assyriological Miscellanies,* vol. 1. Copenhagen: University of Copenhagen Institute of Assyriology, 1980.

———. *Old Babylonian Extispicy: Omen Texts in the British Museum.* Istanbul: Nederlands Historisch-Archaeologisch Instituut, 1989.

Johnson, W. Raymond. "Amenhotep III and Amarna: Some New Considerations." *Journal of Egyptian Archaeology* 82 (1996).

Jung, C. G. *Aion,* C.W.9, part 2. Princeton: Princeton University Press, 1979.

———. *The Archetypes and the Collective Unconscious* CW9 part 1. London: Routledge and Kegan Paul, 1968.

———. *Memories, Dreams and Reflections.* London: HarperCollins/Fontana Press, 1995.

———. *Modern Man in Search of a Soul.* London: Routledge and Kegan Paul, 1961.

———. *Mysterium Coniunctionis* CW14. Princeton: Princeton University Press, 1970.

———. *Psychology and Religion: East and West* CW11. London: Routledge and Kegan Paul, 1958.

———. *The Structure and Dynamics of the Psyche* CW8. London: Routledge and Kegan Paul, 1969.

———. "The Symbolic Life." *The Symbolic Life* CW18. London: Routledge and Kegan Paul, 1954.

Karcher, Stephen. *I Ching: The Classic Chinese Oracle of Change.* London: Vega, 2002.

———. *The Illustrated Encyclopedia of Divination.* Shaftesbury: Element, 1997.

Keynes, Geoffrey, ed. *Poetry and Prose of William Blake.* London: The Nonesuch Library, 1967.

Kirk, G. S., and J. E. Raven. *The Presocratic Philosophers.* Cambridge: Cambridge University Press, 1957.

Kitson, Annabel, ed. *History and Astrology.* London: Unwin Hyman, 1989.

Kristensen, W. Brede. *Life Out of Death: Studies in the Religions of Egypt and of Ancient Greece.* Translated by H. J. Franken and G. R. H. Wright. Louvain: Peeters Press, 1992.

Lehrs, E. *Man or Matter.* London: Faber and Faber, 1951.

Lichtheim, M. *Ancient Egyptian Literature,* vol. 1. Los Angeles: University of California Press, 1975.

———. *Ancient Egyptian Literature,* vol. 2. Los Angeles: University of California Press, 1976.

Liddel, H. G., and R. Scott. *Greek-English Lexicon (Abridged).* Oxford: Oxford University Press, 1974.

Locke, J. *An Essay Concerning Human Understanding.* Oxford: Oxford University Press, 1975.

Loewe, Michael, and Carmen Blacker, eds. *Divination and Oracles.* London: George Allen and Unwin, 1981.

Luckert, Karl. *Egyptian Light and Hebrew Fire.* New York: State University of New York Press, 1991.

Manniche, Lise. *Sexual Life in Ancient Egypt.* London: Kegan Paul, 1997.

Meeks, Dimitri, and Christine Favard-Meeks. *Daily Life of the Egyptian Gods.* London: Pimlico, 1999.

Meer, L. B. van der. *The Bronze Liver of Piacenza: Analysis of a Polytheistic Structure.* Amsterdam: J. C. Gieben, 1987.

Moore, G. E. *Principia Ethica.* Cambridge: Cambridge University Press, 1903.

Morenz, Siegfried. *Egyptian Religion.* London: Methuen, 1973.

Müller, M. D. *Egyptian Mythology.* London: G. G. Harrap, 1918.

Mure, G. R. G. *Aristotle.* New York: Oxford University Press, 1964.

———. *Introduction to Hegel.* Oxford: Oxford University Press, 1940.

Nasr, S. H. *Religion and the Order of Nature.* Oxford: Oxford University Press, 1996.

Naydler, Jeremy. "Plato, Shamanism and Ancient Egypt." *The Temenos Academy Review* 9 (2006).

———. "The Regeneration of Realism and the Recovery of a Science of Qualities." *The International Philosophical Quarterly* XXIII, no. 2, issue 90 (1983).

———. *Shamanic Wisdom in the Pyramid Texts: The Mystical Tradition of Ancient Egypt.* Rochester, Vt.: Inner Traditions, 2005.

———. *Temple of the Cosmos: the Ancient Egyptian Experience of the Sacred.* Rochester, Vt.: Inner Traditions, 1996.

Neate, Geoffrey P. *Akkadian Oracles.* Oxford: University of Oxford thesis, 1973.

Nilsson, Martin P. *Greek Folk Religion.* New York: Harper, 1961.

Onians, R. B. *The Origins of European Thought.* Cambridge: Cambridge University Press, 1988.

Oppenheim, A. Leo. *Ancient Mesopotamia: Portrait of a Dead Civilization.* Chicago: Chicago University Press, 1977.

Palmer, G. E. H. et al., eds. *The Philokalia.*London: Faber and Faber, 1979.

Piankoff, Alexandre. *The Litany of Re.* Princeton: Princeton University Press, 1964.

———. *The Tomb of Ramesses VI.* New York: Pantheon Books, 1954.

Pieper, Joseph. *Leisure the Basis of Culture.* London: Fontana, 1965.

Plato. *Phaedo.* Translated by Hugh Tredennick. Harmondsworth: Penguin, 1969.

———. *Phaedrus and Letters VII and VIII.* Translated by Walter Hamilton. Harmondsworth: Penguin, 1973.

———. *The Republic.* Translated by H. D. P. Lee. Harmondsworth: Penguin, 1955.

———. *Timaeus.* Translated by Benjamin Jowett. London: Sphere Books, 1970.

Plotinus. *Enneads.* Translated by A. H. Armstrong. New York: Collier Books, 1962.

———. *Enneads.* Translated by Stephen MacKenna. London: Faber and Faber, 1969.

Plowman, Max, ed. *Blake's Poems and Prophecies.* London: Everyman, 1970.

Plutarch. *Moral Essays.* Translated by Rex Warner. Harmondsworth: Penguin Books, 1971.

———. *The Rise and Fall of Athens.* Translated by Ian Scott-Kilvert. Harmondsworth: Penguin, 1960.

Proclus. *Elements of Theology.* Oxford: Clarendon Press, 1963.

Ragozin, Z. A. *Chaldea: From the Earliest Times to the Rise of Assyria.* London: T. Fisher and Unwin, 1886.

Rahner, Hugo. *Greek Myths and Christian Mystery.* New York: Harper and Row, 1963.

Reymond, E. A. E. *The Mythical Origin of the Egyptian Temple.* Manchester: Manchester University Press, 1969.

Rickaby, John. "Conscience." *The Catholic Encyclopedia,* vol. 4. New York: Robert Appleton Co., 1908.

Ritner, Robert K. *The Mechanics of Ancient Egyptian Magical Practice.* Chicago: The Oriental Institue of the University of Chicago, 1993.

Rix, Martyn. *The Art of Botanical Illustration.* London: Bracken Books, 1981.

Roberts, Alison. *My Heart, My Mother.* Rottingdean: Northgate, 2000.

Ross, David. *Aristotle.* London: Methuen, 1964.

———. *Plato's Theory of Ideas.* London: Oxford University Press, 1951.

Saggs, H. W. F. *The Greatness That Was Babylon.* New York: The New American Library, 1962.

Sauneron, S. *The Priests of Ancient Egypt.* New York: Grove Press, 1960.

Schwaller de Lubicz, R. A. *The Temple of Man.* Rochester, Vt.: Inner Traditions International, 1998.

Seznec, Jean. *The Survival of the Pagan Gods.* Princeton: Princeton University Press, 1972.

Shafer, Byron E., ed. *Temples of Ancient Egypt*. London: I. B. Tauris Publishers, 1998.

Sharman-Burke, Juliet, and Liz Greene. *The Mythic Tarot*. London: Century Hutchinson, 1986.

Simpson, W. K., ed. *Religion and Philosophy in Ancient Egypt*. New Haven: Yale University Press, 1989.

Snell, Bruno. *The Discovery of the Mind*. New York: Dover, 1982.

Starr, Ivan. *Queries to the Sungod: Divination and Politics in Sargonid Assyria*. State Archives of Assyria, vol. 4. Helsinki: Helsinki University Press, 1990.

———. *The Rituals of the Diviner*. Malibu: Undena Publications, 1983.

Steiner, R. "Das Bilden von Begriffen und die Kategorienlehre Hegels." *Die Beantwortung von Weltfragen und Lebensfragen durch Anthroposophie*. Dornach: Rudolf Steiner Verlag, 1986.

———. *Eleven European Mystics*. New York: Rudolf Steiner Publications, 1960.

———. *The Philosophy of Freedom*. London: Rudolf Steiner Press, 1970.

———. *Theosophy*. Hudson N.Y.: Anthroposophic Press, 1994.

———. "Uniting with the Universal Spirit." *Staying Connected*. New York: Anthroposophic Press, 1999.

———. *Universe, Earth and Man*. Translated by Harry Collison. London: Rudolf Steiner Publishing Co., 1941.

Strabo. *Geography*. Translated by Horace Leonard Jones. London: William Heinemann, 1917.

Swami, Shree Purohit, and W. B. Yeats. *The Ten Principal Upanishads*. London: Faber and Faber, 1938.

Temple, Richard. *Icons and the Mystical Origins of Christianity*. Shaftesbury: Element Books, 1990.

Temple, Robert. *Netherworld*. London: Random House, 2002.

Walker, C. B. F. "A Sketch of the Development of Mesopotamian Astrology and Horoscopes." In Annabel Kitson ed., *History and Astrology*. London: Unwin Hyman, 1989.

Wallis, R. T. *Neoplatonism*. London: Duckworth, 1995.

Westendorf, Wolfgang. "Bemerkungen zur 'Kammer der Wiedergeburt' im Tutanchamungrab." *Zeitschrift fur Ägyptische Sprache und Alterumskunde* 94 (1967).

Whicher, Olive. *Sun Space: Science at the Threshold of Spiritual Understanding*. London: Rudolf Steiner Press, 1989.

Whitehead, A. N. *Science and the Modern World*. New York: Free Press, 1967.

Wilkinson, Richard H. *Symbol and Magic in Egyptian Art*. London: Thames and Hudson, 1994.

Wilson, John A. "The Artist of the Egyptian Old Kingdom." *Journal of Near Eastern Studies,* 6 (1947).

Wolkstein, D., and S. N. Kramer. *Inanna.* London: Rider, 1984.

Xenophon. *Anabasis.* Cambridge: Harvard University Press, 1992.

———. *The Persian Expedition.* Translated by Rex Warner. Harmondsworth: Penguin Books, 1949.

Yates, F. *Giordano Bruno and the Hermetic Tradition.* London: Routledge and Kegan Paul, 1971.

Zaehner, R. C. *Hindu Scriptures.* London: J. M. Dent and Sons, 1966.

# ILLUSTRATION SOURCES

## CHAPTER ONE. THE RESTITUTION OF THE EAR

1.1. The god Enki in his watery abode, the Abzu. From an Akkadian cylinder seal (2340 BC). Drawing by Tessa Rickards. Reproduced by kind permission of British Museum Press from Jeremy Black and Anthony Green, *Gods, Demons and Symbols of Ancient Mesopotamia* (London: British Museum Press, 1992), 27.

1.2. Worship of the god Ptah, who is "great of hearing." Stele of Penbuy, Eighteenth Dynasty. Deir el Medinah, Egypt. Author's drawing.

1.3. The goddess Athena and her wide-eyed owl. Two sides of an Athenian coin (fifth century BC). Author's drawing.

1.4. *Above left:* princess Sedet (Fourth Dynasty), Egypt. Adolph Erman, *Life in Ancient Egypt* (London: Macmillan and Co., 1894), 212.

   *Above right:* Atalanta, from a fifth-century cup painting, Greece. John Boardman, *Athenian Red Figure Vases: The Archaic Period* (London: Thames and Hudson, 1975), fig. 369. Reproduced by kind permission of Thames and Hudson.

   *Below left:* The nomarch Khnumhotep, Middle Kingdom, Egypt. Erman, *Life in Ancient Egypt,* 206.

   *Below right:* a hunter, from a fifth-century cup painting, Greece. Boardman, *Athenian Red Figure Vases: The Archaic Period,* fig. 64. Reproduced by kind permission of Thames and Hudson.

1.5. The dove of the Holy Spirit inspires St. Gregory. Author's drawing of detail of a painting by the Master of the Registrum Gregorii (tenth century AD).

1.6. Albrecht Dürer's demonstration of the perspecive drawing of a lute. From the 1525 edition of Dürer's textbook on perspective and proportion. Willi Kurth, ed., *The Complete Woodcuts of Albrecht Dürer* (New York: Dover, 1963), fig. 338.

1.7. Portrait of Anthony van Leeuwenhoek, 1680. Author's drawing of a contemporary painting.

1.8. Not a telescope but a compound microscope. From Descartes' *La Dioptrique* (1637). Reproduced in Charles Adam and Paul Tannery, eds., *Oeuvres de Descartes,* vol. 6 (Paris: Leopold Cerf, 1902), 207.

1.9. Diagram of the eardrum. Adapted from *Reader's Digest Family Medical Adviser* (London: The Reader's Digest Association Ltd., 1983), 38. Reproduced by kind permission of The Reader's Digest Association Ltd.

1.10. All the senses are engaged by the "listening mind." *Fool and Flower* by Cecil Collins. Reproduced in Cecil Collins, *The Vision of the Fool* (London: The Grey Walls Press Ltd., 1947), plate 17.

## CHAPTER TWO. THE HEART OF THE LILY

2.1. Late fifteenth-century woodcut of ivy. From the Latin *Herbarius* of 1484, (Mainz: Peter Schoeffer, 1484).

2.2. Early sixteenth-century herbal showing rocket (*left*) and opium poppy (*right*). From the *Macer Floridus de viribus herbarum* (1510).

2.3. Mandrake (*top left*) and other plants. From *Le Grand Herbier* (Paris: circa 1520).

2.4. Early sixteenth-century woodcut of a lime tree. From Hieronymus Bock, *De Stirpium* (Argent, 1522).

2.5. *The Garden of Paradise* by an unknown Master of the Middle Rhine (ca. 1420). (Frankfort: Staedelsches Kunstinstitut).

2.6. *The Garden of Paradise* (detail).

2.7. Leonardo da Vinci's study of a lily. Pen and ink and brown wash over black chalk, heightened with white. The Royal Collection © 2008, Her Majesty Elizabeth II.

2.8. Artists prepare an illustration for a medical textbook. Leonhart Fuchs, *De Historia Stirpium* (Basel, 1542). Newberry Library, Chicago.

2.9. The compact single-lens microscope. Replica of van Leeuwenhoek's single-lens microscope. Author's drawing.

2.10. Portrait of van Leeuwenhoek. Author's drawing, from a contemporary portrait.

2.11. Magnified longitudinal section through a plant stem. Photo: Brian Bracegirdle. In D. G. Mackean, *Introduction to Biology* (London: John Murray, 1973), 15.

2.12. Electron microscope and its operator. M. B. V. Roberts, *Biology: A Functional Approach* (New York: Thomas Nelson and Sons, 1976), 16. Reproduced by kind permission of M. B. V. Roberts.

2.13. Lily chromosomes in the first stage of mitosis, magnified approximately one thousand times. From D. G. Mackean, *Introduction to Biology* (London: John Murray, 1973), 182.

2.14. St. Catherine of Siena holding a Madonna lily. By Andrea Vanni (1330–1414), in the Basilica of St. Domenic, Siena. Author's drawing.

2.15. Lily design, from the "Villa of the Lilies," at Amnissos, Crete. From Fred Stoker, *A Book of Lilies* (Harmondsworth: Penguin Books, 1943), 10.

2.16. Women and lilies dancing. From a gold ring found at Isopata, near Knossos, Crete. Heraklion Museum. From B. L. Bogajevskii, *Novoe minoiskoe kol'tso s' izobrazheniem' ku'tovago tantsa* (St. Petersberg: M. A. Aleksandrova, 1912), 3.

2.17. Griffin and lilies. Wall painting in the "Throne Room" of the Labyrinth, Knossos. Author's drawing.

2.18 Woman flies with griffin. From a gold ring. Heraklion Museum. Author's drawing.

## CHAPTER THREE. THE SOUL OF THE WEATHER

3.1. Ani holds a sail, enabling him to breathe in the Underworld. From E. A. Wallis Budge, *The Book of the Dead* (London: Routledge and Kegan Paul, 1985), 197.

3.2. The south wind as a lioness-headed goddess. From E. A. Wallis Budge, *The Gods of the Ancient Egyptians,* vol. 2 (London: 1904), 295.

3.3. The north wind, depicted as a four-headed ram, or ram-god. From Budge, *The Gods of the Ancient Egyptians,* vol. 2, 296.

3.4. Demon of the southwest wind. Akkadian statuette. The Louvre. From Z. A. Ragozin, *Chaldea: From the Earliest Times to the Rise of Assyria* (London: T. Fisher Unwin, 1886), 169.

3.5. Harpy, from a vase in the British Museum. From Jane Harrison, *Prolegomena to the Study of Greek Religion* (Cambridge: Cambridge University Press, 1907), 182, fig. 24.

3.6. Boreas, from the Tower of Winds, Athens. From *A Smaller Classical Dictionary* (London: John Murray, 1910), 119.

3.7. The four archangels and the twelve winds. From Robert Fludd, *Medicina Catholica,* vol. 1a (Frankfurt: William Fitzer, 1629), 113.

3.8. Detail of Raphael, the west wind and its daemon. See 3.7.

3.9. Fifteenth-century diagram of the universe. Hartmann Schedel. *Liber Chronicarum.* (Nuremburg, 1493).

3.10. Sixteenth-century woodcut depicting the four winds and three seasons. Woodcut by Hans Weiditz, *Tacuinus sanitatis* (Strasburg, 1531).

3.11. Robert Hooke's anemometer (circa 1665). *Philosophical Transactions of the Royal Society of London,* vol. 2, no. 24 (London, 1667), fig. 6.

3.12. Robert Hooke's wheel barometer. From his *Micrographia,* (London, 1665), fig. 1.

3.13. The experimental weighing of air. From Otto von Guericke, *Experiinenta Nova* (Amsterdam, 1672). Redrawn by the author.

3.14. Marduk and Tiamat. Drawing of a sculpture found at the Temple of Ninurta, Nimrud, Iraq. British Museum. From Ragozin, *Chaldea,* 291.

3.15. Baal-Hadad riding on his bull. Stele from Arsian-Tash (eighth century BC). Reproduced by kind permission of British Museum Press, from Black and Green, *Gods, Demons and Symbols of Ancient Mesopotamia,* 111.

3.16. Meteorologist at his computer, Meteorological office at Bracknell, *The Weather Book: A Complete Guide to Meteorological Phenomena, Weather Forecasting and Climate* (London: Michael Joseph, 1982), 204.

3.17. A frontal depression, recorded on six graphs, passes over Abingdon, Berkshire, 22–24 Jan. 1956. From A. A. Austin and M. Parry, *Everyday Meteorology* (London: Hutchinson, 1975), 135.

3.18. Satellite photograph of a frontal approaching the west of England (Sept. 26, 1971). From Austin and Parry, *Everyday Meteorology* (London: Hutchinson, 1975), plate 2.

3.19. Satellite picture of global weather conditions. Japan Meteorological Agency.

3.20. Northern hemisphere synoptic chart (Jan. 29, 1955).

3.21. Computerized image of cloud systems over the Atlantic and Europe. From Ingrid Holford, *The Guinness Book of Weather Facts and Feats,* 241.

## CHAPTER FOUR.
## THE REALITY THAT IS NOT THERE

4.1. The premodern geocentric worldview. Peter Apian, *Cosmographia* (Antwerp, 1539).

4.2 . The angels and the sanctified dead portrayed in fifteenth-century cosmological diagram. Peter Apian, *Cosmographia.* Deutsches Museum.

4.3 Chuckchi map of the heavenly ways. American Museum of Natural History.

4.4. Position of our solar system within the galaxy. Reproduced in P. Moore, *Concise Atlas of the Universe* (London: Mitchell Beazeley, 1974), 68.

4.5. Development of a groundsel (*Senecio vulgaris*). Reproduced by kind permission of Hawthorn Press from M. Colquhoun and A. Ewald, *New Eyes for Plants* (Stroud: Hawthorn Press, 1996), 16, fig. 9.

## CHAPTER FIVE. ANCIENT EGYPT AND
## THE SOUL OF THE WEST

5.1. One of a number of very early maps, showing a region of the underworld known as the Fields of Peace. Inner coffin of Gua (BM 30, 840), El Bersha (Twelfth Dynasty, ca. 1850 BC). From E. A. Wallis Budge, *The Egyptian Heaven and Hell* (La Salle, Ill.: Open Court Publishing Company, 1905), 54.

5.2. Truth as the Egyptian goddess Maat. Tomb of Nefertari (Nineteenth Dynasty). Reproduced by kind permission of Thames and Hudson, from Lucy Lamy, *Egyptian Mysteries* (London: Thames and Hudson, 1981), 17.

5.3. The Colossus of Memnon. Reconstruction from *Description de l'Egypte: Antiquités* vol. 2, (Paris: De L'Imprimerie Impériale, 1809), plate 21.

## CHAPTER SIX. ON THE DIVINITY OF THE GODS

6.1. Part of the parade of gods from The Litany of Ra. Tomb of Thutmosis III, Valley of the Kings (Eighteenth Dynasty). Reproduced by kind permission of Princeton University Press from Alexandre Piankoff, *The Litany of Re* (Princeton: Princeton University Press, 1961), 14.

6.2. Anhur with his consort Mekhit. Bronze statue. Late Period. Musée des Beaux-Arts, Budapest. Reproduced by kind permission of Routledge and Kegan Paul from George Hart, *A Dictionary of Egyptian Gods and Goddesses* (London: Routledge and Kegan Paul, 1986), 149.

6.3. The god Ptah. Vignette to ch. 82 of the Book of the Dead. Papyrus of Nu. New Kingdom. E. A. Wallis Budge, *The Book of the Dead*, 265.

6.4. King Seti I joins hands with Hathor. Painted relief from the side of a pillar in Seti's tomb. Valley of the Kings (ca. 1300 BC). Louvre, Paris. Author's drawing.

6.5. King Seti I as Osiris. From his temple at Abydos. Author's drawing.

6.6. Ramesses II attacks the enemy hordes at the Battle of Kadesh. From a relief in the second court of the Ramesseum, Thebes. From J. H. Breasted, *A History of Egypt* (London: Hodder and Stoughton, 1912), 452, fig. 169.

## CHAPTER SEVEN. THE ARTIST AS PRIEST

7.1. The king offers Maat to the god Ptah in his shrine. Bas-relief from the temple of Seti I, Abydos. Reproduced from R. A. Schwaller de Lubicz, *The Egyptian Miracle* (Rochester, Vt.: Inner Traditions, 1985), 41, fig. 9.

7.2. The king offers milk to the goddess Sekhmet. Bas-relief, Temple of Seti I, Abydos. Reproduced from Schwaller de Lubicz, *The Egyptian Miracle*, 41, fig. 9.

7.3. Sculpture of a baboon. From G. Maspero, *The Dawn of Civilization* (London: Society for Promoting Christian Knowledge, 1894), 145.

7.4. Babi, Lord of the Night. Papyrus of Muthetepti (Twenty-first Dynasty). Author's drawing.

7.5. Heka and Maat either side of the sun god Ra-Herakhti. Papyrus of Khensumosi. New Kingdom. Author's drawing.

7.6. Approach to the pylon of Luxor Temple. Photo by Louanne Richards.

7.7. Ramesses II defeats the Hittites. East wing of the pylon of Luxor Temple. Reproduced from R. A. Schwaller de Lubicz, *Sacred Science* (Rochester, Vt.: Inner Traditions, 1982), 129, fig. 23b.

7.8. Seti I defeats the Libyans. Temple of Amon, Karnak (Nineteenth Dynasty). Reproduced by kind permission of Dr. Troy Sagrillo. From R. H. Wilkinson, *Symbol and Magic in Egyptian Art* (London: Thames and Hudson, 1994), 211, fig. 159.

7.9. Tutankhamun hunting desert gazelles. From the lid of a painted chest found in his tomb. Author's drawing.

7.10. Nebamun goes hunting in the marshes. Tomb of Nebamun, New Kingdom. British Museum. Reproduced from J. Gardner Wilkinson, *The Ancient Egyptians: Their Life and Customs,* vol. 1 (London: John Murray, 1853), 236, fig. 249.

7.11. Fishing and fowling in the marshes. Reproduced from J. G. Wilkinson, *The Ancient Egyptians: Their Life and Customs,* vol. 1, 237, fig. 250.

## CHAPTER EIGHT. ANCIENT EGYPT
## AND MODERN ESOTERICISM

8.1. Thutmose III, instructed by Seth and Neith. Drawing of a relief carving at the temple of Amon, Karnak (Eighteenth Dynasty). From Adolf Erman, *Life in Ancient Egypt* (New York: Dover, 1971), 282.

8.2. Thutmose III about to slay forty-two Syrians. Rear of the seventh pylon, Temple of Amon, Karnak. From Heinrich Shäfer, *Principles of Egyptian Art* (Leipzig, 1919), fig. 239.

8.3. King Merenptah defeats the Sea Peoples. Drawing from a relief carving. Reproduced by kind permission of Oxford University Press Inc, from A. Gardiner, *Egypt of the Pharaohs* (Oxford: Oxford University Press, 1966), 286, fig. 11.

8.4. Seth, on the prow of the sun boat, defeats Apophis. Papyrus of Her Uben (B). Reproduced by kind permission of Princeton University Press, from A. Piankoff, *Mythological Papyri* (New York: Pantheon Books, 1957), vol. 1, 75, fig. 54.

8.5. Amenhotep III is in the role of Ra. Tomb of Kheruef. Reproduced from Jeremy Naydler, *Shamanic Wisdom in the Pyramid Texts* (Rochester, Vt.: Inner Traditions, 2005), 206.

8.6. The sky goddess Nut conceals within her body the mysterious inner region. Abbreviated version of the Book of Night on the ceiling of the sarcophagus chamber of the tomb of Ramesses IX, Valley of the Kings. From F. Guilmant, "Le Tombeau de Ramsés IX" in *Mémoires publiées par les Membres de l'Institut Français d'Archéologie Orientale du Caire,* 15 (1907), plate 49.

## CHAPTER NINE. BEING ANCIENT IN A MODERN WAY

9.1. *Barû* extracts liver from a ram laid out on a table. Reign of Assurnasirpal (883–859 BC). BM 124548. Author's drawing.

9.2. Diagram of a sheep's liver, laid out for divinatory purposes. Robert Temple, *Netherworld* (London: Random House, 2002), 243, fig. 37. Reproduced by kind permission of Robert Temple.

9.3. Babylonian clay model of a sheep's liver (ca. 2000 BC). BM 92668. Author's drawing.

9.4. The mythical diviner Kalchas. From an Etruscan mirror (second half of the fifth century BC). Edouard Gerhard, *Etruskische Spiegel* (1884–1897), plate 223.

9.5. An Etruscan *haruspex* studies a liver. Etruscan mirror. Author's drawing.

9.6. The bronze liver of Piacenza (late second century BC). Reproduced by kind permission of Koninklijke Brill, from L. B. van der Meer, *The Bronze Liver of Piacenza*, 10, fig. 9.

9.7. Roman extispicy, from the reign of Trajan (second century AD). From a relief in the Louvre, Paris. Georgius Blecher, *De extispicio capita tria* (Gissae: Impensis Alfredi Toepelmanni, 1905), title page.

## CHAPTER TEN. THE FUTURE OF THE ANCIENT WORLD

10.1. Procession of devotees in honor of the goddess Hathor. Soapstone bowl from Coptos (late sixth century BC). British Museum. Drawing by Barry Cottrell.

10.2. The god Thoth inspires the scribe Nebmertef, Schist sculpture, New Kingdom. Louvre Museum. Photo by M. Chuzeville, Paris. Georges Posener, *A Dictionary of Egyptian Civilization* (London: Methuen, 1962), 254.

10.3. The god Seth teaches Thutmosis III to shoot. Relief from his festival temple at Karnak. New Kingdom. From Adolf Erman, *Life in Ancient Egypt* (New York: Dover, 1971), 282.

10.4. The goddess Nut swallows the sun. Detail from the stele of Taperet (ninth century BC). Louvre Museum. Author's drawing.

10.5. Nut appears in her sacred tree, the sycamore fig. Vignette to ch. 59 of The Book of the Dead. Papyrus of Ani. British Museum. Reproduced from E. A. Wallis Budge, *The Book of the Dead*, 204.

10.6. A Nile deity, in the likeness of Hapi. Temple of Ramesses II, Abydos (thirteenth century BC). Author's drawing.

10.7. Greek river god. Red figure vase (sixth century BC). Louvre, Paris. From J. E. Harrison, *Prolegomena to the Study of Greek Religion* (Cambridge: Cambridge University Press, 1922), fig. 133.

10.8. Storm god. Relief from column of Marcus Aurelius. Rome. Foto Anderson, Rome. Reproduced in Ernest Nash, *Pictorial Dictionary of Ancient Rome,* vol. 1 (New York: Hacker Art Books, 1981), 279, plate 330.

## CHAPTER ELEVEN. CHRIST AND THE GODS

11.1. The celestial self, in the image of Ra. Coffin of Hent-Taui (Twenty-first Dynasty, 1113–949 BC). Metropolitan Museum of Art, New York. Reproduced by kind permission of Princeton University Press, from A. Piankoff and N. Rambova, *Mythological Papyri* (New York: Pantheon Books, 1957), 63, fig. 51.

11.2. Christ portrayed as Helios. From a cemetery at St. Peters in Rome (third century AD). Author's drawing.

11.3. The twelve Olympians in a circle. From a Roman plaque in the Louvre, Paris.

11.4. Helios in his sun chariot, in the center of a zodiac. From a pavement mosaic in the Beth Alpha synagogue, Israel (fourth century AD). Reproduced by kind permission of Princeton University Press, from Erwin R. Goodenough, *Jewish Symbols in the Greco-Roman Period* (Princeton: Princeton University Press, 1988), fig. 10.

11.5. The baptism of Christ. From the Neonian Baptistry, Ravenna (fifth-century AD mosaic). Author's drawing.

11.6. Christ surrounded by twelve angels. Detail from Giotto's scene of the *Last Judgment,* in the Capella degli Scrovegni, Padua. Author's drawing.

11.7. The Earth, the World Soul, the Planets, and the Angels. Robert Fludd, *De Microcosmi Historia,* vol.1a (Oppenheim: Johann Theodore de Bry, 1617), 4.

11.8. Angels surround Christ. Fresco from Lesnovo, Yugoslavia (fourteenth century). Author's drawing.

## CHAPTER TWELVE. PATHWAYS INTO THE FUTURE FROM THE DEEP PAST

12.1. The divine sun boat, whose crew include the succession of gods who ruled over Egypt before human kings. Reproduced by kind permission of Princeton University Press, from Alexandre Piankoff, *The Shrines of Tut-ankh-amon* (Princeton: Princeton University Press, 1955), 109, fig. 37.

12.2. A procession of Egyptian deities makes its way across the heavens. Tomb of Seti I. From O. Neugebauer and R. Parker, *Egyptian Astronomical Texts,* vol. 3 (Providence: Brown University Press, 1960), plate 3.

12.3. Flying to heaven on the back of an eagle. Akkadian cylinder seal. Reproduced by kind permission of British Museum Press, from Black and Green, *Gods, Demons and Symbols of Ancient Mesopotamia,* 78, fig. 61.

12.4. Riding to the stars on the back of a snake. The Book of What Is in the Underworld, Division 11.  Tomb of Thutmose III, Valley of the Kings. Author's drawing.

12.5. The Egyptian initiate standing on the back of the universe. Tomb of Ramesses III. Valley of the Kings. Adapted from a drawing by A. Brodbeck after Champollion, *Monuments de l' Égypte et de la Nubie: notices descriptives,* vol.1 (Paris, 1844), 422–23.

12.6. The High Priest Amenanen wears the mantle of priesthood. New Kingdom, reign of Amenhotep III. From G. Maspero, *The Dawn of Civilization* (London: Society for Promoting Christian Knowledge, 1894), 55.

12.7. Plato and Aristotle portrayed by Raphael. Detail from the *The School of Athens.* Stanza della Segnatura, Vatican, Rome. From Paolo D'Ancona, *Raphael: The Stanza della Segnatura* (London: A. Zwemmer, 1937), 29.

12.8. The baptism of Christ. Detail. From the Baptistry of the Arians, Ravenna (fifth century AD). Author's drawing.

# INDEX

# BOOKS OF RELATED INTEREST

**Temple of the Cosmos**
The Ancient Egyptian Experience of the Sacred
*by Jeremy Naydler*

**Shamanic Wisdom in the Pyramid Texts**
The Mystical Tradition of Ancient Egypt
*by Jeremy Naydler*

**Sacred Earth**
The Spiritual Landscape of Native America
*by Arthur Versluis*

**The Temple of Man**
*by R. A. Schwaller de Lubicz*

**Consciousness from Zombies to Angels**
The Shadow and the Light of Knowing Who You Are
*by Christian de Quincey*

**The Mayan Calendar and the Transformation of Consciousness**
*by Carl Johan Calleman, Ph.D.*

**Galactic Alignment**
The Transformation of Consciousness According to
Mayan, Egyptian, and Vedic Traditions
*by John Major Jenkins*

**Science and the Akashic Field**
An Integral Theory of Everything
*by Ervin Laszlo*

INNER TRADITIONS • BEAR & COMPANY
P.O. Box 388
Rochester, VT 05767
1-800-246-8648
www.InnerTraditions.com

Or contact your local bookseller